EARTH TO GOD

COME IN PLEASE . . .

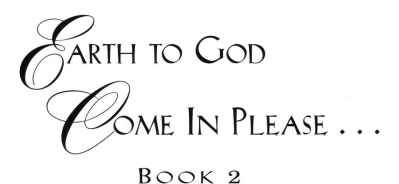

EARTH TO GOD COME IN PLEASE . . .

BOOK 2

HAROLD KLEMP, SERIES EDITOR

ECKANKAR
Minneapolis

Earth to God, Come In Please..., Book 2

Printed in U.S.A.

Compiled by Suzanne Ford, Karon Leach,
and Mary Carroll Moore
Edited by Joan Klemp and Anthony Moore
Text illustrations by Ann Hubert

Publisher's Cataloging-in-Publication
(Prepared by Quality Books, Inc.)

Klemp, Harold.
    Earth to God, come in please—. Book 2, / Harold Klemp.—1st ed.
    p. cm.
    ISBN: 1-57043-116-7

    1. Eckankar (Organization) 2. Spiritual life—Eckankar (Organization) I. Title.

BP605.E3K54 1997   299'.93
                                    QBI97-40565

Contents

Preface ix

1. Protection
Paramedic: A Call from the Other Side 3
Trouble in Delhi 7
The Special Ring 11
Timely Warning 15
The White Bird 17
Accident 21
"Wah Z Caught Me" 25
Saved from Drowning 27
Under the Cloak of ECK 31
Blue Ship 33

2. Meeting the ECK Masters
Protection 41
Kicking the Cigarette Habit 45
The Man with the Glasses 47
Slaying the Dragons of the Mind 49
Experience in India 53
Eyes of Light 55
I Never Walk Alone 57
My Friend "Lamp" 61

3. Sleeping Dreams and Waking Dreams
A Lesson at Chan's 69
The Red Car 73
The Secret of Graceful Living 77
The Tools of Mastery 81
Desert Experience 85
The God Worlds of ECK 89
Red Ants 91

A Lesson in Anger 93
How a Dream of Prophecy Came True 97
Dream Healing 101
A Case of Out-of-Body Travel 103
Setting Myself Free 107

4. Spiritual Help in Daily Life
How the ECK Banished My Fears 113
Traveling to the Seminar 117
Career Change 121
Listen for the Whisper 125
A Miracle of Black Gold 129
Locked Out! 133
Why You Should Follow Your Inner Nudges 137
Help Is on Its Way! 141
Facing a Big Decision: How I Got Sweet
    Confirmation 145
Ginger Ale 149
Getting Off Spiritual Welfare 151
A Business Challenge 155

5. Giving from the Heart
HU, a Love Song to God 165
Halloween Surprise 169
The Little Green Frog 173
A Gift of Life 175
The Red Bicycle 179
Seabird Rescue 183
My Spiritual Tour of Duty 187
Gift of an Open Heart 189
Ride Along, Cowboy 193

6. Family and Relationships
Journey from Faith 199
God, Who Should I Marry? 203
How to Find a Husband: Listen to Your
    Inner Voice! 207
Sharing HU with a Friend 211
Finding Harmony in the Workplace 215
The Same Love Song 221
Reclaiming a Friendship 225

Inner Contract 229
The Touch of Love 233
A Checklist for Forgiveness 235
New Life for an Old Relationship 239

7. Finding Eckankar
A Visitor to the Class 247
Temple Tour 251
"I Met Him Seven Years Ago!" 253
An Inner Call 255
A Dream with Rebazar Tarzs 259
A Special Gift 263
Kathleen 267
My Bridge to God 271

8. Health and Healing
The Perfect Mosaic 277
Getting Advice in Your Dreams 281
Gaining Freedom from Drugs 285
"You Are Cured" 289
The Gift of Life 293
The Making of a Healing 297
Send in the Clowns 301

9. Crossing the Borders of Death
Love Never Dies 309
Farewell to Brian 315
Answers from a Dream 319
Helping Another Across 321
An Unusual Reunion 325
Messages from Hal 327
A Death That Changed My Life 329

10. Past Lives, Present Lessons
Past Lives, Present Healings 335
A Past-Life Recall 343
A Trip to the Mental Plane 347
Close the Slipper Shop 351
A Special Feeling of Love 353
An Important Decision 355
Parent Lake 359

11. Divine Love

The Art of True Surrender 367
Redreaming Your Life with Love 371
Night School 373
Lesson from a Mouse 375
How to Sidestep Trouble 379
The Chemistry Teacher 383
The Crayfish 385
The Secret Power of Divine Love 387
The Last Train 389

12. Experiences with the Light and Sound of God

Hearing the Mysterious Sound of God 393
A Guardian Angel and God's Golden Music 397
My Neighborhood Improvement Plan 401
Soul Travel Surprise 403
Good Morning, America! 405
What Is That Sound? 409
A Spiritual Exercise That Changes Lives 413
The Purple Light 417

Glossary 419

Preface

*D*ear Reader,
How will each of these stories help you spiritually?

That's the question always in mind as I review this collection of stories about how God speaks to you and me every day—to make our lives happier, safer, and more meaningful. Above all, will these stories help you to become a better human being? Will they help you find more love and understanding?

I think they will.

Some of these stories will make you laugh or cry, while others will give you a new understanding of how much God loves you—and others. I hope this book will change you. For the better. To let you see life differently from before.

That's a tall order, especially for a simple, enjoyable book like the one in your hands.

What can you look for inside? Let me give you a quick sketch of three stories that left me inspired about how God's love, guidance, and protection appear in the most humble of circumstances.

In "Paramedic: A Call from the Other Side," Jan feels that the good work she and her partner do as paramedics goes unnoticed. Is it time to switch to another field? Then late one night the answer comes to her at the scene of a serious car accident. High-voltage wires are on the ground, between her and the victims who badly need her help. How to get to them? The answer comes in the appearance of two mysterious beings, who then disappear after other emergency crews arrive.

There's a lesson in that story for you about the ECK Masters.

In "The Red Car," Betsy finds that a dream may be God's way to warn someone of danger. She pays attention to a dream symbol that disturbs her, and it helps her avoid what would otherwise have been a major injury. Possibly, even death. Find out what Betsy learned, because one day that knowledge may prove useful to you too.

"Career Change" by Therese Weber is an example of how God's love surrounds us in everyday life, helping us to make as smooth a transition as possible to another way of earning a living. Maybe one that awakens us to the joy of working. When it's something we love. Therese had an important job in banking, but for all that, it also made her unhappy. Then came a wake-up call from Divine Spirit. From banking to radio? What a laugh! Find out what happened to her after she asked for divine guidance and the roundabout way in which her life changed for the better.

Oh, there are lots of other beautiful stories in this book you're holding. Some chapter titles include: "Family and Relationships," "Health and Healing," "Past Lives, Present Lessons," and "Divine Love." But that's what the book is for; it can speak for itself.

In reviewing these stories, I try to keep in mind a clear picture of who you are. What are your spiritual needs, and what are you looking for?

Here's what I see.

Mainly, although you may be hard-pressed to say it in so many words, you want more of God's love in your life. You also want something better for yourself. And you're pretty spiritual. Yes, one more thing: You've likely had some kind of spiritual experience that no one has been able to explain to your satisfaction.

Look inside. Learn what others like you have had the good fortune to discover about ECK, the wonderful Spirit of God.

Harold Klemp
Series Editor

P.S. Sit back and relax with this book. See the many ways that God's love reaches out to people like you and me.

1

Protection

The Light and Sound are the two aspects through which the ECK, or Holy Spirit, makes Itself known. It comes in many forms to bring upliftment, comfort when we are troubled, or protection when we are in danger.

—Sri Harold Klemp,
Cloak of Consciousness

All I felt was loving trust and the presence of the ECK.

Paramedic: A Call
from the Other Side

Jan Barron

Some years ago, I was working as an ambulance paramedic for the Gary, Indiana, fire department. I was at a point where I was wondering whether to switch to another field.

I asked Divine Spirit to help me. My problem with being a paramedic was that it seemed no one noticed the good work my partner and I did. So I asked in my nightly contemplative exercises, "Show me you're here, show me that you care." I wanted to feel the presence of Divine Spirit and of Wah Z, my inner teacher.

Soon afterward, my partner, Rick, and I were called at 3:00 a.m. to an automobile accident by the railroad tracks. It was misty outside, and a light rain was falling. When we arrived at the scene, we could see that several twenty-five-thousand-volt electrical wires had been knocked down by the cars.

Two of the accident victims were on the other side of these live, high-tension wires.

Both Rick and I knew we couldn't get to the other side—especially in the rain; the wet grass would conduct electricity. Rick went back to the rig to call for assistance while I squinted through the mist at the other car. I could see that a passerby had stopped and was helping one of the accident victims.

As I waited, a police officer walked up to my right side. He took my arm and said, "I will help you across these wires. Those men need you."

I had no fear as the officer flicked on his flashlight and began to lead the way. I didn't look at his face, but I felt his hand on my arm as we stepped across the wires. For one timeless moment I watched the wires as they arced and writhed in the wet grass. But all I felt was an unusual warmth and love. I needed to get to the people.

I put my faith and trust in this police officer and arrived safely on the other side of the wires. As I ran toward the car, I saw that one injured man was being tended to. He had a leg injury, and the passerby was doing a good job of applying a tourniquet to control the bleeding.

I concentrated on the second injured man. He had been crushed against the dashboard, and it was fairly evident he was not going to make it. Inwardly I did my best to be a clear vehicle for the ECK, or Holy Spirit, so he could make his choice when the time came.

Several emergency vehicles were pulling up when I turned around. I looked for the police officer who had guided me across the wires, but he was suddenly gone, as was the gentleman tending the other victim.

They had both vanished!

I was confused. There was no way for them to leave, since the only road was on the other side of the wires. In that moment I realized I had been working with two spiritual Adepts, ECK Masters, who had come to the aid of the Souls in the accident.

No one else on the scene saw either of these beings.

My husband, who is also a paramedic with the fire department, was in one of the other responding ambulances. He was so upset with me for crossing the wires! My partner and everyone else at the scene really chewed me out, saying I could have gotten killed. I tried to explain, but to this day my husband, who does not share my spiritual beliefs, will not speak of the matter.

This experience was a great lesson in inner knowingness and trust. I had sensed that the police officer/ECK Master would protect me as I stood at the threshold of the wires. All I felt was loving trust and the presence of the ECK.

I think of this adventure sometimes when I am fearful or doubt that anyone really cares what happens to me. I can definitely say that the ECK is here to help us. It is a tangible force when It needs to be. We are all surrounded by a saving grace much greater than ourselves. And when I doubt, I know I will be shown. Maybe not in such a dramatic way, but the proof is there when I need it.

Trouble in Delhi

Peter Mihm

he ship docked in Madras. I was glad to be leaving the heat to travel north to Delhi and nearby Agra, the site of the Taj Mahal. The bus ride to the airport, the flight to Delhi, and the visit to the Taj—all was going smoothly. That is until our last afternoon in Delhi.

My friend Leslie and I were the designated trip leaders, each of us responsible for a busload of about thirty college students. Leslie and I had left the larger group of students in Madras to go on this side trip to Delhi. According to our tour guides, the afternoon was to be spent on a shopping tour of the city, then a bus ride back to the hotel. We'd have plenty of time to get to the airport for our flight back to Madras.

Each bus went to a different shopping area. While the students were shopping, I spent time chatting with Shams, the tour guide, and his friend, the turbaned bus driver. We sat by the bus relaxing in the warmth of the day and waiting as the shoppers trickled back.

Fifteen minutes after we were supposed to leave, three students had still not returned. Ten more minutes passed. The driver, Shams, and I were all worried. It would be almost impossible to hunt them down: they had the run of several city blocks of one shop after another. By now, we should have already left for the hotel in order to make it to the airport on time.

I silently sang HU, an ancient name for God, and opened my heart to guidance from the Holy Spirit.

The only impression I had was a nudge to call the hotel, which I suggested to Shams. "Local phones are very unreliable," he explained. "We could waste a lot of time without ever getting through." So we stayed where we were, hoping the three students would return.

I determined the names of those missing. All the while, I was thinking about how I would get thirty people from Delhi to Madras if we missed our flight.

Near panic, I began wishing for an easy solution. Couldn't the Holy Spirit just step in and make this turn out all right? Then a recollection flooded my mind. I remembered a time when I had had the same frightened feeling. Months earlier I was late getting to the airport for a flight. As I hurried to get there, guidance from Divine Spirit reassured me and helped me to meet my flight. The memory brought a strong feeling of love and guidance to the present moment.

Again, I silently asked what to do. I got an even stronger inner nudge to call the hotel.

Now I was determined to follow the inner nudge. This time when I told Shams what I thought we should do, the bus driver overheard, immediately took me to a nearby phone, and got me connected with the hotel. I explained the situation to Leslie and told her the names of the missing people.

"I just saw one of them here at the hotel," she said. Leslie tracked him down and learned that the other two were also at the hotel. The three students had gone to the wrong street looking for the parked bus. When they didn't find us, they assumed they had been left behind and took a taxi back.

At this news, an audible sigh of relief went through our bus. We made it to the airport in time—all because I had followed through on that inner nudge of guidance.

In such moments of fear, perhaps we are most open to recognize the help of the Holy Spirit. This inner guidance may be subtle, but it is vital to know that it is always with us.

The Special Ring

Sharon Etheridge

I like to shop at flea markets. It's one of my favorite pastimes. I don't know who I might meet or what I might find.

One day I went to a flea market near the Texas-Mexico border. An old gentleman from Mexico had a table set out. It had a fresh red tablecloth on it. That seemed unusual to me, because the stalls were usually plain wooden stands.

The old man's table was in a very dark corner. Just a very few items were set out on the cloth-covered table. This usually signaled higher prices. He had gold and silver coins, an old knife, some antique keys, and a stunning silver ring.

The ring immediately caught my eye. I'd worked at jewelry stores, and I knew the prices of such rings. I looked at the gold coins and other items and thought, *No way! I can't afford to even ask him the price on that ring. It's completely out of my price range.*

As I passed by the old man's table, an inner voice began to chime in my head, "Go back. Go back. That ring is for you."

I resisted for a few more steps before giving up. *OK,* I thought, *I'll follow this inner advice. I'll never be able to afford the ring, but maybe I just need to say hello to the old man.*

I turned around and looked at the ring again, pricing it in my head at about one hundred dollars. Then I asked, "How much?"

"Three dollars," he replied.

"What?" I gaped. Maybe it was made of pot metal instead of silver. I picked the ring up and looked at it. It was solid sterling silver, hand-shaped into an Aztec motif. A sun symbol was etched on its large face, with a matrix opal set in its middle. Overall, the ring was very intriguing.

"But it's too big," I whispered inwardly. "And I'll never wear it. Not my style. True, it's a bargain, but what will I do with it?"

"Don't worry about it," came the answer. "Just get it."

I decided to get the ring. Maybe I would give it to a friend. I gave the man three dollars and took the ring home.

That night in contemplation, I remembered my odd purchase. It was a miracle to get a silver-and-opal ring for three dollars. I pictured it in my head and asked the Mahanta, my inner guide, "Why did I buy this ring?"

The inner voice said, "This is a symbol for you of the silver shield of love."

Immediately I had an impression of what that meant. I'd been reading Sri Harold Klemp's book *The Golden Heart* that week. In it, he describes a spiritual exercise of the Shield of Silver Light.

You imagine a large clearing in a forest. The sky overhead is blue with white clouds.

Leaning against an old tree stump is a silver shield that appears to be from medieval times. The Light of God is shining on the shield, reflecting as a brilliant ray of light. The Mahanta uses this shield in his travels on the inner planes, and it is a protection for the children of ECK, those who make the commitment to follow the shield of love. "When you can approach the Shield of Silver Light in the spirit of love, you have the protection of the Mahanta with you," Sri Harold wrote.

I decided the ring was a symbol for this inner protection that always surrounds students of the Mahanta. I accepted the answer and went to sleep.

The next day, I looked at the ring again, turning it over in my hands. I couldn't really wear it—the style didn't go with anything I owned. But I liked holding the ring. It made me feel good. So I decided to take it with me on a three-day trip to Houston. I had a medical appointment there.

I put the ring on my right hand to see if I could get used to it. If I could wear it for three days and not take it off, I reasoned, then I'd know the ring was really mine.

I traveled to Houston and was met by a van from the medical center. All of a sudden, a doctor jumped in the van. He was in a great hurry. Without seeing me at the side of the van, he slammed the door—right on all four fingers of my hand!

My hand hurt so much I couldn't even scream. The driver jumped out of the van, horror-struck. He took my hand very gently to inspect it. Moments ticked by as we looked at my purpling flesh. Gingerly, I tried moving my fingers. Then I noticed that the ring had been bent almost in half by the force of the door.

The ring had obviously protected all four fingers from being broken. The driver very gently squeezed the ring shaft together and pulled it off my hand. I looked at its completely squashed shape. Thanks to the ring, my fingers were badly bruised but not broken.

The injury really stung, but it was nothing compared to what would have happened had I not been wearing the unusual ring. All the while, the doctor didn't budge from his seat, perhaps impatient to get going. I felt a deep enmity toward him. It seemed to come from the past, and I started to fill with rage. Then I remembered the protection of the ring. In that moment, I placed the whole unusual situation into the ECK and let it go.

Slowly I climbed into the cab. The driver had a glass of cold water in the van. I put my fingers in it as we drove to my medical appointment.

As I thought about it later, I felt that the doctor and I probably had a karmic debt from the past. He owed me a bone-crunching repayment of some kind. But because of my love for the ECK, the Mahanta offered me a manifestation of his silver shield of love in return.

In *The Golden Heart* it states that if you accept the Mahanta's protection, "you have the love and protection of the Holy Spirit against every psychic attack, against all harm and all danger. In times of danger, you have the ability to wrap this aura of love so tightly about you that nothing can touch you."

I was grateful I'd followed my inner guidance in the seemingly meaningless purchase of a ring for three dollars. In return, the Holy Spirit helped soften a karmic blow and avoid unspeakable pain. So now I tell people to always consider their inner nudges and guidance. There's always a reason, and it may become apparent in the future in ways you never dreamed of.

I still wear the ring, as a reminder of the Mahanta's love.

Timely Warning

Debbie Kaplan

$\mathcal{M}$y days can be extremely stressful. To relax, I look forward to a quiet dinner at the local sushi restaurant. The sushi is delicious, and my life becomes OK again.

One day it occurred to me that a friend of mine from Japan had made sushi for me at our house. Maybe I could make my own sushi. I was so pleased with my idea. It was going to be wonderful. I thought about it all day, how I would go to the fish market the next morning to implement my plan.

That evening, I was going to the HU Song at the ECK center. I arrived early and started looking for something to read while I waited. I saw a box of books that the ECKists had collected to send to South America. In it was an early edition of *The Spiritual Notebook* by Paul Twitchell that looked interesting.

I picked up the old book. I couldn't figure out why I felt so drawn to it, but I had a strong knowingness that the book was important. Still holding it, I greeted my friends and we sat down to sing HU. As I closed my eyes, I thought, *Why am I still holding this book?*

Suddenly, an inner voice said, "Open the book."

I opened my eyes and stared at the page that fell

open. It was marked by an old newspaper article from 1970. The title of the article was "The Dangers of Making Sushi at Home." The article explained how people can poison themselves by making sushi at home. It takes a trained eye to prepare raw fish. You can easily eat tainted fish without knowing it.

I just sat there in wonder and gratitude. I couldn't believe how far Divine Spirit had gone to protect me. The article might have been in that book for more than twenty years! And I had been thinking about my sushi-making plan when I arrived early at the ECK center. The whole, intricate scenario amazed me.

I thanked Divine Spirit and the Mahanta for the help, and I never made sushi at home. The ECK is always looking out for us if we pay attention.

The White Bird

Irene Dufu

ot long before we found Eckankar, my husband and I grew very restless with our lives. We both felt that it was time to stop serving the world so much, and to start serving God more. But how?

During this same period, my boss grew unhappy with me. I felt I was trying to serve two masters. If I must choose between this job and the work of God, then I'd rather do the work of God. So I gave my resignation.

I was sure God would not let me go without.

I continued, in my small way, to help others. I spent many days helping my brothers get a bank loan for a fishing business. I pledged what little funds we had to help them repay an earlier loan in eight months instead of two years.

One day, the bank manager said to me, "You are the kind of customer we want. There are many people who never repay their loans. But you've paid in eight months what should have taken two years."

So my brothers got their second loan. We acquired a seventy-foot wooden vessel, which we named *Logos*. This is Greek for the "word." At that time, we didn't know why the name was so appealing. Soon after, we became members of Eckankar and discovered the holy name of HU, the ancient name for God. It is a word which expresses God's love for us as Soul.

We employed fifteen men to fish the Atlantic Ocean off the coast of Ghana, where we live. Each fishing expedition lasted twelve hours, with enough food on board for twenty-four hours.

One morning, as the men at sea cast their net, a wild wind blew. The net became entangled in the propeller, and the engine died. They sent one fisherman to go ashore and get help. But none came. Twenty-four hours passed. We finally got word in Accra, Ghana, of the missing boat.

We notified the naval authorities. They sent out a search party. Each day, they returned with no news. By the fourth day, word reached us that the search-party captain had been approached by a priestess. She was a witch, as we still have in Africa. She told the captain that if he set out to look for our boat again, he would never see the shore again.

We depend totally on the guidance and help of the Inner Master, the Mahanta. So we went into contemplation and invited the Mahanta's help. We got the idea to imagine all the tools on the boat, such as wire cutters, scissors, and knives. In contemplation we took these implements and cut the net from the propeller. Then the Inner Master said, "Baraka Bashad," and we thanked him.

The following morning we turned on our shortwave radio. We had not been able to contact the crew so far. But this morning, we heard a faint voice. It was the captain, saying, "We're free, we're free. We're coming home!"

So we called the naval authorities again. Perhaps

they could find the boat and bring the crew food and water. They had been at sea for five days. But the authorities said that they still could not locate the boat. In America, if a boat was lost, it would be found through advanced technology. But in Africa, we had to depend totally on the Mahanta.

When the boat returned, the captain told me about their experience:

On the fourth morning, the crew had decided to sing the HU. They remembered that I had told them that if ever they were in need of help, they should sing this word. They laughed at the time, because everybody in Ghana knows this word HU. We learn to sing it at our mother's knee. Our families tell us that whenever we're frightened or we're walking alone on a footpath, we should sing HU. So they thought I was being funny. But finally on the boat they said, "Why don't we try it? It's better than nothing."

So first they prayed. It was hard to speak because they'd had no water or food for four days. But then they croaked the HU as best they could.

When they finished singing the HU, they saw a little white bird. It came and settled on the mast. They couldn't believe their eyes. So no one said anything. Each thought perhaps he was losing his mind from thirst and hunger.

After about half an hour, someone finally said, "Hey, I see a little white bird. Can it have come all this way across the water?"

The captain said, "Yes, I see it too."

The captain spoke to the bird. "Madam, if you've come to give us confidence that we have a chance to live, please don't go. Stay there so I can catch you. We'll put you on the captain's bridge to cheer us up."

And sure enough, the crew was able to creep up to the bird and put a string around its leg. Meanwhile they resumed singing the HU. Then the captain got a nudge.

"One of you dive again to inspect the propeller."

They did, and to their amazement, most of the net had come free of the propeller. So they ran down to the engine room to turn the shaft. They could grab the few remaining pieces of net off the propeller and cut themselves free.

After they told us this story, I said, "You almost lost your life in this vessel, the *Logos*. Do you still want to fish on it?"

The captain replied, "Madam, what are you thinking? We know that if we had been on another boat, we should never have seen shore again. We want to work for you and your God."

And so now some of the crew have become members of Eckankar, and we have learned the power of the HU in times of need.

Accident

Mike Boaz

y family and I were living in a house about twenty-five miles from school and work. We had to travel back and forth on a little country road. So we decided to move closer to town.

Our decision stirred lots of activity. In order to put our home up for sale, we had to rebuild our wooden deck.

The coming Saturday morning I needed to go to the building-supply store. I planned to use my wife's Ford Bronco, and my father had offered to loan me a small utility trailer to haul the wood I would buy.

I had awakened with a nudge to rent a larger, more stable trailer, but I decided to save money and use my father's trailer. I had asked my wife to go with me, but at the last minute she had decided not to. So I drove away a little upset.

Buying the lumber took forever. It was a do-it-yourself building-supply store. I took a long time making careful selections. I needed about seventy-five good, straight two-by-fours and a lot of other smaller materials. By the time I finished, the Florida sun was blazing hot. When I took the wood out to the car, it wouldn't all fit on the trailer. I had to lash some to the top of the Bronco. The hot metal of the roof burned my arms as I loaded the lumber.

Finally I finished. The Bronco and trailer were loaded to capacity.

I would have to drive home slowly, at about forty-five miles an hour. But the skies were clear, and the roads were dry. So I climbed into the Bronco and turned on the emergency flashers to warn others of my slow speed. What could possibly go wrong?

I began to really feel good. I sang the HU and felt the presence of the Mahanta.

As I drove back through town and got on our little country road, I noticed something very strange in my rearview mirror. A long string of cars was following me from about a hundred yards back. Ordinarily at the speed I was traveling, they would have all passed me. But they didn't pass. None of them pulled closer, even when we got to a straight stretch where they could pass. They just followed behind.

We drove on, until I hit a small bump. The trailer began to swerve violently. I was pulled into the left-hand lane. All I remember having time to think was *Mahanta, I'm going to roll over!*

And I did.

The trailer jerked the Bronco back into the right-hand lane, causing it to roll back across the road. Then it flipped around and landed right side up in the ditch, facing a stunned audience in the cars behind me.

The trailer was under the rear wheels of the Bronco. The top of the Bronco was caved in, especially on the passenger side. All of the glass was broken. I was wearing only a T-shirt and shorts, and splinters of glass and dribbles of blood covered me from head to toe. I looked terrible, but I wasn't really hurt—just a bump on the head and a bruised shoulder. One of my first coherent thoughts was of gratitude: I was so grateful my wife had chosen not to come along.

Within moments, an off-duty paramedic who had been three cars back was in the seat beside me. He checked me out, then called an ambulance and my wife from his car phone. I finally convinced him I was OK and got out and surveyed the scene.

My wife arrived, and after we embraced, she began helping me collect the wood. She discovered that only one piece was broken. Later, I was even able to use that piece in rebuilding the deck.

No one else was hurt, no other cars damaged. We knew I had been through a miracle. We were really grateful.

The situation began to take a comical turn. The sheriff's deputy arrived. She looked quickly around at the wreck; then she looked at my wood lying in the road. "That's just like the wood I used to build my deck. It turned out great. You're going to have a great deck too."

Then a very friendly highway patrolman showed up. He presented his card, and we shook hands. He took one look at the wood and said, "You ever hear of a ring shank nail? You know the kind with the extra holding power?" He dropped down and started drawing a picture of this nail on the wood. He talked on and on. "You know, I had a deck built not too long ago. The guy did a lousy job. He used common nails. He put them too close together and it wasn't months before those boards were wobbling and lifting up every time you walked on them. Use ring shank nails, or you'll be sorry."

Throughout all of this, I stood there asking myself,

"Is all this really happening?"

Finally the tow truck arrived. Two wonderful guys towed off our mangled Bronco. They returned with another vehicle and collected all the wood.

A week later we found just the house we were looking for. But we couldn't afford the down payment. We hadn't sold our home yet. At the same time, the insurance company called to say they were writing the Bronco off as a total wreck. It was not worth repairing. The insurance payoff was just what we needed to make the down payment on our new house. We moved, and now live close enough to ride our bicycles to work.

This experience taught me never to judge the events in my life. They may seem disastrous, but if you have surrendered your life to Divine Spirit, there's always a greater plan at work. Often, a setback will lead you to a giant step forward somewhere down the road.

"Wah Z Caught Me"

Annie Towhill

A seriously ill relative was coming to stay with us. The bedroom she was going to use was on the second floor, but her special bed was just too big to carry upstairs. The only way to bring it up was through a sliding glass door in our second-floor bedroom. This door is usually locked because there is no porch or balcony outside—just an eight-foot drop to the ground.

We had put a small picnic table below the door to stand on as the bed lifted through the doorway. Half the family was outside; the rest of us stood in the upstairs bedroom talking, waiting for the bed.

Suddenly my three-year-old son, Trevan, who had been taking a bath, came running naked into the room. With a gasp I realized where he was headed—right for the open door! He was expecting the door to be shut, so he could lean up against the glass and see Grandpa outside.

I lunged after him. If he had been dressed, I would have caught him. But just as my fingertips touched his skin, he flew out the door with me right behind him. I was stopped abruptly by my sister's grip on my belt.

My heart felt like it was being torn apart. I had

been so close but still unable to prevent my son from falling.

Pandemonium broke out. We all ran down the stairs.

When I got outside, my father was holding Trevan. He hadn't seen Trevan fall. The only injury was a bloody nose.

No one could explain why Trevan wasn't badly injured.

The next day I discovered the real reason. I asked Trevan why he didn't get hurt any worse.

To my amazement he said, "Wah Z caught me." Wah Z is the spiritual name of the Mahanta, the Living ECK Master. I now understood the extent of the protection of the Mahanta.

Saved from Drowning

Isabelle Navarre-Brown

or weeks, I had been looking forward to floating leisurely down a scenically spectacular river in a truck inner tube—a sport called tubing.

When the day of my adventure finally arrived, it was not the perfect hot and sunny day I had hoped for. I thought the weather might improve during the two-hour drive to the river. But it didn't. The sky was still gray, the chilly air gave me goose bumps, and the unusually cold river was flowing dangerously fast from recent rains.

Several of us were determined to get in the water regardless of the weather. So we hopped on our large black inner tubes and pushed off from shore. Most of the others in our group, including parents and children, wisely chose to walk or drive to the rendezvous point a couple of miles downstream.

As soon as I got in, the strong current swept me away, swiftly and uncontrollably. My arms barely reached over the sides of the large tube, so steering would be nearly impossible.

Nevertheless, at every bend in the river I would wildly thrash my stiff-with-cold arms and legs trying to avoid the thick and thorny bushes lining both riverbanks. I was mindful of a recent tubing accident, in which a person had gotten caught beneath such bushes and drowned.

I had no idea how I would finally maneuver to the small beach at the rendezvous point. But that was a problem to be solved later. Now, whenever the river narrowed or curved around a bend my entire focus was on staying in the center—away from the bushes.

The river widened at times, giving me a chance to float without battling obstacles. During these times, I focused on singing HU. As I sang this love song to God, I remembered the spiritual principles I had overlooked.

Though I had eagerly awaited this adventure, I could have practiced more flexibility and discretion in making the final choice to get into the water. I could have asked the Inner Master for guidance—before I got in. I was certainly asking for it now!

Soon after, I saw a fallen tree branch hanging over a narrow stretch of water only a few hundred feet ahead. How swiftly the ECK works, I thought!

But this was not to be my rescue. Though I reached for the branch and caught hold of it, the pull of the current was too strong. Try as I might, I just couldn't pull myself from the water. So I let go.

Sometime later the bushes parted to reveal a rocky shoreline and a member of our group who had landed there to rest. He helped me out of the water. I was relieved. Though short of breath and shivering with cold, I thought all I had to do now was walk back— until my companion pointed out that the rendezvous point was on the opposite shore!

With a sinking heart, I looked back at the river. It seemed to be flowing faster now. My goose bumps also seemed bigger, and I couldn't speak without my teeth rattling.

There was no choice but to plunge back in.

Suddenly I found myself moving swiftly around a sharp bend, kicking and thrashing my arms and legs to avoid the bushes. The next thing I knew I was underwater, caught in a fast current beneath a thick blanket of branches. Thorns quickly deflated the inner tube. It was now wrapped around my arm, pulling me mercilessly downstream.

I was unable to stand up. With my one free arm, I fought to protect my eyes and face from getting scratched and to stay untangled from submerged branches and roots which could snag my clothing and trap me forever.

I thought my life was over. Still, I struggled frantically to remain alive. I anticipated chances for a quick gulp of air, a strong limb to grasp, or the shallowing of the riverbed so I might stand up.

Then it came. The moment when I could hold my breath no longer. I expected my life to pass before my eyes—just like in the movies. Instead, the sight of murky water was replaced by a brilliant white light. I let go.

To my surprise, the great Tibetan ECK Master Rebazar Tarzs appeared in my inner vision! He stepped through the light and quickly showed me a vision of the riverbank several feet downstream. There was an unmistakable break in the bushes—a mere eighteen inches wide—my only hope of escape. I trusted the ECK Master and began to move, though I didn't know how I would overcome the river's pull or if I would be able to lift myself out.

At just the right moment, I thrust my head out of

the water. There was indeed a small clearing. I gasped for air. The inner tube had already pulled my left arm under the next set of bushes. While I braced myself for the possibility that I would drown, a firm grip on my right arm somehow pulled me out.

A brief glimpse of Rebazar Tarzs kneeling beside me confirmed the source of that grip.

I unwrapped the inner tube from my arm and collapsed on the ground—cold, exhausted, and coughing up water. Rebazar was gone, but I was exceedingly grateful.

The urge to sleep was strong; I felt I could have lain there for hours. But one of the children in our group, alone on the shore nearby, had spotted me. With renewed strength I got up and asked him where everyone was. His vague reply hinted that we were both lost.

Together we walked through the woods, as my mind reviewed the amazing sequence of events on the river. With near perfect timing, we reached a road not long before some of our friends drove up in a car. It would have otherwise been a long cold walk to the rendezvous point.

In the car, I again contemplated how perfectly the ECK works—to the benefit of all. Had I not been stuck in the bushes, I would have ridden the river right past that lost boy. I would have floated uncontrollably past the rendezvous point!

What struck me most, however, was that now I knew that the ECK Masters are truly real—I am living proof!

Under the Cloak of ECK

Ed Leary

One summer's night I settled in for an evening of TV when suddenly I heard a crash followed by a tinkle of broken glass. It appeared to come from the family room downstairs. I ran to the lower level. A second crash echoed through the family room. It came from behind the curtains that hid the sliding glass door leading to the backyard.

Fear gripped every muscle in my body, and my mind raced. What should I do? Someone was breaking in. What would await me if I suddenly drew back those curtains: an assailant with a gun? If he was bold enough to break into an occupied house, he would certainly not hesitate to shoot me.

I didn't draw back the curtains. Instead I rushed to the phone upstairs as another crash occurred. The operator's voice brought a momentary feeling of relief. I was able to hear the Mahanta saying: "Don't be afraid. My protection always surrounds you." I shifted my attention to the Inner Master and began to sing HU silently. The operator seemed to take an eternity contacting the police.

Then I saw him. He was young, dark, with black wavy hair and a pencil mustache. He wore khaki trousers, neatly pressed, and a multicolored sport shirt. I continued to sing the HU inwardly as he climbed the stairs toward me.

When he was about eight feet from where I stood by the phone, he stopped. It was almost as though he had seen some invisible barrier that prevented him from approaching any closer. He hesitated with a confused look on his face, then turned around and left the way he had come.

I cautiously went downstairs and looked outside. He was gone. I stood there somewhat dazed, not fully aware of what the ECK had done for me. It's only now, as I look back on the experience, that I begin to realize the protection I received by singing the HU.

Blue Ship

Mark S. Rogers

I work as a systems engineer. Recently, I signed on to a new project on a treasure-hunting ship. I operate a remote-controlled, deep-diving submarine that is designed to recover treasure from the ocean floor. The company had located a sunken galleon that went down in a hurricane on September 5, 1622, about sixty miles north of Havana, Cuba. To recover its treasure, we had to anchor the ship in 1500 feet of water. Mooring cables were tied to buoys that extended more than a mile in four directions from our ship.

But we were in a tropical depression. Forty-mile-per-hour winds, torrential rain, and rough seas hammered the ship, with twenty-five- to thirty-foot waves cresting over the decks. As it was too rough to dive for treasure, we were all in the galley doing our chores.

Suddenly the captain sounded a general-quarters alarm.

You have to think back to old war movies to imagine what this sounds like. It's a very shrill, nerve-racking bell that makes your heart jump into your throat. You imagine fires, severe leaks below decks, or even a man overboard.

We started racing to our cabins, bumping into one

another as we scrambled through our compartments for lifejackets, flashlights, and survival gear. Then we gathered on the bridge.

The captain explained that there was a blip on our radar, about ten miles out. It was headed straight for our ship.

He had been tracking it for several minutes and had tried to establish radio communication. He had no radio response; the vessel was on a collision course with us. In addition, we were unable to free ourselves from the mooring cables. It took about an hour to release each of the four anchor points on the ship. So we might have to abandon ship.

The thought of jumping into 1500 feet of ocean sixty miles from the nearest shore sent shocks of fear into every cell of my body. I comforted myself: Surely someone would pick us up. But the weather was not in our favor. This was hurricane season. Within a day or two tropical depressions routinely developed into tropical storms — or full-blown hurricanes.

"The other vessel is closing in on us at about fifteen knots," said the captain. "Stand by."

The captain swiftly returned to his efforts to hail the ship.

Our radio calls still went unanswered. Then the captain called the U.S. Coast Guard in Key West, Florida, more than sixty miles away. They immediately deployed a rescue helicopter and a cutter, and began signaling all available ships in the area.

"Prepare to abandon ship," they advised. The coastguardsman's voice continued to crackle over the radio, signaling ships in the area that "a collision on the high seas is imminent."

Some of my shipmates yelled that they could now

see the oncoming vessel. The radar showed the ship to be only three miles away. I could just make it out closing in on us through the haze and the rain. I couldn't see the bow or the waterline of the other vessel, just the superstructure, but I could tell it was huge!

Riding on the froth of the angry gray seas, it looked like the ship of death coming straight for us.

With the ship now visible, the captain ordered some of the crew to launch rocket flares. Other crewmen stood on the port and starboard decks with handheld flares. Huge waves were pounding, shaking, and rocking us like cannon fire. We tried to stay upright on the deck, with the flares flashing, and the horn and bell sounding.

I watched the waves breaking on the bow of the huge vessel in the mist and froth. I wondered if I was going to die on this blue-painted treasure-hunting ship in the middle of nowhere.

The captain gave the command, "Stand by your life rafts and prepare to abandon ship!"

I suddenly had a clear image of how we'd spent all of our evenings on the expedition. Fishing. And what did we fish for most? Sharks! I have a great love for all creatures and a tremendous respect for sharks. Then I thought, *If we jump overboard what's it going be? Revenge of the sharks!* Panic rose in my throat. In a flash, I remembered the ECK, and asked Divine Spirit to show me what was happening.

I began to sing the ancient name for God, HU.

Suddenly, the static on the radio was broken. Miraculously, someone had finally heard us! A groggy voice was saying, "Blue ship? Blue ship?"

There was a long pause. "Blue ship off our bow, what is your latitude and longitude?"

From the looks on some of our faces, it was the silliest thing we'd ever heard. We shouted to each other as the captain frantically grabbed the radio.

It was almost too late. The ship was entering the zone of our mooring buoys—the point of no return. Even if the ship slightly changed course and missed hitting us, she would clip our cables and drag us down underwater just the same. I sang HU with all my heart and all my love for Divine Spirit. Suddenly, to our astonishment and stunned silence, the huge freighter made a 90-degree hard turn to starboard!

Somehow, the entire boat had pivoted on a dime. It sometimes takes tugboats many *minutes* to even begin to turn a ship that size.

We all cheered.

No one else could figure out how or why the boat had turned so swiftly. But I knew the HU had saved us—not just my life, but the lives of my shipmates and perhaps the lives of the people on the other ship.

I also knew in that moment, that I had worked out some heavy karma, without having to suffer the worst possible consequences. The HU had buffered the experience so I could catch the lesson without the full allotment of pain I had coming. Long before, I had glimpsed a past life as a Portuguese or Italian sailor. I had lived the cruel life of a pirate or buccaneer, enjoying the freedom of the high seas while crewing on many different boats.

That was why I still loved working on the sea. My shipmates and I had dedicated our lives to recovering treasure plundered by pirates during the Spanish colonial empire. I began to see many of the qualities of these long-ago pirates in my shipmates.

Me and my treasure-hunting shipmates had activated some very weighty karma. Because I remembered to sing the HU, Divine Spirit was able to help me lighten my load as Soul just in time to avert disaster.

2

eeting the
ECK Masters

The ECK Masters work with us quietly. Often they will meet us on the street and we won't recognize them. They come at a time when we need a lesson, when we need insight or inspiration or a little push to help us to the next stage of our spiritual life.

—Sri Harold Klemp,
How to Find God

The presence of these three ECK Masters was as
sure as that of my old friend John silent beside me.

Protection

Debbie Kaplan

I recently spent a week in New York City making the rounds of all the usual tourist spots. Someone suggested a trip to Coney Island, so off we went, my husband and I and John, a good friend of ours.

Unaware of the dangers of travel in that section of the city, we set out to the amusement park by subway. While transferring to another train, my husband became separated from us. John and I rode on through neighborhoods that became worse at every block. Finally we were in an area with dark buildings and empty lots that sparkled with broken glass. Groups of men languished in front of shops with broken windows, and children chased each other between the buildings. We contemplated getting off at the next stop, but my husband would be waiting for us at Coney Island.

The train stopped at the next station, and all the other passengers got off. John and I were alone on the hard benches. Knowing we would be there soon, we tried to relax.

At the next stop, a gang of fourteen boys got on the train. They poured through the doors, screaming obscenities back and forth, arguing about their last episode on the streets. My friend and I were frozen to our seats while they loudly compared notes: which gang had caused more destruction, who had accumulated more stolen goods, and how many women they had harassed in the process.

Their foul language and disregard for human life terrified me, and I began to shake. The argument became even more intense.

Then, one stop before our final destination, the train entered a black tunnel, slowed, and dragged to a stop. It had broken down.

We were completely unprotected, except for the love of Divine Spirit. Remembering this, I sang HU, the holy name of God, silently to myself. I imagined Rebazar Tarzs, an ECK Master from the Himalayan mountains, standing beside me in the subway. I concentrated on every inch of him standing tall and strong in his maroon robe, his walking stick in his hand. Then I was surprised to see him joined in my inner vision by Fubbi Quantz, an ECK Master from northern Tibet. He was regal in his long robe and white beard. Then Wah Z, the inner spiritual form of the Living ECK Master, came to sit next to me. He placed his hand over my trembling one. The presence of these three ECK Masters was as sure as that of my friend John silent beside me.

When I sang HU, their deep voices joined mine, forming a circle of love among us. Meanwhile, the train had started up and began to grind its way toward Coney Island. Twenty minutes later we were there. During the entire time the gang never glanced our way or otherwise acknowledged our presence. We were completely invisible to them.

Once at Coney Island, I sat paralyzed. "It's OK," I heard Wah Z's voice say. "We'll walk off with you." I gripped his firm hand and used it to get my balance and pull myself up. John and I left the train safely surrounded by our three spiritual guardians.

I was filled with gratitude for this protection—a shield of love as real as anything I have ever felt in my life.

Kicking the Cigarette Habit

John London

hortly before the 1990 ECK Worldwide Seminar in Orlando, Florida, I recorded in my nightly dream journal this dream about my smoking habit: *I was parked in my pickup truck smoking a cigarette. I kept dropping it in my lap, on the floor, on the steering column.*

At the seminar, every time I turned a corner, stopped at a light, or bent over in my car, I dropped my cigarette, just as in my dream. I realized the ECK was telling me quite literally it was time to drop the cigarette habit.

But sometimes it's not so easy to quit a long-held habit. One day while walking to my office, I asked the Mahanta, my inner guide, out loud, "Is smoking really that bad? What effect is it having on me spiritually?"

I honestly couldn't see any drawbacks to smoking. I didn't hear an answer to my question that minute. I promptly forgot about it—but the Inner Master didn't.

That night I had another dream. I was sitting on the patio when a friend and his young son walked up. "Come with us," my friend said.

They led me around the side of the house. The yard was covered with cigarette butts, old crumpled packs, and empty cartons.

What a mess! We got busy and filled the trash can

to overflowing. There was still more trash to pick up as the dream faded.

This time I really listened. I knew the Master had answered my question. He had shown me what effect smoking was having on me: it was trashing my consciousness! I have discovered that success with the Eckankar spiritual exercises and smoking are not compatible. The smoke clouds one's spiritual vision.

As a new ECKist, I had been working hard to grow in spiritual awareness. I was trying to prepare myself to receive the Light and Sound of God, while all the time, I had been littering my consciousness with trash!

Wah Z (the inner name of the Mahanta) and the ECK had been working with me, both in the dream state and in my waking life, to help me kick the habit. Thanks to this help, I received the understanding necessary to drop my cigarettes where they belonged—in the trash.

Now I'm a spiritual ecologist—dedicated to keeping my personal environment clean!

The Man with the Glasses

Sarah Butcher

hen I was two years old, something very special happened to me. It was October 22, 1981. October 22 is recognized as the start of the new spiritual year in Eckankar. I was at home in bed in Ohio. It was midnight, and my mom and I were sound asleep.

Suddenly, I sat straight up in bed and elbowed my mom.

"Mom, Mom! Wake up!"

"Sarah, what are you doing awake?"

"Mom, there's a man at the foot of the bed. He's a Master, and he has friends with him."

"Honey, I don't see anyone at the foot of the bed. Why do you say he's a Master?"

"Because he's standing in light!"

"Oh, honey! I don't see anyone."

"Mom, they can hear you!"

"Sorry, honey. I can't see anyone. Could you please tell me what they look like?"

"They're all in light, but one's the most light of all, and he looks young and modern looking."

"Modern! What do you mean by modern?"

"He's wearing glasses."

"Oh, Sarah! If he were a Master, he wouldn't be

47

wearing glasses. He'd get his eyes fixed."

"Mom, he can hear you!"

"Oh, honey, I'm sorry. I can't see or hear anyone, and I'm awfully sleepy. I think I'll go back to sleep and let you talk to the Masters, OK?"

"Good night, Mom!"

The next morning a friend called from an Eckankar seminar in Anaheim, California. My mom answered the phone.

"A new Living ECK Master? Wait, don't tell me. Does he wear glasses? He does? No, I don't know him, but last night Sarah tried to introduce me."

My mom instantly knew what had happened. Months later at an ECK seminar in Chicago, I was in the children's room and Sri Harold walked in. At once I recognized him and ran into his arms, saying, "I knew you wore glasses. I knew it!"

"Yes, Sarah, but I'm getting contact lenses," he told me.

I know the Masters on the inner are real and that they're always with us. Sri Harold had made sure I'd never forget!

Slaying the
Dragons of the Mind

Dorothy Boyer

*A*ll summer I had not felt well. Since I knew several people who'd gotten a long-lasting flu, I assumed I had it too and would be OK again within a couple of months. But two months passed, and I was getting worse—not better. I was terribly exhausted, in pain, and finally, unable to work. Frankly, I'm the type of person who will not go to the doctor until I am practically dead.

As it turned out, that was the condition I was in when I finally made an appointment with my family doctor in August.

After performing a physical exam and blood tests, he sent me at once to an oncologist (cancer specialist), who immediately hospitalized me. During my initial exam and interview, the oncologist kept shaking his head and muttering, "I don't understand why you are not in a coma!" I felt like laughing and telling him I was functioning by the grace of Divine Spirit and conventional rules didn't necessarily apply, but I didn't think he would understand.

The first diagnostic tests showed unexpected results, so further tests were ordered. Finally, exploratory surgery was scheduled to confirm the tentative diagnosis: widespread lymphoma—cancer of the lymph system.

The year preceding my physical malaise, I had gone through a number of stressful situations, and I did not handle some of them very well. Through contemplation, I determined that poorly handled stress, along with accompanying anxiety and resentment, had brought on this disease.

I asked for the support of the ECK Masters and especially the Inner Master, Wah Z.

The day before I was scheduled for surgery, an ongoing vision was with me all day. Hospitals are not quiet, restful places, but whenever my attention was not required by medical personnel, visitors, or phone calls, the vision continued in my Third Eye, where I have learned to focus my attention during my daily Spiritual Exercises of Eckankar.

As I gently turned my attention inward, a title was spelled out in big blue letters: "Slaying the Dragons of the Mind." The inner scene glowed with intense blue light. Suddenly three horsemen appeared. I recognized one as Wah Z. All three carried long swords and sat alert upon their steeds.

Wah Z scooped me up and put me in the saddle before him. I appeared to be in the body of a six- or seven-year-old child, filled with curiosity and wonder.

As we sat astride the horse, Wah Z asked me to call out one of my mental dragons, a fear I had. I called out, "Pain." Together, Wah Z and I visualized the concept of that particular dragon. Then the three horsemen— with me in Wah Z's saddle—charged the dragon in a breathtaking dash.

We rallied, and again Wah Z asked for a mental

dragon; I named "Surgery" and "Poverty." Sometimes our foe would appear as a picture, other times as a huge word spelled out in space about twenty feet in front of us.

Almost always the dragon (or word) would break into many pieces when the horsemen hit it. The pieces floated off into nothingness. Occasionally, a fearful concept did not break up on the first sally, and the horsemen would charge it again until it was demolished. Then we would return to our original position, to call another dragon.

Time and again, all through the day, this active vision of slaying my personal dragons continued, taking away many of my deep-seated, even unconscious fears. I couldn't see who the other horsemen were, but I felt they were the ECK Masters Peddar Zaskq and Rebazar Tarzs.

As the experience ended, I was filled with deep gratitude toward these Adepts. I went into surgery the next day without any fear or anxiety. I felt I had received a deep and thorough healing of the highest order.

Two weeks later, I began chemotherapy at the hospital, along with a very strict diet prescribed by a holistic nutritionist. Two doctors at the medical facility told me my condition was so serious I could be dead within a few days. Even though I felt healed from within, I consulted with my grown children and put my affairs in order. To retain my peace of mind, I constantly turned my life over to the ECK, the Holy Spirit.

Well, I did not die, and the following February the lymphoma was officially in remission. In March, I became the leader of an Eckankar study group; and in April, I was able to attend the ECK Springtime

Seminar in San Francisco. I am enjoying good health and a clearer state of mind than I had before my illness.

Slaying my dragons has helped me live each day serenely, without fear. My experience with lymphoma has given me the opportunity to clear up a much deeper illness of the mind. It has been a gift from Divine Spirit.

Experience in India

Jaswinder Kurr

grew up in a small farming town in India, near the school where my father taught. From my bedroom window, I could see the Himalayas towering behind green pastures. They seemed to stretch into the heavens, as far as the eye could see.

Sometimes when I gazed out deep in thought, I would become aware of a presence in my room. I looked around only to find no one there. Yet I seemed to know where the person was standing.

I discovered that if I turned my head really fast I could glimpse a man in a maroon robe, with dark, clear eyes.

One day my mother said, "Jassie, the next time you see this being in your room, challenge the purity of his intentions by saying, 'Sat Nam, Vi-Guru.' If he is not working for your highest good, he will disappear."

Sat Nam is a name for God. Vi-Guru is a true teacher. In Eckankar this is the Mahanta, my inner guide. These words were very familiar to me because my parents are Sikhs, and these are common terms in that religion.

Anytime I became aware of this man in my room, I would just close my eyes and say, "Sat Nam, Vi-Guru." Instead of vanishing into thin air, his presence would get stronger! Somewhere along the line, without consciously being aware of it, I accepted him as my friend.

Whenever I visited my grandparents, I would walk a mile or so through a beautiful pasture, past a lake with a grove of mango trees. As I walked and skipped along, I would become aware of footsteps right beside me. They would stay with me for a while and then go away.

This continued until I was in my early teens, when I moved to England. I did not feel this presence again for several years. Then a friend gave me a book on Eckankar. I read it and was really impressed. Finally someone was speaking my language!

One day, as we sat discussing the book in my friend's home, I looked across the room and saw a painting on the wall. Walking up to it, I pointed to a figure in the painting.

"Who is this man?" I asked.

My friend smiled and said, "He is the great Tibetan ECK Master Rebazar Tarzs."

"This is the man who used to appear in my room years ago."

At that moment of recognition my whole being vibrated. All the many experiences I'd had with Rebazar Tarzs flashed before my eyes.

I realized that no matter what path we follow, what we believe or don't believe, these spiritual giants, the ECK Masters, work to uplift us. They guide and protect us and are right beside us, waiting for a spark of recognition or an opportunity to take us a spiritual step forward.

If you want to meet one, try singing HU tonight.

Eyes of Light

Virginia Reynolds

*I*t seemed my spiritual life had dried up over the past few months. I wasn't recognizing any spiritual experiences.

I was new to Eckankar and had gone to a meeting at the local ECK center. Before the meeting started, I talked with a fellow ECKist and mentioned this. "Maybe something will happen during the HU Song," she said.

I knew that singing HU, the ancient name for God, aligns us with the Holy Spirit. *Perhaps she is right,* I thought.

The couch I sat on faced a wall with pictures of several ECK Masters: Gopal Das, Fubbi Quantz, Rebazar Tarzs, and Lai Tsi. When I glanced up briefly after the HU Song ended, these pictures appeared the same as before. As far as I could tell, nothing had happened during the HU Song.

I continued talking with my friend. Looking up, my eyes scanned the pictures again. I stared, amazed. The picture of Gopal Das seemed to be alive—alive in the sense of molecules moving around before my eyes. And the room was suddenly brightly illuminated.

Then my eyes met those in the picture. Gopal's eyes blazed.

I continued to talk as if nothing out of the ordinary

were happening. Yet, the whole time I was talking, the light from those eyes was so intense I had to avert my eyes. The light seemed to bore into my being, purifying me.

I don't remember how long this lasted or when the picture returned to normal. Just as I was leaving, though, I took one last look at Gopal Das. This time, his picture was back to normal, hanging on the wall with the others. The next week when I came back to the ECK center, the picture remained a normal picture.

After this experience, I began to look at several situations that I had refused to examine before. The light from the ECK Master's eyes had not only illuminated the room at the ECK center, but the next step in my spiritual life as well.

I Never Walk Alone

Val Sellars

I had experiences with an ECK Master many years before I found Eckankar. The first time was one evening when I had gone to a party at my friend's house.

As I entered the house, I saw that a man was looking at me. He was short and stocky with a blue navy cap pushed back on his head. He had a full, round face and he was chuckling.

I never saw him again that night.

* * *

I met my present husband through his sister. We were golfers together, and she often said to me, "You remind me of my brother. You must meet him sometime." This went on for some time, and we finally met at a Christmas party.

We got along great, and it turned out that he and I had been living in the same Australian suburb since birth. Though we had never met each other, we knew the same people and had the same friends, although at different times. So we finally married, and in due course had a little girl.

We three went to Katoomba, northwest of Sydney, for a few days' holiday. Our daughter was four years old at the time. The year was 1964. We were wandering through the bush one hot day when I felt someone looking at me from above. So I looked up into a cavelike opening in the cliff face that we were passing. There I saw a short, stocky man with a wide-brimmed hat on. I was stunned, but I quickly looked away and hurried on after the other two.

Again I didn't recognize Peddar Zaskq (the spiritual name of the ECK Master Paul Twitchell). And I didn't yet connect him to the man I had seen at the house party years earlier.

We came across this man again, farther along the path, as we stopped at a picnic spot for refreshments. He chatted with my husband, Noel, for a while. He didn't look directly at me, but I wondered at his sky blue eyes.

* * *

Years went by. By this time I was searching for a spiritual path, because I didn't feel I fit in anywhere.

One Christmas a friend gave me a book. I looked at the man's face on the back cover and memories came flooding back. When I read the book, *In My Soul I Am Free*, Paul Twitchell's name stayed in my head and I recalled the unusual man I had been dodging all these years.

Every time I lay down to go to sleep I began seeing other beings in my inner vision. At the time I wondered who these unknown men were. Paul Twitchell wasn't one of them. But I could feel that something good was happening as I slept so soundly.

I told my friend about this, and she gave me an Eckankar newsletter. It had pictures of the ECK Masters. They were the men I had been seeing in my dreams! I started practicing the Spiritual Exercises of

ECK shortly after that because I wanted to know more about these wonderful beings.

From this point on I felt my spiritual education was in good hands. Because of the presence of the ECK Masters, and particularly the Mahanta, the Living ECK Master, I know I never walk alone.

My Friend "Lamp"

Richard J. Roberts

I n 1960, I was a five-year-old boy living with my family atop a hill in suburban Birmingham, Alabama. The subdivision was new, and the road ended right in front of our house. An arch of green trees at the end of the road marked the entrance to my kingdom: the woods. I built a string of forts as I explored and blazed trails in the virgin green. Such are the dreams of conquest of five-year-old boys.

Until one summer morning. Piles of lumber, bricks, and sand appeared in the lot across the street. Each morning found me hurriedly downing breakfast to run across the street to a noisy, new world of hammering, power saws, and the fascinating magic of a house going up. The woods were forgotten.

I was a whiz at building with my Tinkertoys. The frame of the house looked like a large-scale replica of them to me. So I figured I could help.

One day I asked the workmen if I could. They all laughed and told me to come back in a few years.

After they'd had their joke, one fellow spoke to me in a warm and unusual accent. "There's always a way to help if you really want to. Pick up all the small triangles of wood we're trimming off the rafters. That will save us the trouble, and you can have them," he smiled.

I liked this fellow instantly. His dense beard reminded me of pictures in my books of Civil War heroes. As long as I didn't ask too many questions, he would answer them, although his accent sometimes confused me.

Watching this fellow drive nails fascinated me. He would tap the nail once to set it in place, then drive it nearly all the way in with the next blow. Another tap finished it. One, two, three. Bang, BOOM, bang. Set, drive, home.

Not wanting to go home even for lunch, I told my mom I wanted to eat with the workmen. She said I had to get their permission first. With a yes from my bearded friend, my mom handed me my peanut-butter-and-jelly sandwich in a brown paper lunch sack. I carried it proudly across the street.

My friend and I ate and talked in the cool shade of the trees. He explained things to me, like how a triangle always has three sides and how the frame is like the ribs of the house. He seemed to know so much! I was sure he must know everything—even more than my dad. I asked him who he was.

His odd accent muffled the response. It sounded something like "Rebeler, the living something-or-other." None of which made any sense to me.

"Did you say your name was Rebel?" I asked hopefully.

"No," he replied patiently.

"Limb? Lamp?"

"Hmm. OK. You can call me Lamp. That's not exactly my name, though," he laughed.

The men went back to work, and I took my wagon filled with triangles back to our driveway. Playing with them, I hit on an idea. All those pieces could be assembled into a single, long board if I could lay them out and nail them together a certain way. So I got out Dad's big hammer and some nails, and went to work.

It was slow going. The nails were big, and the hammer was so heavy I had to hold it near its head. I looked across the street at my friend Lamp. Bang, BOOM, bang. He held the hammer near the end of its handle, I observed. Bang, BOOM, bang. And he swung it with his arm extended.

That's how I have to do it, I thought. I carefully held a nail with my left hand and raised the hammer high over my head with my right. I swung with all my might—landing squarely on my thumb!

The scream that followed seemed to come from all around. Through my tears, I saw Lamp jump from the top of the house where he had been attaching rafters to the frame. Landing on his feet, he rushed toward me faster than I'd seen any grown-up run before. His nail apron jingled with each stride.

"Let me see it," he said. I held my hand up just a little bit. It hurt so much I was afraid to move. He took my smashed thumb in his hand.

"Open your eyes, and look at me," he commanded.

I did, looking instead toward my throbbing hand.

"No," he said, "Look me in the eyes, and it won't hurt anymore."

I looked, and instantly forgot my thumb, the pain, and everything else in the warmth and love that flowed from those shining, dark eyes.

My mom, who was seven months pregnant, arrived at the same time as the rest of the workmen. Lamp released me to my mother's embrace and joined the others.

The foreman examined my thumb and sagely declared its bone unbroken, though I'd probably lose the thumbnail. I glanced toward Lamp. He met my gaze from the corner of his eye as a grin spread across his face. Whether his eye twinkled or winked I couldn't say; but there was no more pain from my thumb, even when I did eventually lose the nail.

As my childhood unfolded, I never forgot Lamp.

*   *   *

I didn't recognize my childhood friend Lamp when he walked up to me in a church parking lot in Fort Lauderdale, Florida, some eleven years later in the early seventies. Not even after he invited me to an introductory talk on Eckankar, given by Paul Twitchell, its modern-day founder. Even when he said he built houses for a living, I still didn't make the connection.

It was his suggestion at this time that I pursue the music, art, and poetry that have since become such a large part of my life. Many important changes in my life can be traced to this second meeting.

But it would be nearly two decades before I connected it to our first meeting.

I spent those years making my life as a musician and as an artist. In the spring of 1992, my wife and I began building our home. Using extra lumber left over from the construction which would otherwise be burned, I built a screened-in porch on the back of the house.

This is not the kind of work I was used to doing. I was tired and sore when it happened—when I finally finished making the connection.

I smashed my thumb with the hammer.

I was surprised at the deep cut on my thumb, because I hadn't hit it all that hard. Instantly, I realized this must be some spiritual lesson with a much deeper meaning. I quickly searched my memory. Had anything like this ever happened before?

With my voice now deeper, what came out of me was a bellowing of my wife's name, not the blood-curdling scream of my youth.

The memory of my earlier thumb-smashing and my friend Lamp hit me harder than the hammer. I recognized him without a doubt as the mysterious Tibetan ECK Master Rebazar Tarzs from our meeting in the early seventies in Florida.

This time, however, it was my wife who came running. As she exercised her skill as a registered nurse, cleaning and bandaging my wound, I realized I'd come full circle.

Like many spiritual lessons, the realization happened quickly. The mind tried to deny the meaning of it simply because it had happened so fast. Another lesson was needed to anchor it.

As I was finishing the porch, I made an entire board for a ribbon joist out of several short pieces of wood which had been cut at forty-five-degree angles. I found myself arranging them exactly as I had tried to do with the triangular pieces when I was five. This time it worked. I looked at it as I nailed it into place, and the entire realization was undeniable. Even to the mind. It had all been truth patiently awaiting my awareness.

I've often wondered if I will ever meet Rebazar again in the physical body. It would be like the third blow when he hammered nails, a tap home; a chance to say thanks, that I finally got it right. I keep an attitude of open expectancy . . .

3

$\mathcal{S}$leeping Dreams and Waking Dreams

You are the creator in your dream worlds, whether they are on the inner planes or out here in the physical. The Dream Master tries to show you how to use your creativity, how to make your life better out here because of what you learned on the inner planes.

—Sri Harold Klemp,
The Dream Master

Every person and creature I was ever to serve deserved nothing less than my total, loving touch.

A Lesson at Chan's

Patrice Wagman

ome dreams linger long after I awaken, leaving me subtly impressed with the truth they offer. I had one of these dreams not long ago.

In my dream, I began working in a Chinese restaurant for Chan, a well-loved employer. He was respected by all who knew him, and I was eager to be part of his world. I wanted to do my best and learn all I could.

Chan began training me for my first customer. He had two food trays, one filled with noodles and the other with a different dish. He proceeded to place the trays on my hands in a most unusual and awkward manner. One tray was balanced on my upturned right palm, propped above the shoulder, with my fingers pointing behind me. He placed the other tray in my left hand, positioned down by my thigh.

I thought, *There is no way I'll be able to safely carry these trays without a spill.* Nevertheless, I went along with this odd arrangement. There had to be a reason why Chan had set me up with this impossible task.

As I suspected, a slight shift of my right palm caused the entire tray of noodles to spill down my neck and shoulders. The second tray also tumbled to the floor. What a sight—food everywhere! I stood there with two empty hands, feeling that I had definitely been tested and found wanting.

Suddenly the absurdity of the scene flashed before me. I was convulsed with laughter. Then I realized that Chan and his wife were laughing uproariously with me.

Chan said I had passed the test and was welcome to stay and work with him. Though he had given me an impossible task, I had trustingly tried to accomplish it. My lightheartedness buoyed me through a potentially stressful and embarrassing incident. Chan said this proved I would serve his customers with an attitude of calm and humor.

He then asked me to help him serve his next customer—a special customer who deserved great care and service. I was intrigued with the idea of serving royalty and watched carefully as Chan placed a fine red cloth over his arm. Then he picked up a beautiful silver tray with a domed cover.

Chan entered the dining room with me following closely behind. We approached a table where a man was seated. Chan said hello to him, and I thought, *Being here is truly an honor.*

Then, unexpectedly, Chan turned his attention to the floor.

In a cardboard box sat a small, black, mongrel dog. It had no pedigree—this was a thin, common, hungry mutt waiting to be served by his friend, Chan.

Chan smiled at me then served the animal with every ounce of his loving care. With his actions he showed me that every person and creature I was ever to serve deserved my total, loving touch. No living Soul deserves anything less.

This dream returns to me whenever I meet with those I am to work with. It awakens my senses when I face those I might consider lesser, and I remember the truth and love of the dream.

The Red Car

Betsy Lange

or years, a red car has symbolized a warning for me. When I see a bright crimson car in my dreams—or if it catches my attention on the road while driving—I know it means, "Pay attention!"

My first conscious experience with this personal symbol took place about ten years ago. I was driving down a winding country road near my home in Connecticut. As I crested a hill, I almost hit a red sports car that was backing out of the driveway.

I screeched to a halt, the other driver jammed on his brakes, and we narrowly missed a bad collision.

At the time, the experience really caught my attention. I wondered what it meant.

About a week later, I was backing up in my station wagon. It was a rainy day, and the back window was fogged. Suddenly I heard a crunch. I got out and saw with dismay that I'd bashed in the side of my husband's red Porsche.

Then I read the Eckankar book *The Secret Language of Waking Dreams* by Mike Avery. I started to piece together other key symbols in my life. The book confirmed many of my perceptions and expanded my awareness and understanding of the Mahanta's guidance in small daily occurrences.

Recently I was driving to a doctor's appointment when I noticed five bright red cars coming toward me in the opposite lane. At the end was a light blue car. Immediately I said aloud, "This is a message. And that blue car at the end is telling me where the message is coming from."

To me, light blue symbolizes the presence of the Mahanta, the inner guide. The Mahanta often appears as a light blue pinpoint or globe of light on the inner screen of consciousness during the day or in contemplation. In my dreams, a blue car also symbolizes the presence of the Mahanta. Whenever someone would arrive in a blue car, he or she would have wisdom that I needed.

So as I drove on toward a country intersection, I was thinking about this message.

I tried to pay careful attention to what was happening around me. Was the five-car symbol warning me about another car-crunching encounter ahead? I rounded a blind corner and spotted two more bright red cars coming toward me. I knew they were reinforcing the message.

But I arrived at the doctor's office without further incident. On the way home, I continued to remember the message or symbol and was cautiously aware. As I came to a bend in the road, a quiet voice said, "Slow down."

Because I was alert, because of the waking dream symbol of the red cars, I was able to hear the voice. So I thought, *OK, I'll slow down from the speed limit of fifty-five miles per hour to forty miles per hour.*

Just as I rounded the blind curve, I saw a small side road on the right. A woman in a station wagon was slowly pulling out of the side road without seeing me.

I stood on the brakes and barely managed to avoid hitting her. Had I been traveling at the speed limit, there would have been no way to avoid her. There was no shoulder, and oncoming traffic prevented me from swerving around her car. The moment I saw the car in the road, I knew that this was what the warning was about. Had I not heeded that little voice, we would have been in a serious, if not fatal, collision.

Red cars continue to be a symbolic message of divine protection. I am so grateful to be able to see some of the guidance I'm receiving from the Mahanta through waking and dream symbols.

The Secret of Graceful Living

Beth Richards

*I*t all started with a persistent but frag-
mented dream. In the dream, I saw myself
starting a new project at work. I wrote the
dream down and wondered if the program
could work.

A short while later, my boss and I began discussing
the possibility of the plan I'd dreamed about. I was
allowed to begin putting it into place within the company. I felt very gratified at being able to follow my
dreams and thanked the Inner Master, Wah Z.

Then my dreams took a new turn. They began to
warn me of obstacles and discord ahead.

Several months later, I took a vacation. As I relaxed, my dreams became clearer. One had a stunning
message, which I recorded in my daily dream journal:

*My boss is sitting patiently but hopefully wait-
ing for me to quit my job and leave the company.
I go to her and ask if she is ready to let my coworkers know I am leaving at the beginning of the
month.*

*As I speak to her, a wave of anxiety comes over
me. I do not have another job lined up. How will
I make the mortgage payments on my house? Then
a voice tells me I am experiencing fear. "There is*

*no room for fear," the voice says. I start jumping
for joy, realizing I am going to my next step in life.*

When I woke up, I felt confused. I had followed my
earlier dreams and started a new program at work, but
no one else in the company knew enough details to
assume the task. If Divine Spirit did not want me to
work at the company, why had It directed me to implement this complicated program? Were my dreams true?
And how could I let my boss down when she had trusted
me so much?

And more importantly, what would I do without a
job—especially since the beginning of the month was
only one week away? I felt foolish and unstable.

So I decided to wait and take no action. I would
allow the dream to manifest in the outer arena of life.
Meanwhile, I kept my eyes open for clues. Slowly,
conflict arose at work. Several confrontations with a
powerful administrative committee resulted in one
officer saying, "We may need to eventually get rid of
you, if you don't cooperate." From that moment on, I
felt under attack by various people in the company.

Five months later, the situation was intolerable.
My dreams were coming true. I realized Divine Spirit
was telling me: You are no longer needed at this particular job. Your presence is unbalancing here.

I gathered up my courage and stepped into my
boss's office. We discussed the situation quietly. Then
I took a chance and told her about my dreams, before
quietly resigning. My boss, stunned by my revelations,
said, "You're very perceptive, Beth. I can't say too much
more, just that you're right about needing to move on."

Then she continued in a more thoughtful vein, "I
don't know why, but I have always really liked you. I
can't put my finger on why that is or why others in

the company are opposed to you." We agreed I would leave as soon as they found a replacement for my position. I promised to make the transition as comfortable as possible for the company.

From that moment, my boss and I became closer. But weeks passed and neither the company nor I seemed able to part. I was having real trouble finding a new job. Everyone seemed to procrastinate in finding a replacement for me. Problems arose in every direction with the clients I was serving, delaying my departure.

Various people in the company seemed to want me to stay. But no one would say anything. It was as if they were waiting for me to change my mind. I had difficulty reconciling the idea of being forced out of a job I loved, with clients I had served faithfully. My decision to leave my comfortable, tailor-made job seemed quite irrational. Was I heading for disaster?

Others had been forced out of the company just like me, and clients had suffered unjust abuses. Shouldn't I stand up for my rights and help put a stop to this kind of behavior? Every time doubt set in, anger and resentment would creep into my heart. I consulted several lawyers to see what recourse was available. Doors closed one by one, and I really did not want to pursue litigation. It was too financially and emotionally draining.

Meanwhile, a persistent image of "jumping for joy at my next step in life" had taken residence in my mind.

Each day, I contemplated on the situation. The answer and feeling I always got was, "Leave!" Not too subtle. I decided a peaceful resolution was the answer, despite my misgivings and anger. I needed to trust that the ECK always worked in my best interest. My dreams had never failed me before.

I finally set a deadline. In two months, I would leave the company, even though I was still uncertain about my future. This was truly a test of faith.

My boss gave me a nice letter of recommendation. In turn, I wrote her a personal letter of gratitude for the opportunity to serve. I included two Eckankar books with my letter. She was delighted!

My attitude changed, and I began to pour love into the entire situation. I cleaned and organized everything in my office. Every loose end was tied up. I made peace and chatted amicably with two staff members who had repeatedly conflicted with me.

When the time came, I left as quietly and inconspicuously as possible. Unexpectedly, the company gave me two weeks of severance pay.

Exactly two weeks after I quit, I found a new job. I am entering my next step with such joy and satisfaction! I now have an inkling of what Sri Harold Klemp meant when he said we must live gracefully in accord with Divine Spirit.

The Tools of Mastery

David Purnell

I have a friend I'll call Gordon, who shares a house with his father. Gordon was experiencing intense spiritual distress. Nothing in his life seemed to be going right.

It came to a head one night while Gordon was driving home.

His car began making dreadful sounds. When he got home, he went to the garage to look for tools in his father's toolbox. But the garage light wasn't working. With the dim light coming from the kitchen, Gordon found the garage lightbulb and replaced it with a new one. Clicking the switch again, there still was no light.

It was late, and he didn't want to wake his father. But Gordon had an important meeting the next day and needed to fix the car before morning. As gently as he could, Gordon woke his father and asked if he knew where there was a flashlight so he could look for the toolbox.

Groggily, the older man replied that there were some big flashlights on a top shelf in the garage. But to reach the shelf Gordon would have to get out the ladder. His father said there was also a small penlight flashlight in the bottom kitchen-cabinet drawer. But he cautioned Gordon that it wouldn't provide much light. He suggested that the larger flashlights would work much better.

In the kitchen, Gordon stopped at the cabinet drawer. He wasn't in the mood to haul out the ladder to climb up to find the big flashlights. He just wanted to find the toolbox so he could check his car. So he opened the kitchen drawer and, after a minute of rummaging, found the flashlight crammed among assorted gadgets and gizmos.

It didn't offer much light, but Gordon decided he could get by with it.

In the garage, he spent the next hour fumbling in the dark, struggling with the little flashlight. Pointing the tiny cone of light, he could see an area of only about 5 inches in diameter at a time. He thought he knew the garage, but in the darkness it seemed as though he was stumbling through the back of some strange theater.

He knocked over a tin of nails, tacks, and screws that scattered across the concrete floor. He hit his head several times on pipes and boards that were jutting out. Still, he was determined and dedicated to get by with what he had. Finally he stepped on an upturned tack. It punctured his shoe and pierced his foot. Teetering off balance, he crashed into a pan of what he later found was transmission fluid. The slippery oil oozed along the floor beneath his foot. Arms flailing, he annihilated an army of unseen objects that were dozing on tables and shelves. The concrete floor came up fast, and it was merciless.

Bruised and scraped, Gordon made a few more feeble attempts to find the errant toolbox. Finally, he had had enough and decided to call it a night.

Gordon's final thoughts before dropping off to sleep

were, *What is the waking dream here? Mahanta, what are you trying to tell me?*

The next morning, seated at the breakfast table with his father, Gordon bemoaned his late night fiasco and failure to find the toolbox. "First of all," his father said, "you could have saved yourself a lot of aggravation if you had just taken the time to find the ladder and get the big flashlights."

After a pause, he added, "When was the last time you opened your trunk? Don't you remember that we put the toolbox in the back of your car about three months ago? You're been driving around with it all this time."

After this, Gordon took a long hard look at what the Mahanta was trying to show him through the waking dream that night.

The first connection he made was that he had been skimping on the Spiritual Exercises of ECK for a long time. He realized the ladder was a symbol for the spiritual exercises. The ladder would make it possible to reach the bigger flashlights—allowing him to see what he needed to see. Allowing more light into his world.

The final realization was that he already had the tools to make the needed repairs — on his car and in his life. A little more light makes all the difference!

Desert Experience

Dale Childs

t was going to be a long, hot summer. In my job, I was facing certain people and situations I had managed to avoid for many months and years. Circumstances I had long feared were being placed squarely in my path. Everything in me resisted these experiences, and my inner and outer lives had become quite chaotic. I was depressed and full of self-doubt.

My retreat from this emotional storm became the desert mountain behind my home. Climbing eight hundred feet above the valley floor several mornings each week gave me a precious half hour of solitude.

Many days at sunrise, I sat on the mountaintop in contemplation, asking the Mahanta why this series of uncomfortable events had entered my professional life.

"Do I have to go through this?" I pleaded aloud. "How will I survive? Where are these experiences leading me?"

The answer came a few days later, as I walked the mountain on a warm June morning.

I had reached a ridge near the summit and followed a trail down its opposite side. I was surprised to encounter several acres of desert terrain charred by a recent brush fire.

Damage extended down a steep slope. It ended near a housing development not far from my home.

The fire was a mystery to me; I had heard neither sirens nor any mention of brush fires from my neighbors.

I entered the burned desert at a point where charred vegetation met the trail. About thirty yards into the devastation, I leaned down to take a closer look. Everything in the fire's path—tiny ground-level plants and grasses, as well as larger bushes, trees, and cacti—was black. The air held the pungent odor of burned wood. Sadly, I snapped a twig from a blackened mesquite tree. My gaze wandered down the hill and across the desolate panorama. I tried to imagine the orange heat and crackling explosions of violent flames that had rushed through this area just days before. This had been no small fire.

Suddenly the ECK, or Holy Spirit, brushed my consciousness with a sense of knowingness. I knew this scene was somehow personally significant to me.

Pictures of my work troubles flashed into my mind. I saw clearly that my recent professional turmoil was like a brush fire. Events were burning karma, my past debts. It was not bad; it was necessary. At some point in another life, I had earned the experiences I was currently enduring. Now, during this particular life, my slate was being burned clean. It might sear my senses, but it was healing to Soul.

I dropped the twig and rubbed the black residue from my hands. My mind pondered this sudden insight as I continued my hike around the mountain. I knew it would help me face the present adversity.

The waking dream continued. July brought cleansing rains to the mountain. Each time I visited the burned site it looked greener, as minute plants sprouted from the ashes. Even the mesquite trees showed new signs of life; apparently they had survived their trial by fire.

On the first day of August, I was thrilled by a magnificent sight: The entire area of damaged desert—from the trail all the way to the homes below—was covered in a thick carpet of tiny, bright-golden flowers. Again, I left the trail to walk to the spot where two months earlier I'd held the charred mesquite branch. I breathed deeply of the early morning air. It smelled not of charred wood but of the sweet and rare fragrance of freshly bloomed desert flowers.

Again the ECK spoke to me. The message was even stronger and clearer than on the day I had discovered the fire site.

This summer's experiences were not only burning old karma, but leading me toward new spiritual growth. This growth would grant me the strength I need to manage my current work challenges. It would also advance me to the next step of giving as a Co-worker with the Mahanta.

The summer is nearly over, and all outward signs of June's fire have vanished from the mountain. Changes have also come in my work life. Many issues have been resolved that months earlier seemed insurmountable.

Early in my study of Eckankar, I had mistakenly assumed these teachings would make my life much easier than it was before. Rather, Eckankar has provided great insight into the meaning of my life and its apparent obstacles. In that sense, life is easier. I am more fulfilled and far less frustrated. I feel I am making spiritual progress. I know that problems are but lessons to be learned if I am to better serve God.

The God Worlds of ECK

Lauretta McCoy

t was the weekend of the annual ECK Worldwide Seminar, and I was very disappointed I couldn't attend. But being a creative Soul, I promised myself during a spiritual exercise that I would visit the seminar in the dream state and through Soul Travel exercises.

That night I had a dream. I was standing in a place of soft, white light. Suddenly a man drove up in a beautiful antique, black Model T Ford. It was in mint condition.

Wow! I really love this car, I thought. The car had a certain mystique. It was timeless, better than any modern-day car. It was like Soul, and nothing could keep it from its journey or destiny.

The driver of the car approached me. Greeting each other, we expressed our admiration for the black Model T. I noted he was an average-looking man about my height, dressed in a suit.

"You want to go for a ride?" he asked.

My heart stopped. Just the thought of riding in this car was beyond my wildest dreams. My heart said, "Yes." But doubt crept in. I looked at him. Who was this man? I didn't know him.

So I said, "No". But he didn't seem bothered by my

answer. He seemed to know exactly what was in my heart.

Taking my hand in his, he said in a very kind voice, "Come on, take a ride." The invitation was extended with so much love. I looked at his gentle face, and my doubts faded away. I knew it would be all right to go for a ride. "OK," I said, and we approached the Model T. Before we got in, he motioned for me to follow him to the rear of the car. He pointed to a bumper sticker. It read, "The God Worlds of ECK."

"Wow! The God Worlds of ECK!" I exclaimed and immediately woke up. *What a wonderful dream,* I thought.

A few days later, my friends returned from the ECK Worldwide Seminar. They were excited. Eckankar had a new Living ECK Master. One of the million questions I had was, "What does he look like?" No one seemed able to describe him. I thought that was strange.

I finally drove down to the ECK center to see for myself what the new Living ECK Master looked like. There it was, a picture of the kind gentleman who had offered me a ride to the God Worlds of ECK in his beautiful Model T Ford. Sri Harold Klemp, the Mahanta, the Living ECK Master. I knew he was truly the Living ECK Master, able to help me grow and explore the inner worlds of God.

Red Ants

Michael Fleming

/ came home to my apartment one day to find a long stream of tiny red ants marching from under the counter to a speck of cereal left over from breakfast. I gently scooted them out of harm's way and cleaned up the spill, singing HU and telling them they did not have my permission to inhabit my kitchen. With the kitchen spotless, the ants left.

A few days later, I left dishes in the sink. I came home to find ants eagerly sampling leftover pancake syrup. I shooed them away again and cleaned. Once more, I requested them to go someplace else for their meals. With no incentive of leftover food, they stayed away.

Over the summer, as long as I kept my kitchen immaculate, the ants would not come. If I left so much as a spot of juice or a dirty spoon in the sink, they returned.

My patient, loving requests gradually gave way to assertive warnings. "You've got one day to get out of my space before I use bug spray!" But even chemicals didn't help. There was no quick fix.

Inwardly, I wondered what the spiritual lesson was. At times I thought it must have to do with cleanliness and order. I'd clean my kitchen until it sparkled. Yet it didn't matter to the ants how great a job I had done when the next day rolled around. If my discipline faltered—they were back.

It wasn't how well I had cleaned yesterday, it was the attention I put on it today that mattered.

Through this waking dream, I decided the ECK was trying to show me why I had felt stuck lately. It was asking, loud and clear, Did I want the higher consciousness enough to persist in my practice of the spiritual exercises? I might go for three weeks doing a daily spiritual exercise and writing down my dreams, but then I'd get bored and slack off for equally long periods of time.

The red ants came to teach me that sustained, daily attention was the key. I realized I can't climb the spiritual ladder or reach a certain initiation and rest on the glory of my past efforts. The ants in the kitchen of my consciousness are always waiting!

A Lesson in Anger

George Benny

I have been learning how corrosive anger can be. My lessons began on May 24, 1990, when my neighbor parked his car in front of my gate. Much to my annoyance, he left it there all night and the next day.

At 11:00 a.m., I left my house and got into my car. I was angry to see his car still there, but said nothing. As I edged out my driveway past his car, I accidentally bumped into it.

I had been driving for over twenty-two years without an accident, calmly coming and going from the same driveway for over fifteen years without incident. But I had to learn my lesson about anger. And I had to repair both cars at my expense.

In November 1991, my grandfather clock stopped working. I engaged the services of a local repair person who quoted me an exorbitant price. I reluctantly agreed and gave him a 10 percent deposit.

In the meantime, another repair person came by and serviced the clock for one-tenth the price of the first quote. The following day, the first repair person telephoned to finalize arrangements. I told him I no longer wanted him to fix my clock and asked him to refund my deposit.

He bluntly refused. I became angry and slammed the telephone receiver down. At the time, I felt I was absolutely right. He had done no work and was trying to extort money out of me by charging exorbitant prices! I overlooked the fact that I could have gotten other quotes before putting my deposit down.

A few hours later, I was backing my car down the driveway when I struck one of the posts on my gate.

In March of the following year, my wife and I were on the way to a funeral in the south of Trinidad. My wife runs a service station, and we stopped to check the tire pressure before our trip. Normally customers put air in their own tires, but my wife requested one of her employees to help with the task. The employee balked a little, and I blew up. "How dare he treat my wife, his employer, that way!" I fumed. She smoothed the situation over, apologizing for assuming the employee's help, and I angrily filled the tires with air.

On the way back from the funeral, in the middle of a very busy highway, the left rear tire blew out. The car veered out of control. I barely missed hitting several cars as we skidded off the road.

These events taught me to be more aware of my thoughts and actions. Thoughts are things. And when you charge them with anger, they can become harmful. I was lucky my anger didn't hurt others. It could have caused me to create more karma or spiritual debts to repay.

In all cases, I could have applied an extra measure of initiative, forethought, or patience to right the situation. I could have requested that the neighbor move his car. I could have researched the clock prices before surrendering hard-earned cash. I could have let my wife deal with her own employee.

Each was a test, to show me new ways to be more neutral and filled with the love of Divine Spirit, which is endlessly creative. I've learned that anger hinders or delays me as Soul in my progress toward spiritual freedom. Needless to say, since then I have been diligently practicing alternatives to becoming angry.

How a Dream
of Prophecy Came True

Bruce Weber

*T*he company I work for had been going through a rough period and announced one-fourth of the employees would be laid off. But six months passed, and still no one had been fired. Anxiety ran high.

I made a decision not to worry about getting laid off. But deep down I wasn't really certain if I would survive the cutbacks.

One night in a dream, the Mahanta let me glimpse the direction I should take in this period of uncertainty. In the dream, I was in the lobby of a skyscraper. I got in an elevator. One of the women from my workplace was the elevator operator. In the dream her name was Cassandra. I also sensed an unseen person in the elevator with us.

The elevator zoomed to the top. Then Cassandra opened the doors and said, "Here is your destination: Hebron."

What did that mean? I wondered as I stumbled off the elevator. I had to watch my footing, because the building consisted only of open beams, without walls or flooring. I could see the sky and feel the wind blowing.

Another fellow from work was leaning against a beam. Oddly enough, he had on a safety belt and a chain. He was chained to the structure. He was laughing and flying around, borne by the breeze filtering through the building.

The entire tone of the dream was very lighthearted. I walked toward my coworker who was blowing in the breeze. I told him, "Well, that looks like a pretty good idea."

As soon as I spoke, I saw I had a safety belt around my waist too. I picked up the end of a chain lying on a floor beam and hooked it on to my safety belt. Then I latched the other end of the chain to an iron ring in the wall. Soon my coworker and I were laughing and swaying around together in the wind on the open floor.

I woke up and wondered what the dream meant. I decided to do a little research and looked up the name *Cassandra*. She was a prophetess in Greek literature. She resisted the advances of Apollo, so he doomed her prophecies never to be believed. But they were accurate nonetheless.

I decided Cassandra was signaling a forthcoming event. The destination was Hebron. I thought it might be a biblical word; something to do with the Hebrews. I found a concordance for a Bible and found a reference. The wife of Abraham had died, and he was about to bury her. He had nowhere to bury her, so he approached the people of Hebron. They knew he was one of the elders of their religion, so they didn't want to charge him for a grave plot. They kept trying to give it to him, but he insisted on paying for it. They finally relented, and Hebron became the burial place for the family of Abraham.

The message I felt coming through the dream was

that this new floor, or land, was already paid for. I had a resting place. It was not bought with money but earned through other means—such as service and contacts with other workers in the company.

The image of being secured by a safety belt meant hang tight. If you want this job, you can have it. The winds of change are blowing, but you have the spiritual foundation and the job security to enjoy them.

Even though I had suspected this in my heart, the dream helped me immensely. I was able to relax, be patient, and soothe my coworkers.

Then I realized that the unseen person accompanying me in the elevator was the Mahanta. He was leading me into a completely new realm of consciousness, where I gained a greater perspective of my own future. He was with me while the strong wind of ECK blew in both my dream and my daily life.

True to the dream's prophecy, my position was retained. Still part of the company after a layoff of 25 percent of the workforce, I am deeply grateful for the peace this dream gave me during a very rough time in my career.

I always tell people now to ask the Mahanta for help in their dreams with their deepest questions in life. With his guidance, it's very possible to glimpse just the answer you need!

Dream Healing

Dorothy Thomas

y family had been grieving over three recent deaths. Then on New Year's Eve, my brother died a tragic, sudden death. I felt like I could not cope with yet another loss.

On the eve of my brother's funeral, I asked the Inner Master to give me strength in the days ahead. That night in my dreams, I met my brother in a large, white ballroom. We waltzed while the Dream Master stood looking on. When I awoke the next morning, I felt a calm and peace within. It reassured me I had the strength to face my brother's funeral with confidence and courage.

After the funeral, I postponed my return trip and sent my family on ahead. I wanted to spend some time with my mother. We had all pitched in two days before to help her dispose of my brother's belongings. But there were a few items remaining.

As my mother and I sorted through them, Mom's grief soared. I was almost overwhelmed by it. As I tried to comfort her, my thoughts went back to my dream. I wished I could tell her my brother was fine, that there was no cause for concern.

Suddenly she stopped weeping. She walked into my

brother's room, sat down, and put her head in her hands. I sat quietly beside her, feeling powerless and inadequate. When she finally looked up at me, I could tell that something was occurring beyond what I could see or understand.

I asked her to tell me what she was seeing or feeling. To my amazement, my mother confided that just moments before, she'd had a vision. It was so vivid, it had banished all sense of time and physical reality. She said, "I saw your father and several other deceased relatives. They were celebrating joyfully. I also heard your brother's voice join in with them, even though I couldn't see him. Then he spoke to me!"

As I listened and watched her acknowledge the reality of her experience, I saw her face soften. A peaceful calm swept over her. I knew the Inner Master was helping not only me but my loved ones cope with my brother's death.

A Case of Out-of-Body Travel

Vic Shayne

or a few years after finding Eckankar, I made a concerted effort to prove to myself that Soul Travel was real. Every night I would get out of my body in the wee hours of the morning.

I would try to wake a family member or leave some physical proof of my out-of-body travels. This went on for some time until I got tired of trying. I had not yet realized that Eckankar points the way to Soul Travel experiences for deeper, spiritual purposes.

One morning, at about 3:30 a.m., I was in the midst of a dream. I was on the steps of a courthouse or government building, chasing a small, reddish-haired boy up the steep steps and around the railing.

We played chase like this for a couple of minutes until I found myself at the side of my bed, looking at my own and my wife's body asleep under the covers.

This was amusing. When I looked to my left, I noticed the ten-year-old boy from the dream standing beside me at the side of the bed.

While we were standing there, my wife, Janice, woke up in the physical. She looked at me with the strangest expression. The next thing I knew, I was being shaken from a deep sleep.

In my grogginess, I mumbled something like, "What are you doing? I was having the most amazing dream. It had something to do with courthouse steps and . . ."

Janice interrupted me, "Never mind your dream. I just saw you standing at the side of the bed, out of your body!"

"No kidding?" I replied, still staring at the inside of my eyelids. Finally it registered. "Really?" I asked.

Then I said, now coherent enough to quiz her, "Was anybody with me?" (I thought she'd never guess this one in a million years.)

"Yes. A small boy with red hair was standing next to you."

I was amazed! Not only did Janice confirm that I was out of my body, but she also described my companion! We discussed this incident only for a minute; then we both rolled over. However, I was determined to repeat this wonderful feat.

I concentrated on a deep humming in my head as I left my body again. This time I appeared at the opposite end of the bed. Not yet asleep, Janice sat up startled in bed and stared at my nonphysical form. I tried to speak to her, but all I could manage to do was gesture that I was fully aware of what I was doing and had complete presence of mind.

Later that morning we discussed this experience. She remembered seeing me and described my gestures. I decided that my personal keys to achieving out-of-body clarity included focusing on the Sound Current and relaxing the mind. (The Eckankar book *How I Learned Soul Travel* describes the out-of-body experience in detail.)

This particular experience proved to me that the dream worlds, the physical world, and the out-of-body state are linked by Divine Spirit. As Soul, we can move quite easily among these different levels of awareness.

Setting Myself Free

Larry White

ight after night, I was having the same nightmare. I was being chased by a man with a knife. It didn't matter where I was or who I was with in the dream. This man would always pop out of nowhere and begin following me. Around corners, down unlit streets and alleys, through abandoned buildings, he chased me.

To make things even less pleasant, the faster I tried to run, the slower I would actually travel. It felt as if I were trying to run underwater. My legs would grow heavier; just before I was captured I would wake up in a cold sweat.

Since my line of work demands an alert state of mind, sleep deprivation was threatening my job security. My boss asked if I had a second job. He felt I had been sleepwalking through the days. I finally decided to put an end to the madness.

I decided that the next time I felt I was chased in my dream, I would turn round and ask, "What do you want from me?" After all, the Living ECK Master has always emphasized how much one can learn from dreams. Confronting a dream situation face-to-face is always better than running away, I reminded myself.

That night as I lay in bed, ready for action, I repeated to myself, "Tonight I am going to confront the man with the knife. Tonight I am going to ask him what he wants from me."

Eventually I slipped into sleep. In no time I woke refreshed from a full night's rest—without remembering any dreams.

I had a better day at work than usual, and that night I repeated my directive to confront the man in my dreams. Again nothing happened. Was this good? Was getting rid of one silly nightmare worth wiping out all my dreams? My boss didn't seem to care; he was happy to have his employee back.

The third night I repeated the postulate. But I felt much more detached. Suddenly I was in the dream state, flipping through record albums in a record store. I was searching for one in particular. I didn't know what it looked like, but I knew I'd recognize it when I saw it. I was about to give up and leave when I spotted it on a wall rack. The name of the album was *Look at Yourself.* The cover was a mirror. I felt strange when I saw my reflection: a very sad face looked back at me.

The reflection also held another person. He was screaming, "You'll never amount to anything!"

It was the man with the knife.

I left the store, running as fast as I could through the mall. I heard familiar footsteps behind me; and the faster I tried to run, the slower my legs moved. In an instant I remembered I was supposed to confront this mysterious stranger. I stopped.

"What do you want from me?" I asked.

"Thank God," the man sighed. "I thought you'd never stop running away."

I closed my eyes and heard a grating sound. When

I opened them again, I saw the man at my feet. He was using the knife to cut each of my legs free from a ball and chain. He looked up with a compassionate face and said, "You've got to stop blackballing yourself. There. Now you're free."

I woke up and wrote down the dream. I realized I had been holding myself back. I knew of an opening for a much better job at another company, but I hadn't felt I was good enough for it, so I didn't bother to apply.

Echoes from my past included You'll Never Amount to Anything, a message set in old, well-established grooves of thought, a recording played over and over again. But was that any reason to keep sabotaging my life?

The next day after work I sat down and listed all the skills I had. When I finished, I was honestly surprised. I created a résumé from the list and submitted it to the other company. They called me in for an interview that morning.

I was hired right away.

Since this experience I have given up a lot of my old recordings of fear and replaced them with the unconditional love of the ECK. Whether hideous or beautiful, my dreams have been blessings full of truth.

4

Spiritual Help in Daily Life

ECK is all about learning to help yourself. Of course, if the problem gets to the point where you simply cannot help yourself, the Master can always come and help you out. But the principle behind the ECK teachings is to learn to use our own creativity to achieve a solution.

—Sri Harold Klemp,
The Dream Master

Finally something in me let go. "Mahanta, if you have a plan for me, then I want to let it happen."

How the ECK
Banished My Fears

Brad Peterson

bout two years ago my boss called me into his office, late in the day. The building was almost empty, and I was on my way home. Things had been going well at work, and I wanted to celebrate.

That is, until I heard what my boss had to say.

"Brad," he said, "you've got a new job." This was in a time of sudden cutbacks and layoffs. "You're to assume responsibility for our subsidiary company." He went on to tell me that this was not a choice but an assignment. I would take it if I wanted to stay with the parent firm.

We had acquired the subsidiary company two years before. It had cost us a lot up front, but the hidden problems that we had found since the purchase had cost a lot more. There was much talk among the managers of simply dumping the company, since it appeared beyond salvation.

That night I explained the situation to my wife. We joked that the only bright spot in the picture was the company's location—in Minneapolis, just a few miles from the Temple of ECK. Since the new job would require plenty of travel to and from Minnesota, I would

113

at least be able to see the Temple.

Back at work on Monday, my friends urged me to make a deal with the boss. This was a nearly impossible assignment; who could make it work? On the other hand if I succeeded, I should be rewarded, they argued. But I felt an inner nudge telling me that such an attitude would bring nothing but heartache. Better to just start working.

But within twenty-four hours, I came down with a severe case of pneumonia. The doctors were puzzled by how fast it came on and how it took me months to regain my energy. That's when I had a hint of a divine purpose in my job change: During the fevers I saw the next several months clearly laid out in front of me, with success at the end of the road.

The first month I was named president of the subsidiary, our revenues only covered half of our expenses. The accounting department called me repeatedly during one weekend, each piece of news worse than the last. Bizarre expenses popped up out of nowhere; revenues evaporated. And of course, I was now responsible.

I have always feared failure in my work as a black hole of extinction. This situation was putting me right on the edge of my deepest fears. As an ECKist I knew I had a special responsibility not to become personally embroiled in the karma of the sinking company. But how could I stay detached when my job was on the line?

Divine Spirit kept reassuring me that everything would work out.

The next month was a repeat of the first. Our losses continued to be enormous. There were rumors that the parent company had lost patience with my management and was selling the subsidiary company. As if suddenly realizing I was a sinking ship, people who had been my friends and close associates stopped talking to me. A longtime friend called me to go to lunch, only to warn me to resign now rather than waiting for the ax. He had heard the rumors in our small business community.

I responded by telling him about Eckankar and how the ECK speaks to us. I held on to the knowledge that no matter how awful things got, Divine Spirit was still running the show. It was a test, my own dark night of Soul. As long as I kept listening, things would work out.

By this time I was traveling six days a week, on the run from early morning to late at night. I was sleeping only a few hours a night; the rest were spent tossing and worrying. My heart had started beating irregularly, and I was having trouble breathing.

Then something amazing happened. We broke even the next month—and the next, and the next! Although we were juggling millions of dollars and problems that would require years of effort to cure, things were beginning to shift. The month's revenues would look abysmal, then on the last day a large order would come in out of the blue.

Thirteen months went by, and most showed a small profit. I started to think we were doing a pretty good job. As I mentally patted myself on the back, I thought that I should get a real whopper of a bonus—not giving the ECK any credit at all. Things immediately went downhill again. Four months out of the next five showed large losses; problems I thought we'd solved rose up again.

Finally something in me let go. "Mahanta, if you have a plan for me, then I want to let it happen. I won't keep worrying about it anymore."

As I surrendered this last hold, it felt as if a refreshing breeze blew over me. I could easily believe there was a divine plan! After all, we finally had the right people in the right jobs, doing all the right things. Things couldn't get any worse, they could only get better.

When I went in to work the next day, I was greeted by unbelievable news. The figures had totally changed; we were having a record month. It was just the opposite of two years ago.

Personal transformation came for me by way of the challenges of my job. I don't know if we're out of the woods yet or what next month will bring. I do know that I will survive no matter what, because I have a different trust in the Mahanta. Soul continues on Its journey in spite of worldly problems.

The ECK created my own personal drama to prepare me for the next step. It could hardly have been more difficult. But I don't think I will ever have the level of anxiety about my life that I had before.

What will the ECK bring next? I suppose that It's just giving me a breather before the next round.

Traveling to the Seminar

Marilyn Keim

few years ago, while living in the high plains of rural Montana, our family decided to drive to an Eckankar seminar in Anaheim, California. My husband, Ardi, left Monday morning for the long drive to work with his head full of plans for our vacation through Death Valley and southern California. The sun was just rising over the Bull Mountains.

A short while later, I received a call.

"Honey, it's Ardi."

"Ardi, why are you calling me? You just left for work!"

"I'm in Lavina. I just hit a deer out on the highway. The car is pretty bad."

"Oh, no! Are you all right?"

"I'm OK. But the deer is dead. And I'm not sure what we're going to do about the car. It looks like it's totaled. Even if it can be fixed, it sure won't be ready in two days."

I hung up the phone in a daze. Ardi would try to hitch a ride to work. His job in Billings was forty-five miles away from Lavina. Only a hundred people or so lived there. But a few did work near him.

A couple of hours later, I got another call. Ardi had

gotten to work, then contacted our insurance agent and a repair shop. He'd also called a rental agency. The news wasn't good. The car was not repairable, and we couldn't afford to rent another one.

That evening, we looked at our options. Since Ardi had to work tomorrow, the girls and I would go to town to look for a used car. A friend, Willie, graciously agreed to help me in the search. At dinner that night, Ardi and I went over a list of what we needed in a used car.

"Good gas mileage." ·

"At least thirty miles per gallon. I put six hundred miles on it a week just to and from work."

"Low miles — not more than thirty thousand with all the wear and tear of these gravel roads."

"Good quality."

"Ah, Japanese-made, of course."

"Japanese?"

"Well, yes. It's got to be inexpensive and sturdy to stand up to these bad roads."

"OK. What about the price?" I asked.

"Well, we can't afford much more than four thousand dollars."

"You know," I suggested hopefully, "we've never had a car with air-conditioning."

"It doesn't get hot that much of the year, and it'll cut down on gas mileage. I'm afraid it's a luxury we can't afford."

"OK." I had my detailed list of what to look for. The next day I headed into town with Willie and my two daughters. I hoped to line up several cars for Ardi to check out when he got off work at 3:30 p.m.

Each car salesman was so happy to see us at first. We'd tell him about the vacation to California, and he'd suggest several nice cars in a higher price range with options like air-conditioning and four-wheel drive.

Then I'd pull out the list. Each time our selection narrowed considerably. One salesman even told us flatly that we'd never find what we wanted at that price.

We took a break to stop at the bank, to try to preauthorize a loan. There I got more questions. "What type of car? What make and year? What dealer?" I had no answers. I just knew we needed to drive it to California the next day.

Meanwhile Ardi was having his own doubts. I checked in with an update while he was at work. "You know," he said, "I'm just not sure we can make this trip. I've been talking to some of the guys. They think we're crazy to take a used car on a three-thousand-mile trip. We're just asking for trouble."

"I know it's going to be OK, Ardi," I said. "In my contemplation this morning, I talked to the Inner Master. I carefully outlined the situation. If we're supposed to go on this trip, we'll find a car. That's what I saw in my spiritual exercise. If it doesn't manifest, we'll know we don't need to make the trip. The girls and I are happy with whatever happens."

That was the key to the whole situation. We'd all let go of the outcome and placed it in the hands of Divine Spirit. As ECKists, we knew we could rely on the Inner Master's guidance and the support of Spirit in every detail of life.

Willie and I had three cars lined up at three different dealerships when Ardi got off work. Willie left to get everything out of our old, wrecked car. The bank closed at 5:00 p.m., so we only had an hour and a half to strike a deal, finalize the loan, and get some money out of the bank for our trip!

We test-drove the first car to the second dealership,

and the second car to the third. After a mechanical checkup, we picked a nice little hatchback. By 4:45 p.m., the deal was done, and Ardi and the girls were rushing to the bank one more time to get money for our vacation.

I stayed behind at the dealership to sign the final papers. Later that evening, we met with our insurance agent, who, amazingly enough, handed us a check for our wrecked car. We put it in the night deposit at the bank to cover the down payment on the used car. Then we headed home. Divine Spirit had shown Its hand in every last detail.

The next morning, we got up early, packed, made lunches, and left just a little behind schedule. We averaged over forty miles per gallon on the trip. We'd been very specific about what we wanted, and the Inner Master helped us find a way.

We learned a lesson of trust in Divine Spirit from this little episode. Our family vacation through Death Valley, the seminar, and the new car—each were a gift from God.

How did we know it was a divine gift? By the timing of the whole experience and the slightly detached, neutral feeling we each had. If you proceed from that viewpoint, which is Soul's, everything works out as it should. It didn't matter whether we went to the seminar or not. Only that we stayed in touch with the flow of life, Divine Spirit. Try it yourself the next time you face an obstacle or challenge!

Career Change

Therese Weber

I'd been in banking for a number of years and was very unhappy. The banking field was going through a very difficult time; many banks had gone under. My job gave me a lot of responsibilities. I dealt with captains of industry and top executives in my state, in an area of banking known as private banking. Everyone who knew me thought I should be happy, but I didn't feel I was expressing myself in my job. Yet I had good people skills.

One day, as I was driving into work, I was listening to the radio. I thought, *Wouldn't it be fun to be on the radio!* I surprised myself with the strength of this thought. I realized I'd held this dream in the back of my mind for years, without letting it to the forefront of my attention.

Was this unexpected thought a message from Divine Spirit, the ECK, that I should change careers? I asked for a sign.

Over the next several months, people began saying to me, "You know, You have a wonderful voice. Did you ever think about being on the radio?" Others said, "You should have a talk show," or "You know, you're soothing to listen to. I could talk to you for hours."

I started thinking seriously about a career in radio. What kind of radio program would I like to be on? I decided I'd want to be in talk radio.

I continued with my job in banking, because it paid me good money and my family was counting on me for that. I thought it would be good to take a class in radio broadcasting, but I didn't know how to start finding one. So again I asked the ECK, "Can you give me some guidance?"

Not long after that, I was talking to a friend about my dream to work in radio. I told her I wanted to research some radio-broadcast schools, but I wasn't exactly sure how to go about it. Very unexpectedly, my friend decided to take this on as a research project. She looked into every type of school and brought me all kinds of information. There was a very famous school near my home. People came great distances to attend, but the location was extremely convenient for me.

The school was expensive, and I would need to attend evening classes while working during the day. So I talked it over with my husband. He thought it was a great idea, even though it would require quite a bit of money.

Each applicant had to audition. This was a hurdle for me, but I made it through. I also did very well in the class. My instructors were so pleased that they recommended me for a few TV specials. My confidence soared. I realized I was becoming a much more positive person; I was truly happy for the first time in a long while.

But I was still unsure about radio as a career, so I talked it over with one of my close friends. I told her I was interviewing for another job in banking, because I believed I couldn't make much money in radio. I said,

"After all, I have a responsibility to my family." To my surprise, she replied in a very offhand way, "What about your responsibility to yourself as Soul?"

Her comment shook me. But despite what she had said, I stayed in banking.

It was horrible. I was so unhappy that one day I said out loud to Divine Spirit, "Have I missed my window of opportunity? Can I still get into broadcasting? If I can, give me a sign that even I couldn't miss." This was months after graduating from my broadcasting class.

That day I was at my desk at the very back of the bank. A man came in at lunchtime. He walked back to my desk and said, "Miss, can you tell me where there's a cash machine in this bank?"

I looked up and recognized the man. He had been in my radio class. "What are you doing here?" I asked him in surprise.

"I don't actually know. I was going in the opposite direction, but something nudged me to stop. I realized I didn't have any cash, so I came into this bank."

We went to lunch. Immediately he asked me, "Why aren't you doing anything with your broadcasting skills? You of all people! You were the best student in the class." I was amazed that all this was occurring the very same day I had asked Divine Spirit for a sign— a sign even I couldn't miss! So I just grinned at him. I knew that this conversation was my sign that my window of opportunity was still open. I decided to act, even though my husband and I didn't know how we would make ends meet without my income because I would have to intern at a radio station for free. But an unexpected part-time job came up that would bring me a little money while I interned. So I sent out audition audiocassettes to radio stations in my area. I mailed each package with the ECK blessing, "May the blessings be," because I didn't want to feel attached to any particular outcome. I knew that Divine Spirit would have Its way.

To my surprise, almost immediately I got a job offer at a radio station!

I worked up in the field to the point where I had my own five-hour radio talk show. Sometimes I could talk about things that had a subtle spiritual principle or message. I never mentioned Eckankar, but I often encouraged people to look at their lives from a broader perspective.

Not long after, I decided to leave that radio station and look for work in producing TV talk shows. But my bosses did not want to let me go; they offered me an hour-long evening show once a week to cover any topics I desire.

Someone once said to me, "When going to work is easy, you look forward to it, and it's fun, you know you've listened to Spirit. You're in the right place at the right time." And that's how I feel. It's a new sensation for me because I've never had this before in my life.

If I hadn't paid attention to the signs that practically hit me over the head, I wouldn't be having all this fun right now. I'm not making the money I used to, but everything has worked out; the bills have been met. And I know for sure that Divine Spirit had a hand in the whole design of my career change—from drudgery to dream job.

Listen for the Whisper

Rich Miller

$\mathcal{A}$ change of careers put me into the world of computer-information services. I attended a special school for my training, graduated at the head of the class, and was pleased when the school hired me to automate a few of their departments. Everything was going well. Then after about a year I received a little whisper from the ECK, the Holy Spirit. "It's time to move on to another challenge," It nudged me.

But I was a reluctant. I was comfortable where I was and unsure of what my next step might be.

So I told Spirit, "I'm in the middle of a project. I can't drop it right now, so I'll wait a little while."

I had some teaching experience prior to entering the data processing industry. So I started teaching computer programming at night school while continuing to work during the days. *This is more challenging,* I thought. *This is probably what Spirit had in mind.*

It wasn't long after I began teaching that I was called into the office of the school director. Without any warning, he asked for my resignation.

"Go clear out your office and come back here to return your keys," he said.

I was stunned and shocked. It felt like somebody

had pulled the rug out from underneath me. As I walked back to my office my mind and emotions started to babble at me, "What are you going to tell your friends and family? How are you going to face them? What about your financial responsibilities? What are you going to do for a job?"

I knew that Spirit would not abandon me, ever. I had told others of my faith and confidence in the integrity and justice of Divine Spirit. Now I had an opportunity to live my beliefs.

So I took a few deep breaths and started singing HU. By the time I reached my office and packed my things, I felt more relaxed.

OK, God, what now? What's the next step? I wondered as I walked back to the director's office.

"Sit down," he said. "I want you to understand that this does not reflect on you. I was caught in an awkward position with our budget. I had to make a decision about what was best for the whole. So that's what I did. But I'm sure something even better will come along for you. I understand you're in the middle of a project."

."Yes."

"I'd like to hire you as a contractor to finish that project, so keep your keys."

I left his office feeling a little bit better. The fee for the contracting job was considerably more per hour than I was making as an employee. But it was just a part-time job and a short-term contract.

Meanwhile, I was still teaching night school. In the middle of class one night, I was asked to go see the director of education. By this time, I was prepared for anything.

He smiled at me. "Rich, when you were working at

the school as a daytime employee, I couldn't give you any job referrals. But I can now. I think this is tailor-made for you. It's a creative, challenging teaching opportunity. You'll be designing a course to teach hearing-impaired adults computer programming."

I thanked him. My emotions were a blur; all my mind heard was "job opportunity."

At the interview, it only took me a few moments to realize that this wasn't just a job opportunity. This was a spiritual opportunity beyond my wildest dreams. The interviewer kept asking me questions, and all I could say was, "Yes."

Have you ever been in a room, maybe at a meeting or a party and walked outside? You take a deep breath of fresh air and realize you hadn't known how stale and stuffy the room was. That's what I felt like. I had been in a tedious job and hadn't even known I was in a rut. Then this new opportunity came along. I said to God, "If it's good for the whole, I would love this job."

They called me back for a second interview. Before my first interview, they had already completed their interviewing process. They had even picked their finalist. But the director of education from my night school had called and urged them to interview me. They agreed to do a final interview with two applicants.

At the final interview, I realized how new this job would be to me. I had never worked with hearing-impaired people before. So I silently sang the HU and decided I would just let Divine Spirit help me. I would simply talk from my heart with love.

During the second part of the interview, I was asked to talk to prospective students. But I didn't know sign language. I had no idea how to do this so I just talked Soul to Soul with them, using very clear lip movements. I didn't talk to them as disadvantaged individuals or handicapped individuals, but as Soul.

A couple days later, I was offered the position. They said the students had chosen me because of the way I talked to them and treated them.

This job proved very creative and challenging and more financially rewarding than I had ever imagined.

But more importantly, it was an opportunity to experience new dimensions of love and grace. I was reawakened to the blessings of Divine Spirit. Miraculous things happen all the time. The Holy Spirit is continually trying to communicate to us if we would but listen to Its whisper.

A Miracle of Black Gold

Gbubemi Omare

My company transferred me to Lagos, Nigeria, from my station in Abuja, almost five hundred kilometers away. The call came during a severe gas shortage in Nigeria.

Cars were kept waiting at filling stations for upward of twenty-four hours. We called the gas black gold. A twenty-five-liter jerrican that would normally sell for about twenty naira often went for over two hundred.

Luckily, before I left for Lagos a friend waited at the filling station for several hours and got some gas for my car. It would be enough for the first half of the journey.

On a Friday morning, my friend and I began the long drive to Lagos. By noon, my fuel gauge showed less than a quarter full. We hadn't found fuel in any of the small villages we'd passed, and now the larger town of Okene was also dry. The filling stations had abandoned vehicles lined up for half a mile. The drivers were waiting for petrol tankers to deliver to the filling stations. Even the roadside bootleggers had exhausted their supply of gas.

It appeared that I was stuck. I looked at my watch; it was 1:00 p.m.

The next major town was over 120 kilometers away, linked by a very lonely and deserted highway. Running out of gas on such a road would be pretty risky—one would get no help, and armed bandits roamed the countryside at night.

With a sigh, I parked at the end of the line to a gas station. My friend said we should be prepared to spend the night in Okene. We hoped the tankers would come with fresh supplies in the morning. But I was pretty worried. I did not want to sleep in Okene. I had already committed to be in Lagos on Saturday.

So I surrendered the situation to Divine Spirit and my inner guide, the Mahanta.

At about 2:00 p.m., I suddenly had an inner nudge. "Continue with your journey."

I immediately hit the road, even though my traveling companion insisted we should stay put. As I watched the needle on my fuel gauge drop toward empty, I wondered if he was right. But as we drove into the small town of Ihima, I saw the miracle the Mahanta had in mind.

Two boys and an elderly man were refueling a taxi from a large container of gas. I jumped out and asked where I could buy fuel. "Nowhere, sir," replied the old man. "I bought this yesterday, so I could drive my taxi for the afternoon shift."

I asked the man to sell the fuel to me. I would pay him for the gas, plus what he would make in an afternoon. We haggled, and he settled for 200 naira. The fuel was mine!

The exhilaration that coursed through me was indescribable. I marveled at the timing and sequence of events. Had I not listened to the inner nudge from the Inner Master, I would have passed the night in

Okene, with no guarantee of fuel.

I arrived in Lagos at 7:00 p.m. and returned thanks to the Mahanta for always being with me.

Locked Out!

Catherine Kirk Chase

ot long ago, I was preparing for a long journey by car. I had many details to wrap up and things to pack before I left. I started to go through an old drawer when I found an extra key to my car. I held up the key and remembered my last trip.

I had been driving through rural Kansas, tired and bored, when I pulled into a gas station. I quickly jumped out of the car and slammed the door, locking my keys in the car. Just as I began to look around in a panic, a station attendant came up. He had one of those magic sticks that goes down into the window and opens the door. Within seconds, my misery was over.

As I drove away, I resolved to get an extra key made. I would buy one of those little magnetic boxes, hide it on the car with the extra key in it, and never be caught in this situation again. When I got home, I had the extra key made, then forgot about the magnetic box. Until now.

The day before my trip, I went out and bought a magnetic box for the extra key. I checked it off my to-do list and went out to attach it to the car. But the key was too big for the little magnetic container.

So I put the task back on my list and resolved to

complete it by the end of the day. But I forgot.

I couldn't sleep that night. I tossed and turned. I had a feeling that the Voice of God had spoken to me. There was something I was overlooking. But what?

After a late start the next morning, I got caught in two hours of bumper-to-bumper traffic in Chicago. Then in Detroit, I got lost on a detour and didn't get back on the highway for another few hours. My twelve-hour trip turned into an eighteen-hour nightmare.

About two o'clock in the morning, I pulled off the highway into a gas station. I was tired; I was bored. I stepped out of the car and slammed the door. Time stood still. My keys were still in the ignition of the locked car.

I screamed, "Oh no! Not again!"

Just at that moment, an attendant came walking up. I asked him, "Sir, do you have one of those little magic wands that opens cars?"

"No, ma'am. They're illegal in this state. The best I can do for you is call a locksmith in the morning."

What was I to do? I was tired, I had very little money, and I was a good distance from my destination. I also had the heavy knowledge that I had been clearly warned by Divine Spirit. I sunk lower and lower as the weight of the situation began to crush me. But then I remembered to sing HU, the holy name for God. As I sang, I began to remember something else. *I'm a creative Soul,* I realized. *I can figure a way out of this.* I turned to the car and realized I'd left the window open about a quarter of an inch. It would be just enough to get a coat hanger down inside.

I ran into the station and asked the man if he had a coat hanger. He did, but no matter which way I bent the hanger, it would not cooperate.

Suddenly I heard a voice say, "Do you have a rear-hatch release on that car?"

I raised myself up. There in front of me stood a friendly young man who had just appeared out of nowhere.

The young man explained that the hatch release might be easier to reach than the door lock. I quickly examined the car. The release for the back of the car was directly below the coat-hanger hook!

The man stood beside me, putting his fingers into the cracked-open window to open it just a little bit more. I reached for the rear-hatch release and almost unlocked the car on the first try. My new ally coached me and cheered me on, "One more try. You almost got it!"

The next time I tried, I caught the latch. I ran around to the back, opened the hatch, and jumped into the back of the car. In no time I had crawled to the front seat and pulled the keys from the ignition. When I stepped out, the young man had gone.

A realization came over me: This had been a very important test, symbolic of a problem I'd had my whole life. Every time I was in a situation, I would get gentle guidance to help me prevent trouble. If I overlooked the guidance, Divine Spirit would get my attention again, to show me how to be more creative.

I resolved to begin using my inner ears to listen better. Like the young man at the gas station at 2:00 a.m., the sweet Voice of God is always there helping and cheering me on.

Why You Should Follow
Your Inner Nudges

Peggy McCardle

One way God speaks to me is through the little inner voice that some people call intuition. But in my busy life, I have to make sure I take time to consult and follow my inner nudges.

I teach at a university in a large metropolitan area. One hectic week, I reviewed my schedule. I had a lecture in two weeks to prepare for, but guest lecturers would be addressing the class in the intervening sessions. There was plenty of time to prepare, but for some reason I felt quite anxious about my upcoming lecture.

I had taught the subject before. Why the sudden worry? It didn't make sense.

By Monday, I gave in to my feeling, cleared my schedule, and spent the whole day working on the lecture. By Tuesday morning, I'd finished digging through new material and needed only to edit and refine it.

Around 10:30 that morning, the department secretary called. "Peggy," she said with trepidation in her voice, "I hope you're sitting down. Your guest lecturer for this afternoon just canceled!"

This was not good news. The class had to meet, and there had to be a lecture. I looked at my notes lying on the desk in front of me, and it was suddenly clear why I'd been so anxious.

The lecture was already prepared! Not as polished as I would have liked, but far enough along to salvage the situation.

"Thanks!" I said aloud.

"What?" said the surprised secretary.

"Oh, nothing," I replied hastily. "Thanks for letting me know. I think it'll work out OK. I'll do the lecture myself."

I chuckled. The thanks hadn't really been for her, but Divine Spirit. It had nudged me so strongly I had to act, even if I didn't know why! The lecture went fine.

But my week was not over.

My car was making noises. The mechanic said it was probably covered by my warranty, so I called and made an appointment at a dealership for Friday. When I looked at the paperwork on my extended warranty, it didn't seem complete. But I was too busy to worry about minor details.

After my impromptu lecture I was quite tired. When I got home that evening, there was a message on my answering machine. I was to call a toll-free number for the company that built my car, regarding my extended warranty.

I was puzzled. When I called, a pleasant representative told me that unfortunately I'd been the victim of a clever telemarketing scam. In fact, I did not have an extended warranty on my car! The warranty was useless, even though I had paid for it. She went on to assure me the car company was quite concerned. It intended to provide warranty service or refunds. But it would take some weeks for all this to be resolved.

She knew nothing about my impending repairs, but the timing of her call gave me sufficient warning to make other arrangements for the work that had to be done immediately on my car. I would put off the rest of the repairs until the details of the warranty had been worked out.

It saved me quite a large sum of money. Had I gone ahead, I would have had to pay cash to the dealer and been placed in a very awkward situation! Again, I said, "Thank you."

By the end of the week all I could do was smile. Clearly, the overriding lesson for the week was, "Pay attention to your nudges. You don't need to understand why. Just follow Divine Spirit's subtle directions."

God is talking to us all the time. I was almost too distracted to pick up on the subtleties of Its message.

Now I try to pay more attention. But I trust that on those occasions when I get distracted, the ECK will find more creative ways to get my attention and guide me through lots of little daily hints.

Help Is on Its Way!

Karin Archos

For many years, I prided myself on not needing anybody's help to make decisions in my life. Then in the middle of a bad recession in Australia, my job of three years took a sudden turn for the worse. Management became indecisive and strangely secretive. The staff felt like pawns in a high-stakes game of takeovers and rumored changes.

My contract and those of a handful of other independent contractors expired without explanation. Yet management expected us to report to the office each day as if nothing had happened. They said they just hadn't had a chance to organize our paperwork.

We had no legal contracts, so we could not invoice the company. Essentially working without pay, I decided to accept some part-time work offered by a competitor. I spent a number of half days away from my original employer, working at the part-time job. My old boss made it clear he was not at all happy about my absences. But he still didn't get around to giving me a signed contract!

An emotional few days followed as I struggled to decide whether I should just leave the first job. I would not be able to survive financially on part-time wages.

Jobs were extremely scarce in Brisbane, Sydney, and Melbourne.

Finally I realized I was not seeking help from the right source. I resolved to set aside the next day, Saturday, as what I call a "clue day."

In my spiritual exercise I asked the Inner Master for help with my job situation. "Please give me some clues tomorrow," I requested aloud. "I want to make the decision that's spiritually best for me and others." My part of the bargain would be to pay special attention all day, so I wouldn't miss Divine Spirit's clues!

I woke up Saturday and walked into my living room, wondering where to turn my attention first. I absentmindedly turned on the television. As the picture came into view, I saw my first clue: the words *The Inner Circle* were on the screen.

What did this mean? I wondered as I ate my cereal. *Did it have anything to do with my fellow initiates in Eckankar, who comprised an inner circle of sorts in our mutual love for the Mahanta?*

Suddenly the phone rang. A dear friend and member of Eckankar was calling. "I've been reading an article by Sri Harold Klemp, and I felt I just had to call you!" she exclaimed. "I don't want to intrude, but I can't get rid of this urge to share a bit of his advice."

I replied, "I'm all ears. Tell me."

"Well," she said hesitantly, "the article goes something like this: Remember to connect the spiritual diamonds in your life—all the gifts, skills, and opportunities you already have. Use all your creativity to connect the points that bring love and goodness to you. This will help you live the life you dream of—one that brings spiritual happiness and success.

"Of course, I don't know why I'm telling you this,"

she said, trailing off.

I reassured her. "I'm so grateful you cared enough to follow through on your urge to call. I promise to start looking for the spiritual diamonds in my life right now," I replied, although I didn't exactly know what a spiritual diamond was. Something that brought goodness into my life. I pondered the possibilities. Were there connections I was failing to make?

That afternoon, I was due at a business meeting with my part-time employer. The job I was doing for him was challenging and exciting. It was also a bit scary, since it plunged me into new territory.

As I drove to the meeting, I worried about missing the connections between different aspects of my life. How could I tie all my skills and opportunities together? It seemed hopeless to worry about it mentally, but I really felt at a loss. At that moment I turned on the car radio and heard the words of a song: "Hang on—help is on its way!"

I burst into tears.

Not because I had an answer to my situation, but because I suddenly realized how much trouble the Inner Master was going to, to help me with my clue day. He was there, knowing my every doubt, offering reassurance. Drying my eyes, I decided to just surrender it all to Divine Spirit, the ECK.

An hour later, during the business meeting, the boss paused to read a proposal I'd worked up for him. In the minutes of silence, my ears began to ring. Suddenly, my friend's words boomed loudly: "Connect the diamonds!"

I jumped in my chair, hoping the boss had not heard anything. It was so loud! But he hadn't flinched. So I settled back and pleaded silently, "Which diamonds am I to connect? Please, I don't know what you mean!"

At that moment, my part-time employer turned to me and asked, "How are you going to manage all this work for me, when you have a full-time job already?"

To my surprise, I said in a calm voice: "They aren't paying me in my old job, so it's not likely I'll be there much longer."

My brain went numb. I had firmly decided some time ago not to discuss either of my jobs with my employers. Was this a connecting diamond or a disaster?

The boss's response was resounding. "That's great!" he said.

"It is?" I asked meekly. "Why?"

"Because I can employ you full-time, of course! There's so much to be done," he said, rubbing his hands together in glee.

I slumped in my chair, dumbfounded. It had been less than a day since I had asked the Mahanta for clues. Through his love and that of my dear friend, I was able to blurt out a single sentence in that meeting which changed my life.

The diamonds were my love for the Mahanta, my friend's love, and my enthusiasm for a challenging new task. Only Divine Spirit, the ECK, could help me connect them all for such a wonderful solution.

Facing a Big Decision:
How I Got Sweet Confirmation

Steve Scott

*I*t was a bright spring morning, and I decided to take my dog Fritz for a long walk. There was much to think about. My winter semester at college was drawing to a close. I had applied to the school of nursing and was hoping to be accepted for the fall term. But after almost a year of courses in science I was still plagued by doubt. Was I cut out to be a nurse? I asked the Holy Spirit, the ECK, if It could offer confirmation.

I decided to let Fritz take the lead while my mind chewed over my career choices. Finally I gave up. It was time to turn around, point the puppy toward home, and put my cares in the hands of the Mahanta. Life would let me know.

On the way home Fritz decided to go down a shady alley. We walked behind old houses shrouded by overgrowth, their yards strewn with odd cement statues watching like silent sentinels. My attention was taken by the mysterious setting, and I didn't notice that Fritz had stopped.

I looked around. Barely discernible in a bed of rusty, fallen sea-grape leaves, a red Doberman lay in wait. I backed off, hoping for the best. I knew such dogs could be deadly if they chose to attack. Fritz seemed confused as we retreated carefully out of the alley. A near escape. Or was it?

The adrenaline from my sudden fright diffused as we walked home. I reviewed the scene. Fritz hadn't even growled. Had the Doberman? The dog's image replayed itself in my mind. *That dog looked awfully thin,* I thought. *And he didn't even lift his head as we approached. Was he alive?*

I had to go back and see. I put Fritz in the house and gathered a few cans of dog food, a leash, and a bottle of water to take with me, just in case. The alley seemed even darker. But my love for dogs pushed me on.

All fear melted as I knelt by the emaciated animal. "Hey there, puppy," I cooed softly.

His eyes lifted to mine, but that was all. He was in very bad shape and had picked his place to die. I held his only hope in a can of dog food. His head perked up as I opened the cans and set the food next to him.

SLURP. Good-bye, dog food. Maybe he'd make it, I thought as I watched the dog food disappear. But I still had to get the trembling Doberman to the vet. Would he let me put a leash on him?

With quivering hands, I reached for the dog's head. He offered no resistance as I slipped the chain around his neck and helped him to his feet. After a moment he followed me, very shakily, to the car. Fortunately we got an emergency appointment with my vet.

"This guy's pretty far gone," she said. "He needs a lot of care." She looked me in the eyes. "And I can't promise he'll even make it."

I had to give him a chance.

During the next few days the world faded away as

I focused on my patient, whom I named Zachary. With time and a little love, Zachary made great progress. I began to look forward to his daily improvement. I had never enjoyed myself so fully. That's when I realized I was *nursing* him back to health! The confirmation couldn't have been sweeter! I humbly thanked Divine Spirit for such a clear answer to the question about my career.

Ginger Ale

Kristin Joseph

*E*ight months pregnant, I was trudging around the grocery store with my husband and our two preschoolers. A rowdy clamor seemed to hover over our two shopping carts, as we made slow progress up and down the aisles. Most of the other shoppers would make eye contact and smile at the antics of our little ones: the four-year-old likes to scrub the floors with his tummy, crawling commando-style; the two-year-old studiously examines hot-dog packages with her teeth when we're not looking.

I saw, however, as we kept passing him every other aisle, one particular dad with his son who never seemed to notice our crew. He was middle-aged, harried looking, and he seemed less than sure of himself. His son asked him about doing something the coming weekend, and he responded with an absentminded, "Maybe we can." On one pass, he impatiently wheeled around us, as we took up space making a decision on the brand of peanut butter to buy.

After checking out, I was avoiding the drizzle, standing under the eaves of the store while I waited for my husband to pull up with the car. I was chatting idly with the bag boy. Suddenly, the harried dad walked from the parking lot, carefully carrying a damp sack

149

of birdseed that had split down the middle. He trotted up to where the bag boy and I were standing.

Treating him as I would any casual acquaintance, I quipped, "What, back so soon?"

He looked at me and the young man and explained hastily that his birdseed had dropped out of the car and he had run over it. I looked sympathetic, and the bag boy directed him into the store for an exchange.

My husband arrived with our car, and I got into the front seat, grabbing a two-liter bottle of ginger ale from the bags in the back. I had in mind to pour some over a cup of ice for the ride home.

But as soon as had I shut the door, the plastic bottle fell over between my feet and sprang a leak along its seam. Sticky soda spewed out over my purse and feet and the car's carpet.

"How did that happen?" wondered my husband. I just rolled my eyes.

I knew the ECK was talking to me. I couldn't quite get the message, though. I knew I'd gotten into the harried dad's space and was reaping near-instant karma. But why and how? I was just being cheerful and friendly.

A couple of days later, after contemplating on the matter in a spiritual exercise, I realized what I had done. There I had been, a burgeoning symbol of motherhood, challenging someone who lacked confidence in a motherly chore. "What if he had never shopped for his household before?" the gentle voice inside my head prodded. "What if his wife, the boy's mom, is in the hospital or divorcing him?"

I learned two lessons that night. One: never interject my point of view, humorous or not, into a situation at another's expense. And two: always open the bottle of soda in the parking lot before getting into the car.

Getting Off Spiritual Welfare

Beverly Foster

*I*t looked like I had finally used up all my miracles. My husband and I had always lived on the borderline financially. If we had money, we spent like kings. If we didn't, we lived like paupers.

In between, we did the best we could to control our finances, but we couldn't seem to figure out how. During those years we leaned on the Holy Spirit. Sure enough, each time we were headed for disaster a miracle intervened.

One year I quit a well-paying job. We hadn't planned how to make our house payments, but my retirement savings and gifts from my family added the needed amount to my husband's income. A few years later my husband started his own computer business. One of his projects was to develop a piece of software. At the same time I changed careers to freelance writing.

From then on whenever we faced certain financial ruin I would sell an article or someone would call from out of the blue to order a computer program. Windfalls, unexpected inheritances, gifts when we most needed help—the evidence mounted to prove that God was taking care of our every need.

Last summer we were perched about as far out as

we could get on the usual cliff. This time, though, the miracles were slower in coming.

I'd quit another job, and now we were faced with another financial crunch. If we were lucky, if I found a way to make some extra money, if we could control our spending a little more, we might survive. If not, there was a good chance we might not be able to pay our next house payment.

I was waiting for a sign from the ECK that all these ifs would become reality when I went to Sunday's worship service at the Temple of ECK. Sri Harold Klemp was the speaker that day. Excited, I closed my eyes and opened my heart to him. "Are we going to be better off now?" I asked inwardly. He would know what I meant. Then I sat back and waited for confirmation of my hopes. Instead, three words in his talk went straight to my heart.

"Tighten your belt."

While Sri Harold spoke this from the stage, the Mahanta added in a very loud voice to my inner ear, "This means you!" Certainly the sign I'd been waiting for, but not what I wanted to hear.

I headed straight for my office after the service to look over our finances. Grimly I asked myself where I could cut spending. We had almost stopped buying new clothing. We never went to movies. We only ate out in restaurants once in a while. I shopped at the cheapest grocery store. What else could I do?

As it turned out, there was plenty I could do. I added up every paycheck for the next six months and subtracted the bills, then divided the balance by the number of weeks. That was how much we could spend. No more. The only way we would be able to meet our bills was to stick to this plan. At the end of five months we would be caught up, and there would be some extra money for Christmas.

For the first time in our marriage, we had a budget. Actually, the budget figures were quite generous. My husband's income was more than adequate for our needs, but living within it was hard, and we didn't get any breaks. The kids continued to wear out shoes at a horrendous rate, we did not lose our appetites for those occasional expensive restaurant meals, and this time no surprise checks or lucrative job offers came through. Still, we managed to stick to the budget—no matter how tight it seemed — for all five months.

At the end of that time, it occurred to me to ask the Inner Master what I had done to create this lifetime of financial problems. Gradually, the answer started to come through my dreams and contemplations.

Then one morning before my spiritual exercise I asked the question again. I closed my eyes and sang HU. When I opened my eyes to my inner vision a beautiful young woman stood before me. Her blond hair was cut short in the bobbed style of the day. Her green eyes were smudged with dark eyeliner.

In a gentle, almost childish voice, she spoke of the corrupting influence of money. "Look at my father," she pointed out. "He used his money for power and didn't care who got hurt in the bargain." As she spoke I could imagine the cruel and capricious parent who had oppressed this woman beyond her limits. To escape she had run away to finish that lifetime in the gutters of Paris.

When I realized this woman was me in a past life, I could go back and forth between her world and mine, seeing the truth from both points of view. I had had the benefits of great wealth in that lifetime, but money was not something I appreciated then. Wealth was like air, or water, or my own beauty — always there. When I did allow myself to think about it, it was with feelings of guilt for having so much while others around me had so little — and feelings of shame at how my father used his money for control.

Because of this belief from the past there were many opportunities for wealth that I had thrown away in this lifetime.

I saw how often I had relied on others to take care of me. I thought relinquishing control over money would absolve me of any of the past responsibility and guilt. I spoke to the woman, showing her how her attitudes had traveled through time to restrict me in this lifetime.

I came out of the contemplation with a great sense of relief.

The cushion in our budget is a little softer now, but things have not really changed. We still need to work hard and watch our spending. After years of going around with our hands out to Divine Spirit, it's not always easy. But with each step toward financial independence we feel greater pride in our own abilities.

So at a time when I thought we had run out of miracles, I received the greatest one of all — proof that the Mahanta loves me enough to teach me to stand on my own two feet.

A Business Challenge

Ed Spaulding

y job was going well. I was a salesman for a printing company and had landed a number of large accounts. My commissions were increasing every month, and I was happy and excited about the future.

Then the owner of the company, Dave, called me into his office one day. "Ed," he said brusquely, "I want you to sign a new contract." It retroactively lowered commissions which he had yet to pay me. I would lose over ten thousand dollars. The new contract greatly limited my future earnings.

When I protested, Dave told me bluntly, "You're making more than your job is worth. I have to restructure your commissions."

In shock at the sudden turn of events, I muttered something about needing time to look over the contract then stumbled out of Dave's office.

I put off signing the contract for several days. The more I tried to negotiate with Dave, the angrier and more intimidating he became. When I sat down to do my spiritual exercises, I realized I was caught in a web of emotional and mental turmoil.

Trying to talk with Dave was emotionally draining.

I was hurt by his unwillingness to communicate. Finally he gave me an ultimatum, "Sign the contract, or you're fired!"

I realized I didn't trust my boss anymore. I couldn't keep working for him.

Silently within myself, I began to sing HU, to keep my balance. Then I told him, "Dave, I quit. But I want to be paid what is owed me according to the old commission structure."

Dave flew into a rage. His face turned as red as a beet. He physically shoved me out of the building. I felt lucky to escape without harm.

As I drove away, I felt relieved. But I also felt cheated out of a lot of money. I was so terrified of Dave that I didn't know if it was worth going after my lost commissions.

Partly out of avoidance and partly because I needed a break, I stopped thinking about the situation. I calmed myself and started a new business in another area of the printing field.

I was driving to my new office one day when I noticed a large rusty car following me. Waves of fear and anger washed over me. Dave was having me followed. A game of cat and mouse ensued as I let the other car pass and then tried to catch up with it, but I lost him in traffic.

Later I looked out my office window and saw the same rusty car at a stop sign. My heart started to pound. I chanted HU to myself, asked for divine protection, and ran out to confront the driver. Questioning my own sanity, I knocked on the window of the rusty car.

The man swore loudly at being caught. Then he rolled down the window and shouted, "I should be beating you up right now."

In my most calming voice I said, "Why is Dave paying you to follow me?"

"Dave says you're out to destroy his business. He told me you needed to be watched. He even offered me a two-hundred-dollar bonus if I would beat you up!"

I stared openmouthed as he continued, "My brother said you were a nice guy. He knows you from work and advised me not to do it." As the man drove away, I stood wondering, *Why has my life suddenly been transformed into a bad TV movie?*

There was no avoiding Dave now. My anger was stronger than my fear. I called and said, "You better stop having me followed!"

He denied everything and told me instead that I was stealing his customers. If I didn't stop, he was going to sue me.

As I hung up the phone, I realized I needed to see a lawyer. I needed to know my rights in order to compete fairly with my old boss. I picked a law office out of the phone book and made an appointment.

The night before I went to see the lawyer, I had a vivid dream that I was back in Dave's office. Dave's wife came up to me, her face filled with fear and desperation. "Please, Ed," she pleaded, "don't you and the lawyer put us through this again." She even mentioned the lawyer's name.

Then Dave came up and said, "I'm going to sue you!" I was surprised he didn't throw me out of the office. Instead he said, "As long as you're here, the least you can do is help out." I noticed he was working on one of the jobs I'd sold, so I joined in.

To make the job work, I had to fold up the contract paper he'd wanted me to sign. I wedged it under a chart to keep it from slipping.

Then the dream shifted, and I was at home. I received the same piece of paper back from Dave in the mail. On it was written the amount of money that would settle our differences.

When I awoke, I wrote the dream down and felt encouraged. But I had to rush off to meet with a lawyer from the law firm I'd found. When I got there, I was shocked to discover the attorney who would be helping me had the same name Dave's wife had given in the dream!

I showed the lawyer my documents and described the situation. His eyes lit up with dollar signs. "This will be an easy case to win," he gloated. Perhaps he sensed some reluctance on my part, because he said, "I'll even waive the normal retainer to get us started. Just sign here."

I just sat there, thinking about my dream and what it meant. It seemed to me that if I sued Dave I would be repeating something from a past life. If I found another way to work things out with Dave, our karma could be resolved once and for all.

I told the lawyer I needed to think things over and left.

Later, in contemplation, I expressed my frustration to the Mahanta. I asked if I could see the past life that had resulted in such intense conflict between Dave and me.

The Mahanta said, "You'll see these past lives in time. For now, I'll arrange a meeting with Dave, Soul to Soul, to begin to work out your karma."

In my contemplation, the Mahanta opened a door. In walked Dave, smiling and full of light. It was great to see him happy and willing to talk with me. Here in a higher state of consciousness, we shared the goal of resolving all karma between us.

I asked Dave about the behavior of his human consciousness. He said, "I'm afraid of you!"

I found this amazing since I was so afraid of him. I then asked, "Well, how can we work things out on the outer, since I can't speak with you?"

Dave smiled and said calmly, "A way will be provided."

I thanked him and the Mahanta, because I now was beginning to feel things could really work out.

A few days later, I received a very threatening letter from Dave's lawyer. But at the end of the letter it said if I had any questions I could call him. "Aha!" I cried aloud. "This is the way Dave has provided for communication."

The meeting with my lawyer had convinced me I was in a position of legal strength. So I called Dave's lawyer and explained my case to him. I told him all I wanted was the commission I was owed.

Later in the day, Dave's lawyer called back. Although he'd obviously had a pretty rough session with his client, he had convinced Dave to pay me in full!

For the next year, I received monthly checks from Dave in the mail. This monthly income enabled me to sustain myself while I built my own business, a goal I'd had for some time.

I realized that the experience with Dave had strengthened me. It had given me the courage to take the risk of forming my own business. Next to the risk of enduring another difficult boss, starting a new venture seemed easy.

After a year, Dave's lawyer called. "Dave's willing to meet with you to reach a final agreement," he informed me.

As I prepared to call Dave and set up an appointment, I realized I was still terrified of him. So I went into contemplation and met again with him Soul to Soul.

I asked, "Would you please tell me what you need to keep your composure when we meet?"

When I called Dave, the first thing he said to me was, "We'll sit down and go over the books. But I can't handle any discussion. Please respond to me in writing."

I realized this was what he needed to keep his balance, so I agreed. We had two tense meetings. I kept my agreement not to argue with him in person. We resolved our differences on paper, struck an agreement, and went our separate ways.

Shortly after our last meeting, I had a vision. I saw Dave and me in a past life. He had cheated me in a business situation, and I had responded vindictively, ruining his business. Suddenly I saw that Dave's tremendous anger in this life was simply a mirror of my own hatred from the past. It was just coming back to me in the present setting.

I had to work off the karma for ruining his old business by helping Dave build his present company into a success. When he cheated me in this life, it was a golden opportunity for me to grow spiritually. I could work things out in a balanced way, while facing my own anger at myself and him from the past. As I forgave Dave, I was forgiving myself.

A year and a half later, I ran into Dave on the street. I was surprised when, instead of getting into his car, he came over to me. He smiled and shook my hand.

"Just after our last meeting, I had a severe heart

attack," he said. "I nearly died. The doctor told me I had to sell my business if I wanted to live."

Dave had spent the past year traveling around the world with his family, having a wonderful time. He commented, "It's great to get to be the nice guy in life. My only regret from the business was how I treated you."

Quietly, Dave apologized to me. I accepted his apology with tears in my eyes, and we were both swept with a wave of emotion.

I felt the presence of the Mahanta. With it came the knowingness that, at long last, our karma was completely healed.

As I stood there looking into Dave's eyes, I recognized the beautiful Soul I had met in contemplation, now outwardly manifested.

5

iving from the Heart

When you step onto the path and ask Spirit to come into your life and give you greater unfoldment, It will; the Sound and Light pour into you whether or not you're conscious of it. It will pour in for perhaps a year or two, sometimes longer; then when you get filled up, you have to learn what to do with It. This is the next step, this learning how to give in some way that suits you.

—Sri Harold Klemp,
How to Find God

During the workshop, I led them through a short imaginative exercise in which they went to an inner river of Light and Sound.

HU, a Love Song to God

Mike DeLuca

My sister recently married a man whose five-year-old son from a previous marriage had died suddenly. Her husband had carried tremendous pain from that loss for many years. One evening my sister, her husband, and I were having a discussion about dreams and the HU.

I told them how we work with dreams in Eckankar, that we can sing the holy word HU to help us remember and understand our dreams. My brother-in-law looked very interested, so I said that HU can also bring healing from painful experiences.

"I've often had the beginnings of dreams with my son," he said, "but fear and anxiety shut off the dreams before I can actually meet him."

I suggested he try singing HU before he falls asleep.

A few days later he called me, very excited. He'd tried singing HU and had a dream where he actually met his son. He was able to tell the young boy many things he'd never been able to say before. His son replied that he was truly happy now. This relieved his father very much.

Soon after this, my brother-in-law started a local chapter of a national support group for bereaved parents. Because of his positive experience with singing HU, he asked me to do a workshop on dreams and the HU for these parents. A couple from Ireland attended. They were Roman Catholics who had moved to the United States a few years earlier. Their eldest daughter had suddenly fallen ill and died in their arms. The experience had shattered them.And because their families were back in Ireland, they had no support.

During the workshop, these two were able to try singing HU. I led them through a short imaginative exercise in which they went to an inner river of Light and Sound. When the wife came out of the exercise, she said it was the first time in a long while that she had felt some peace.

When they got home, they decided they had nothing to lose by trying the exercise again. Maybe it could bring them some understanding about their daughter.

So they sang HU together and went to sleep.

That night, the wife traveled to a hospital in her dreams. She was very conscious of all that happened. When she arrived, she was told that her daughter was no longer there; she knew this meant the child was no longer in pain. Later in the dream she saw her daughter surrounded by a circle of children.

"I'm fine," the daughter said to her mother. "I don't hurt anymore. I feel happy, and I have a job to do, working with these children. It's just wonderful here."

The mother said, "I just can't wait to bring you to your dad and tell him all this."

"Mommy," the girl replied, "I can't go with you. This is where I belong now. But you can come visit me anytime you want."

"How?" asked the woman.

"Just do what you did to get here. It will bring you

here again," the daughter told her.

Before she knew it, the wife was back home. Excitedly she told her husband all that had happened. Then they told their other children, who began having dream experiences with their sister.

Later that week the couple went to their Bible study class and told how they had found healing through this spiritual exercise. They later told my brother-in-law that they want everyone to know how important it is to try singing HU and ask for assistance in their dreams.

The HU and the Mahanta are here for everyone.

Halloween Surprise

Cameron Fox

he Halloween committee met every week for six weeks to plan the party for the hospital employees. We wanted everyone to have plenty of time to decide upon their costumes.

Many of the hospital jobs revolve around crisis intervention and other stressful life-and-death situations. These parties are a time when all departments can share their lunch hour, dress up in bizarre costumes, laugh, and regain a playful, childlike spirit.

The music began promptly at eleven o'clock on the day of the party. Several committee members placed baked goods on the table to be judged. Then the judges — the hospital director, the dietitian, the chaplain, and others — went from item to item tasting the delicious food. Hospital employees started coming in — many more than we had expected. The room soon filled with laughing people dressed in costume. This year the costumes were especially creative. One person, dressed as a bag of dirty clothes, had so many rags covering him no one could guess who he was.

After prizes were awarded for the baking contest, the judges took their seats so they could see the contestants in costume as they walked across the stage.

The room was crowded with contestants, committee members, and other members of the hospital staff. All eyes were on the stage. One by one, contestants began to walk slowly across the stage. Some performed a skit to go along with the costume. Raggedy Ann did a short dance, the rock singer sang for us, and the soldier marched.

I found a comfortable place to sit toward the back of the room. I closed my eyes for a moment and began to inwardly sing HU. Singing this love song to God is something I often do. It gives me a sense of peace and purpose, and lessens the anxiety I sometimes feel during a busy or stressful day.

After singing quietly for a few moments, I opened my eyes and gazed around the room. I had the feeling I might be dreaming, yet I knew I was not. I looked down at my Gypsy costume. I had dressed as a Gypsy every Halloween for years. As a child I had even performed in a chorus of Gypsy dancers for a ballet recital. I closed my eyes for a moment and saw a vivid picture, much like a picture postcard. It was a view of me dancing around a fire with others dressed as Gypsies. I realized that by choosing this outfit again and again, I was stepping back to a time in the eleventh century when I was learning lessons of survival as a Gypsy.

Many times in my job as a counselor I am called on to assist patients to find meaning in life. This requires my teaching basic survival skills such as physical, mental, and environmental health. As counselor, I often find myself around highly emotional, even unpredictable people. I am not upset by this. I know I learned survival skills and an ability to balance uncertainties during that Gypsy lifetime. They continue to be useful to me even today.

Sitting in the back of the room, I felt as if I were surrounded by light. That light projected to several other co-workers in the room — the gorilla, the pilgrim, the cat, the Indian, and the soldier. Of all the costumed workers, these were the most comfortable and believable in their roles. I wondered if they had chosen their costumes for the same reason I had chosen mine — for the chance to step back into the past.

When these contestants took their turns upon the stage, everyone in the room applauded. The judges, too, were obviously impressed. These five were each awarded the top prize — dinner for two at the best restaurant in town.

After this, Halloween has taken on a whole new meaning! It will never be quite the same for me again.

The Little Green Frog

Carol Shellenburg

n an ECK spiritual exercise I asked the Mahanta if I could work in the inner worlds in the dream state. I hoped to be of service by working with Souls translating from the physical plane. I had almost forgotten my request when I received a telephone call from my daughter.

"My mother-in-law, Karen, asked me to thank you," she said. "She is feeling much better about Justin."

Justin was Karen's grandson. He had fallen to his death from a high-rise hotel while the family was on vacation. Justin had been a very troubled little boy. His temper and emotions were often out of control and grew worse as he approached his teens. The family was left agonizing over the question on whether he fell or jumped to his death.

I recalled the last time I saw Justin. He had made a little green frog out of paper for me—a very clever craft for one so young. His gift touched me deeply. I put it away, never dreaming Justin would not be with us much longer.

So why was his grandmother thanking me? My daughter's next words left me stunned.

"Mom, Karen said that you came to her in a brilliant, vivid dream and told her that Justin's death had been an accident. It was just time for Justin to leave."

Although I did not recall the dream, the experience was both gratifying and humbling. The Mahanta had allowed me to realize the importance of asking when one wants to be of service to the ECK. I treasure the gift from a young boy, and I am grateful for the ever-constant gifts from the Mahanta.

A Gift of Life

Henry I. Bunting

I know that life continues after death. Before I stepped on the path of Eckankar, I felt I was destined to live a short life and die a violent death—this was to be my payment for certain past-life karmic debts. However, karma is changeable. My relationship with my spiritual teacher, the Mahanta, the Living ECK Master, saw to that.

One evening I prepared to leave my home in Port Harcourt, Nigeria, when a scuffle ensued in the street. A short, thickset policeman in civilian clothes drew a pistol and fired twice at his opponent, a naval officer also in civilian clothes. He missed him by a hairbreadth. Pandemonium broke out on the street as everyone ran for their lives.

I quickly grabbed my six-month-old niece and yelled urgently to other family members, "Get into the house!" They immediately took cover.

I managed to get inside and was about to lock the door when I saw a sudden flash of white light and felt an excruciating pain in my lower back. My eyes shone in shock as blood flowed down my legs. A bullet had pierced the door and hit me.

"Good God! Mahanta, Mahanta, I have been shot.

175

I am going to die," I said inwardly.

My legs buckled, and I slumped, dropping the screaming baby into a chair. Then I began to lose consciousness.

At that time, I had heard of Eckankar but had not yet had the opportunity to become a member. *Will the Inner Master, Wah Z, wait for me at the border of the next world?* I wondered. *Why hadn't he forewarned me that this would happen, or better yet, prevented it?* A nagging thought dwelt in my mind: What about my mission to be a Co-worker with the Mahanta here on earth?

Somehow Soul took over from mind. As I lay in a growing pool of my life's blood, I began to silently chant the holy name of God, HU. I started drifting into a blissful sleep, as my eyelids became heavier and heavier. Sweet, gentle death beckoned me.

I managed to glance in my brother's direction, and I saw fear flood his face. He was frightened that the family might lose me. I felt a strong love bond holding us together.

"No, not yet!" something within me screamed. I suddenly felt a surge of new life. If I was to die, I wouldn't die in the house like a helpless baby. I would die fighting.

I managed to stand up, open the door, and stagger into the street. The Mahanta's hand was at work, because a passing taxi drove up at that instant, and my brother helped me in. I was taken to a clinic where I stayed for a week. Fortunately, the injury wasn't a crippling one.

While I was at the clinic, anger welled up within me as I cursed the man who harmed me. I wanted compensation. I threatened to take him to court.

Months later, I asked the Mahanta, "What was that all about?" In my dreams, I realized that in a past lifetime I had avenged the death of a girlfriend by killing her murderer. I escaped being caught in that incarnation. In this lifetime, my girlfriend had reincarnated as my small niece. I had saved her life this time, but I had been shot by her past murderer, who was the police officer in the street.

As I wondered at this dream, I received more spiritual insight from the book *Soul Travelers of the Far Country* by Harold Klemp. In it Paul Twitchell instructs him, "One who is destined to find ECK in this life may be spared an 'accident' no longer needed to repay a karmic debt from the past."

From this, I recognized my blessings: I had been spared an early death by the grace and protection of the Master, and through the essence of God's love I was given the gift of life.

The Red Bicycle

Todd Cramer

It all started one evening as I was talking with my wife. We were appreciative of how blessed we were. We had a beautiful home and two healthy children. We could worship God in our own way, we had enough to eat, and there was great love in our lives.

"It would be so nice to give some of this love back to life," my wife commented.

"Yes," I agreed, "but I don't want to just write a check to some charity. It would be more rewarding to personally help someone."

"It would," said Valerie, "but I wouldn't know where to start."

"I guess you couldn't just go down to some corner in Philadelphia and start handing out hundred-dollar bills," I mused. "It wouldn't really change anyone's life for long." So we consciously handed this goal over to the Holy Spirit, the ECK—and promptly forgot about it.

I didn't find out until three months later that as we spoke, a family from another part of the world was praying to God as hard as they could for someone to help them.

One afternoon, my children came in from the

backyard and said, "We made a new friend. His name is Sasha. He doesn't speak any English, and he's from a town we can't pronounce."

The next day, the boy came to play and the children became better friends. I still didn't understand who he was or where he came from. On the third day, I finally met the eight-year-old boy. From what I could make out, he was from Ukraine. He and his family had just immigrated to the U.S. To him, our house was Disneyland, so he began to spend more and more time with us.

Since his English was nonexistent, we communicated through sign language and smiles. Later I discovered that his family had arrived just a few weeks before and had been given temporary refuge down the street from us. When we said good-bye to him, I waved to his parents down the street, but we still didn't talk.

One summer afternoon, I saw Sasha standing in my driveway. He was watching my daughter and son ride their bikes up and down the sidewalks. There was a look in his face that an eight-year-old boy has when he doesn't have a bike and everyone else does.

Then and there, I decided to get Sasha a bright, shiny red bicycle. I left for the store without saying anything to my family.

When I got back, my kids were watching TV. Sasha had gone home. So I asked them to take the bike to Sasha's house and give it to him as a present from them.

About an hour later, there was a knock on the door. I met Sasha's father. He had only two words in English, but he used them to good effect: "Thank you! Thank you! Thank you!" he beamed.

That marked the beginning of our friendship.

Over the next few months, we learned they were religious refugees. Devout Pentecostal Christians, they and their fellow worshipers had sought asylum in the U.S. Sasha's family had been temporarily placed with a family on our block. Sasha's parents were at their wits' end. They had no jobs, no money, nowhere to live, no English, and Vera, the wife, was pregnant.

One day I saw Vera talking to my wife. They were both crying. Vera had come to say good-bye. The social-services agency had found the family a place to live downtown. It was not a very nice apartment, but they could get by for a while.

That's when it clicked.

We'd been asking for a way to give help, and here it was. My wife and I looked at each other. Sasha's family would stay with us in our large house!

The Ukrainian family lived with us for one year. Our project was to help them become a happy American family. That's when the miracles really began in our neighborhood.

It started with the red bicycle. Soon there was a chain reaction of giving among the people in our community. As they came to understand the Ukrainians' story, they caught the spirit and joy of helping somebody else.

In the first year, the Ukrainian family received countless appliances, a mountain of food, and eleven color TVs. That meant ten other Ukrainian families received new TV sets.

A friend of mine called and wanted to get in on the action. He asked, "How can I help?"

Fascinated, I replied, "Well, we're really getting a little tired driving the family around. They don't have a car."

So he gave them a car.

The counselor at school heard their story. Her mother-in-law had passed away recently. Rather than sell her things, she gave the Ukrainian family the entire contents of the apartment. So we stored all sorts of furniture in our basement until Sasha's family was ready to leave.

I noticed that they had better stuff than I did.

My dentist fixed their teeth for free. And the gifts went on and on. To me, it was a stunning example of how a single act can start a chain reaction.

When you give, you can open the lives and hearts of many, many people.

I'm grateful for learning that. When you give, you can live your dream of the best possible life: one in which you uplift yourself spiritually while reaching out a hand to help someone else.

Every word and action from an awakened heart lives forever. Do you have an opportunity to give a "red bicycle" to someone you know?

Seabird Rescue

Johanna Kothbauer

have always been skeptical of miracles. As a doctor in Munich, Germany, my miracles are to discover exactly how the eyes work and can be healed, for instance, or how they interact with the brain.

But once during a long journey to the other side of the world, a different sort of miracle occurred.

I spent eighteen days in a little village on the northern coast of New Zealand. One day I noticed that one of the seagulls had one foot caught in several angler's lines and hooks. The foot was so bound up, it could not reach the ground. I guessed there must be a hook lodged under the wing at the side of the breast, which held the lines that bound the leg. The bird was able to fly, but it could not walk.

Each day, I fed the bird, crawled very close to him, and spoke to him of his problem and an easy way out of it if he would let me help. Sometimes I had the scissors with me. But the bird did not allow my hand to come within a yard of his leg.

For some reason, the bird's dilemma was totally compelling to me. I went out and bought a piece of fisherman's netting, and enlisted the help of a hotel neighbor, Win. I had high hopes for getting the bird free. Win was a former military test pilot and had once sailed from San Francisco to Auckland. He told me he'd once freed an albatross from a hook. But even with Win's help, I could not catch the bird.

Soon helpful Win and family had to return to Auckland. I sat down to give the bird's plight some careful consideration. Perhaps I could give him some medicine in his food that would make him drowsy. My scheme did not work. The bird could still easily out-maneuver me. A sadness washed over my heart. I could not help the crippled seagull except to feed him.

As I studied the seagull, I decided he must be plagued by at least three hooks. One large hook was fixed in his breast. It anchored a smaller line whose hook had pierced the right leg and bound it. A third line was ensnared with the second. Its hook hung halfway down the tangled leg.

Each morning at dawn, the bird waited in front of my window. I blessed him in the name of God, Divine Spirit, and my spiritual guide, the Mahanta.

I became so upset, I faxed a letter to my friend Sigrun in Munich, telling her about the bird. Sigrun faxed me a letter back: "Perhaps another bird will help." Maybe she imagined a very kind bird would bite away the lines.

As I fed the bird some cheese, I pondered Sigrun's words. All at once a small, greedy seagull swooped in to steal the food. But one of its wings caught on the small, dangling hook.

The larger bird flapped skyward, with the small seagull hanging from his leg, trying to fly with its free wing. What a mess! Both birds plunged into the water with a large splash.

I shouted for help as I watched the birds spread

their wings to hold their beaks above water. They looked like two wet rags. I ran for the net and the scissors from my cabin. After much chasing and shouting, I eventually drove them into a bush and got the net over them.

First I freed the small seagull from the hook. He immediately took wing. Then I turned to the cripple bird's leg. What a joy, after two weeks of longing, to finally hold that cold little foot!

The bird eyed me quietly, perhaps knowing I meant no harm. Gently I located a big hook at the side of its breast. It was difficult to remove. The hook was stuck firmly between the feather quills, with a kind of glue formed by fat and dirt. But finally I got it free! I quickly removed the other lines from his legs, and the bird flapped its powerful wings and headed toward freedom.

Over the next day or so, I continued to watch his progress on the beach. At first, he could not reach the ground with his once-bound leg. I wondered if the bird would ever overcome the atrophy of the muscles and tendons.

About that time, I had to leave, but I was scheduled to return about five weeks later. When I came back from my trip, the hotel owner said, "Oh, it's you! You know, that seagull you helped has waited each day for you in front of your old window!"

I took my old room, and watched for the bird. Soon I saw him running along the strand, only limping a tiny bit! It was a wonderful miracle.

My Spiritual Tour of Duty

Walt Wrzesniewski

he day after the United Nation's deadline for Iraq's withdrawal from Kuwait, my wife and I sat down to supper in the United States. Suddenly I felt as if I were surrounded by exploding bombs. I could feel the terrific concussions and hear the explosions. I could see the dirt fly up. As Soul, I observed this with a dispassionate, yet compassionate, spiritual vision, feeling no pain or fear.

I turned my attention back to my wife, still sitting at our tranquil supper table, and announced that the bombing had just started. The war in the Persian Gulf had begun. A short time later the television newscasters confirmed this.

Over the next few months in my thoughts, dreams, and contemplations, I spent much time Soul Traveling throughout the Middle East. This was my spiritual tour of duty.

One morning I awoke and told my wife that Saddam Hussein was hidden in a bunker below his presidential palace. I knew he was unafraid, even calm in the midst of the chaos of war. In time, television broadcasts would confirm this.

One day I found my attention on a battlefield. The bodies of Iraqi soldiers were scattered about. Some

Souls lingered near their lifeless physical bodies, not quite sure what they should do. Other Souls swayed, drifting almost completely out of the body then back inside again. The rest of the soldiers were in great shock and pain, but here and there some felt relief.

I was not alone in my spiritual mission. Moving about the battlefield were other Souls from many different faiths, working, like myself, with strength and compassion. We were all working together with the purest love to help the soldiers. Some of the soldiers were guided across the veil of death, some were given strength to handle pain, and some found the comfort they needed to regain their composure.

Once, in my inner travels, I came upon a mother and her young son hiding under a stairway. She enveloped her child in her arms as the nearby bombing filled the air with dust. Backed into a corner, she prayed fiercely for help. These prayers were answered. Although the bombing continued, she felt the comfort and knew the serenity of the Light and Sound of God.

Battlefield duty was only a small part of the spiritual service for which we were commissioned during the war in the Persian Gulf. We guided downed airmen and pointed the way for the rescuers searching for them. We reached out to comfort families and other loved ones when news of a loss arrived. And we helped lighten the fears of those people who huddled in desperation while the world shook terribly around them.

Throughout these experiences, I was filled with gratitude to the Mahanta, the Living ECK Master that I could be of help in this way. Serving God is the highest duty, and duty was never so gratifying.

Gift of an Open Heart

Bonnie Anderson

*B*abies can be wonderful little channels for divine love. I experienced this with the birth of my second daughter, Debby Louise. We weren't planning to have a baby, but Debby came with perfect spiritual timing. We had moved to Minnesota from Oregon and begun new jobs. My husband and I and my ten-year-old daughter, Julia, were comfortably settled in our new routines, but Julia kept pestering us to provide her with a sister or brother. Since I had finally begun to make some progress in my career, we didn't seriously consider having another child.

"When are you going to have a baby so my kids will have an aunt or uncle?" she asked over and over. I began telling her, "Ask the Mahanta. You'll have a sister or brother when God gives you one."

When Julia went off to Oregon to visit her dad that August, she teasingly asked, "Are you going to start a baby while I'm gone?" We just smiled at her audacity. Yet when she returned she told me of a dream where I had had a baby girl. I didn't suspect I might be pregnant, but sure enough, within three weeks the doctor confirmed it.

We took Julia out to dinner that night and told her the news. At first she thought we were kidding. Then her eyes got big and round. "Really?" she said. Yes, we told her, we're going to have a baby in May.

Because of her dream, Julia was certain she would have a sister. "I'll love the baby just the same if it's a brother, Mom," she'd tell me, "but it's going to be a sister." The approaching birth united us as a family. We had been mother, daughter, and stepdad before. Now the baby became a focal point of love, which brought us together as never before.

Debby finally arrived two weeks late. A cesarean section was done. We sang HU during the cesarean to help us stay calm and focused, and to celebrate the spirituality of the birth. Debby cried when she was born until the nurse brought her to me. When Debby heard my voice, she quieted and looked into my eyes.

From four to six weeks of age, Debby "spoke" to us constantly. She was very serious about it and by her facial expressions was obviously trying to say something very important. It was as if she were telling us the secrets of the universe, if only we could translate what she was saying. Six weeks after her birth we celebrated her ECK Consecration Ceremony in the Temple of ECK. Then she stopped using her special language. Maybe she was content now that this significant spiritual event had taken place.

When I held Debby in my arms, I felt as if my heart would burst with love. A small stream inside began to open my heart wider and wider until it was a rushing torrent. I marveled at the effect this tiny baby was having on me.

The time came to return to work, and I placed Debby in a day-care home. There I experienced more learning about love. Sandi was a woman near my own age who really loved the children in her care. I, on the other hand, was often uneasy around other people's children. Now when I visited the day-care home to nurse Debby on my lunch breaks, I watched Sandi care for the toddlers. She resolved tot-sized conflicts with firm but loving discipline, involving simple explanations followed by hugs.

A three-year-old named Lara was clever at provoking the younger children when Sandi's back was turned. I'd watch her as I nursed Debby, marveling at the way Sandi handled the toddler. "Lara, don't hit Tina," she'd say. "It hurts her and makes me sad." I was slowly learning my own lessons on how to care for children by watching Sandi. They responded well to her love and simple logic. I saw when each child was treated with love and dignity, it brought out the best in them. Children are each unique as Soul, doing the best they can.

As I write, Debby is now thirteen months old and beginning to walk and talk. Her antics have brought smiles, laughter, and joy. To me she is a gift from God, one that has opened my heart wider than I could have ever imagined. She's a little miracle of love.

Ride Along, Cowboy

Graeme Crawshaw

hen I was a small child my father used to sing a lullaby that went "Ride along cowboy, ride along to the big corral."
I didn't know it at the time, but in a way, preparation was being made for our last shared experience together in this world.

Recently, after a very brief illness, my father was admitted to a nearby hospital, where his condition suddenly deteriorated. In a few short days, I was informed that he would live only a matter of hours. I rushed to the hospital with other family members. After talking briefly with them, I left my unconscious father and went off to a quiet room to contemplate. I sang HU for a while. Then an inner scene appeared in my mind's eye.

A huge wall was suspended in time and space. Many doors opened on the wall. A number of Souls were waiting near the wall, including my father. He was in a terribly confused state, near panic.

I was there long enough to catch his attention. Relief flooded his countenance as I held up my hand to him and said, "Be calm." Then I was drawn out of contemplation and back to his bedside. I squeezed his hand and assured him outwardly again that everything was going to be OK.

Returning once again to the quiet room, I went back into contemplation. The wall reappeared, and I found Dad astride a dancing white horse. He seemed very relaxed, almost back to his usual mischievous self! You can imagine my relief when I saw he was OK. "Wait for me," I told him. "I'll come with you in just a few minutes." He nodded his head.

I returned to Dad's room to find the situation was critical. With a sigh, his body ceased to function. I stayed with the rest of the family who were beginning their grieving for the "lost" life. During the emotional minutes of reaction, I forgot about my inner appointment.

But as soon as I could, I slipped away to the little room again, and back to the inner wall.

As soon as I arrived, it was obvious the proceedings had been waiting for my return. Immediately, we were accelerated to a phenomenal speed. We streaked through a particular door like two beams of flashing white light.

On the far side of the wall was an immense space, almost without end. It dropped away below us and extended out in front with no horizon. I found myself suspended lightly above and behind my father, who was still on horseback. A path appeared in front of us, and we began to swoop like a roller coaster over its surface. The path curved around to the left and back to the right again. Our destination became brightly lit, a space-age "mother ship" with thousands of twinkling lights.

Like a bullet, my traveling companions flew into their landing bay between two of the lights. Suddenly, thousands of Souls gathered around me for an instant to witness the event. As soon as I sensed the completion of this moment, I was delivered back to the easy chair in the quiet hospital room.

I felt a great wave of joy at having been honored with this exquisite inner experience.

I quietly walked back to gather my relatives. I found that gently sharing my story with individual family members has helped them through this time of my father's passing. They feel reassured that he is happy and well.

I am grateful for the opportunity to accompany my father on his last great journey. After all, he helped me adjust to the adventure of my present life, singing sweetly to his son, "Ride along cowboy, ride along to the big corral."

6

amily and
Relationships

Soul gains experience, thereby gaining expression of Its divine self. In the process, Soul must learn to receive love and to give love.

—Sri Harold Klemp,
The Dream Master

Put all of yourself in your task, and God will be there too.

Journey from Faith

Mary Carroll Moore

I grew up in my grandmother's religion. She was a leading Presbyterian at Brown Memorial and had a unique understanding about God. She combined faith healing, bake sales, homemade sermons, and weather predictions. Her faith made her a rock in the church community and the strongest person I knew.

At age four I began spending weekdays with Grandmother while my mother worked.

Mom dropped me off each morning about seven. I tiptoed into the apartment. Grandmother would be having her quiet time. During this hour, I was informed, my grandmother talked to God.

Grandmother's chats with the Divine helped her approach each day with an organized mind and spirit. In a fifteen-cent spiral-bound notepad by her chair, she would record what God told her to do. Celestial messages ranged from "Call the butcher about Saturday" to "Write a card to Angie about her son."

To my way of thinking, God gave her very ordinary instructions, but she believed that God liked it when you carried through. At four, I was learning a basic spiritual principle: Clean up your life as you go, so you don't have to do it later.

Grandmother took charge of cleaning up other people's lives too. Her business and life's mission was a summer hiking-and-canoeing camp for children. She never advertised; she had faith that word of mouth and God's will would bring the right children to her door. The camp was rarely lacking for applicants, and many came back every summer of their childhood. Although we made fun of her all-purpose connection with God, we only half-scoffed when Grandmother's faith brought sunny weather and a good wind right before a sailing race.

A year before Grandmother died, Mom called cross-country one evening to tell me someone had mugged my grandmother: they had knocked her down and stolen her purse. She had lain there in the cold, hurt and frail, waiting for God to help her. But it was an hour before anyone came. Later she was angry. Angry that such a safe section of town should be prey to such activity. Angry that her husband sat alone upstairs awaiting her return instead of being at her side, sheltering and protecting her. Angry, most of all, that the God she talked to each morning had let her lie helpless on the pavement.

When I saw her about a month later, fear had replaced the anger. Her faith had been mortally shaken, and she simply waited to die.

Her faith, based on a physical strength and a mental ability to carry through, had shattered around her like pieces of brittle glass at the first serious doubt. Now she wondered if God really could protect her when she had nowhere else to turn.

I was to face the same doubt, ten years later.

Like my grandmother, I had always depended on a special connection with God. Grandmother's faith had rested on outer proof, like good weather and a full camp roster. Mine had been shored up by outer miracles, brilliant inner experiences, and a strong sense of knowing what to do next.

My faith had been untested for fifteen years. Then God tapped me on the shoulder when my life was at an all-time high. The tests began slowly. At first, it was simply a feeling of losing my spiritual anchor points. I stopped remembering my dreams. Then I lost my inner guidance: I would ask God what to do and end up in a mess when I followed my instinct.

For a year, I watched my world change. Outwardly all was normal. Inwardly, I walked in a place totally unfamiliar to me. Like Grandmother, I struggled with the same fear that God had left me high and dry. But there was one difference between us: Grandmother's religion had not readied her for the natural transition away from human faith to spiritual knowing. But I had the teachings of ECK. Inwardly I asked the Mahanta for help.

Suddenly, after months of blankness, I began to remember a recurring dream. I would be with my grandmother, setting up for a dinner party in her apartment. As we placed the china and silverware along the table's edge, Grandmother would be discoursing on a lesson she had taught me as a child, like carrying through. "To carry through, dear, just concentrate. You know you can do it. Pay attention to how you're placing that dinner plate, how you put the forks on the table. Put all yourself there, and God will be there too."

Night after night I would return in my sleep to her

apartment for instruction, inspiration, and hope — all the things she had given me as a child. She soothed my troubled spirit in the mundane activities that accompanied the dream — brownie-making, dusting the piano, transplanting an African violet.

The dreams lasted for less than a year, and so did my doubts about God.

One day I realized the doubt was gone. During that year I had learned to recognize God in the joy I took in small tasks, like setting the table or reading a poem. I no longer desperately sought evidence in brilliant inner experiences that God loved me. Now I knew God was indeed in all of life, even in the most subtle of things.

About that time, I stopped seeing Grandmother in my dreams. Instead, one night a brief picture of her hallway appeared, accompanied by her voice from the kitchen: "This is the past. I've moved on now."

It took me several months to realize she was giving me her last bit of instruction — and that I too had passed from my crisis of faith and now stood firm in knowingness.

God, Who Should I Marry?

Dennis Calhoun

n college I met a woman I was sure I would marry. From the moment we met, it seemed as if we had always been together. But after we graduated, she got a job in Chicago, and I ended up working in Houston. We maintained a long-distance relationship.

One day during my spiritual exercise I told the Master I was ready to get married.

I explained that I wanted companionship. If the ECK (Divine Spirit) could work it out, and if it were for the good of the whole of life, well, that's what I wanted.

Time passed with no resolution to the situation. Finally my girlfriend and I decided to date other people. It just didn't seem likely that I could transfer to Chicago or that she would move to Houston. Shortly after that, I met a woman, Jaye, and we began dating.

Four months later my company announced they were opening an office in Chicago. I was going to be transferred! I thought, *This is perfect.* I had let go of the situation, and the ECK had provided a way for me to move to Chicago and marry my college girlfriend.

Before I left Houston, Jaye shared her feelings with me. She believed we belonged together. She was certain I felt something for her, too—and I did. But in my mind, in my thoughts, I was headed for my old girlfriend in Chicago.

I moved to Chicago and became engaged. The relationship was peaceful and calm, as if we had been married before. But then all of a sudden, things began to fall apart. Somehow, it just didn't feel right to either of us to get married. Sadly, we broke off our engagement.

Once again I took the situation into contemplation. The answer I received was clear: Follow your heart. Go see Jaye.

I had followed my head, and that hadn't worked out. So I called Jaye. A wonderful feeling rushed into my heart. I knew I wanted to marry Jaye, but I still didn't understand why. I was making a big decision purely on the feeling in my heart.

About a month before we were to be married, Jaye and I went to New Orleans. As we walked, we discussed some wedding details. While in the French Quarter, we turned a corner and looked into a breathtaking courtyard.

In that one moment, I glimpsed an entire past-life experience.

I turned to Jaye in astonishment and saw that something had happened to her too. We began to talk and discovered we'd both had the same vision of a shared past life!

In this previous incarnation, I had been a young man in the southern United States of the late 1850s. In about 1859, I moved north to find a job to pay for medical school. I met a northern woman (my college sweetheart in this life), and we married. Her parents were very wealthy and put me through medical school.

Soon after, the Civil War broke out. I returned to the South to serve as a doctor for the Confederacy. During the time I was stationed in New Orleans, I met a woman (Jaye). We fell deeply in love. But I was married, and so we did not act on our love.

The war ended. I left New Orleans and returned to my wife in the North. Jaye and I lived out our lives without seeing each other again. I spent the rest of that life living comfortably with the woman I almost married in this life.

After the brief glimpse of this past life, I understood why my relationship with my college girlfriend had been so easy. We had been married before. I also understood why I thought we should be married again. The mind likes familiar and comfortable paths.

But I needed fresh experiences and growth in this life. My heart wanted to move on and fulfill the love I had left behind in New Orleans in that life. Jaye and I have been very happy together in our marriage.

Now if I hear two voices—one from my head and one from my heart—I know which is guidance from Divine Spirit. The heart is often more aligned with Soul. Thoughts are from the mind. The mind is a good servant, but a poor master.

I always tell my friends, "When in doubt, follow your heart!"

How to Find a Husband: Listen to Your Inner Voice!

Kathia Haug Thalmann

fter months of carefully planning an extended vacation in the United States, I was finally at the Eckankar seminar in San Francisco. I anticipated seeing friends after the seminar and traveling. But Saturday evening, after listening to Sri Harold Klemp speak, my plans abruptly changed.

I was doing my evening spiritual exercise when, all of a sudden, I knew I had to return to Switzerland tomorrow, as soon as the seminar was over!

Maybe I'm sensing an emergency at home, I thought. But when I called, all was calm. It seemed crazy to have come all this way from Switzerland to San Francisco and not be able to continue my vacation, especially when I had budgeted the time and money to stay. It didn't make sense!

But I have been a member of Eckankar for many years. I've learned to trust the inner instructions that come from the Holy Spirit, the ECK. So I canceled all my flights within the States, called all my friends and told them I couldn't visit; then I resignedly flew back to Switzerland.

Once home, I waited for something exciting to

happen, anything that would explain this sudden interruption of my travel plans. But nothing did.

Then a day or two later, I received a phone call from the brother of my sister-in-law. I barely knew this man. Over the years, we'd met perhaps six times at the baptism, birthday parties, and wedding of our common nephew.

"Kathia, how are you?" he said. It was taking me a few moments to place his name and voice. "I'm going to be in your area to attend a tennis training camp soon," he continued. "I'd like to have dinner with you, if you're free."

I was a little surprised at this invitation, since I hadn't seen the man in at least six years. But then I thought, *Why not?* I casually agreed to join him at a nearby restaurant later in the week.

Over dinner, our conversation took an unexpected turn. This man I barely knew opened his heart and poured out a story of personal drama that had unfolded over the past year. His wife of sixteen years had left him quite unexpectedly for another man. His life had been so secure, planned out in every detail; he had not been prepared for such a shock.

He had been living alone for the last six months. Just the day before, he had received the final divorce papers from his lawyer. "I don't know why I'm telling you all this," he concluded. With sudden conviction he added, "Today a new life is beginning for me!"

My inner voice was nudging me again. It was telling me very firmly: This is why you came home. This is your future husband! I was so shocked I almost fell off my chair! I had no intention of marrying. I tried my best to hide my sudden insight. "So," I asked feebly, "what made you think to call me?"

"You know," he grinned, "it was just a sudden thought. I haven't been out this way in ages. But I just knew I had to get in touch with you. I'm so glad you were home!"

"Me too," I agreed dryly. If I told him what I was thinking, he would get up and run out the door!

Since then, Kurt and I have enjoyed each other's company very much. Without any prompting from me, he became a member of Eckankar. And recently we were married in an ECK wedding ceremony at sunrise on the top of a mountain.

This is not only a love story; it has proven to me that anything can happen when you're open to the guidance of the ECK. It has given me valuable lessons to remember: That the Spiritual Exercises of ECK allow me to listen and perceive the guidance of Divine Spirit; that I must trust and follow this guidance; that Divine Spirit points the way, but I am free to make my own decisions, which then form my life.

I'm glad I didn't scare Kurt at dinner that day with my personal flash of insight. But I did make a commitment to step through the window God had opened for me—and now I feel like I am reaping the gifts of heaven!

Sharing HU with a Friend

Donna Harman

I lost track of my high-school best friend, Pattie, when we went to different colleges. But later, I moved back to Rochester, New York, and we picked up our friendship where we'd left off. Pattie got into Transcendental Meditation, and I became a member of Eckankar. We'd get together with our husbands and talk about spiritual matters. Our relationship continued to grow, even though we had different philosophies and beliefs.

Then Pattie got very sick. She was diagnosed with a tumor of the pituitary gland. It was in a very delicate spot in the middle of her brain, so before attempting surgery, the doctors wanted to try some medication that ended up being very hard on her body.

During the treatment, Pattie asked me if there was anything in Eckankar that might help her.

I told her about singing HU. We discussed how to do a spiritual exercise and the value of watching your inner experiences and developing your own visualizations. I talked to her about her feelings about herself and the tumor.

Pattie was having the most trouble with the fear of death. It was so strong at night that she couldn't sleep. So we made up a little visualization she could practice before she went to bed. She would sing HU, look into her Third Eye at a white light, and imagine that she was well, safe, and taken care of.

Pattie tried the exercise every night and began to see results. She expanded the visualization and imagined that her tumor was shrinking. Her husband, Ted, became fascinated with her exercise and began to sing HU too.

A few weeks later, she had to go back to the doctor for an adjustment in her medication.

The doctor was very surprised: The tumor was shrinking. Pattie started smiling. She knew it was due to singing HU.

The doctor said, "I'm going to slow down your medication. We're going to observe this a little longer. I've got you scheduled for surgery if you need it, but we'll have to take your whole pituitary gland out. We can't separate it from the tumor. So you would have to be on medication for the rest of your life. Let's see if we can avoid that."

A few weeks later, the tumor was still shrinking. Eventually, the gland was free of all signs of cancer. The doctor was puzzled. "You know," he confided, "the medicine we gave you wasn't really supposed to make your tumor go away. It was just supposed to help you control your symptoms until we could operate."

Pattie just grinned. She told me later, "Singing HU and the spiritual exercise was what healed me."

To this day, twelve years later, Pattie and Ted sing HU. Singing HU is an important part of their lives. They are still curious about Eckankar. When they have problems, they ask us, "What kinds of things do you have in Eckankar that might help us?"

Recently I spoke with Ted, and he told me that Pattie's mother has pancreatic cancer and may die soon. As we talked about how this news was affecting the family, we shared some memories and feelings from all the years we had been friends. Before we hung up, I said, "And remember, Ted, you can sing HU when you feel down or need to feel safe and protected." He immediately said, "Oh yes, I always sing HU. As a matter of fact, I was just thinking of you last week, because I saw a car with a license that read *HUUUU*. I smiled when I saw it and said, 'I bet Donna knows the woman in that car!'"

We laughed together for a moment. After we hung up, I realized that I didn't feel that I needed to tell Pattie and Ted anything anymore. Spirit was working with them directly.

Finding Harmony
in the Workplace

Gerald Nonez

I work for a large company that installs alarm systems for New York City businesses. It's a very competitive field, and each job has to be done perfectly for our company to survive.

Last year, we had a complete personnel reorganization. When I learned who I would report to, I groaned inside. My new boss and his general manager both had terrible reputations for being unkind.

The first day was very difficult, as I grumbled about the new assignment. Finally I gave up and said to Divine Spirit, "OK, if this is where you want me, I will try my best to find harmony and divine love in the situation."

Things settled down, and I found the new boss wasn't as bad as my coworkers had said. He just wanted the job done right.

The first week my new boss did a special inspection of a couple of my jobs. He wanted to see how I worked. The next week he seemed pleased. "I won't have to keep checking you," he said gruffly. "From now on, I think I can trust you to get the job done."

Soon a coworker and I were assigned to install a

very large alarm system. When we'd finished, the client called my boss. "The men you sent out did a really lousy job," he complained.

The general manager, not bothering to find out what had really happened on the job, told my boss to discipline me for poor work. But my boss felt something was wrong. "I don't think this guy needs to be reprimanded for sloppiness," he told the general manager. "There must be a mistake somewhere."

My coworkers and I were astonished. My boss had actually stood up for me!

But the general manager wouldn't let the incident pass. He asked my boss to write me up for having made a mistake. My boss came to me with the unhappy news.

"Can I meet with the general manager myself?" I asked. I knew union regulations specified that the manager had to meet with a worker if requested, before putting a reprimand in his file. Both sides have to be able to have their say.

I pulled the computer diagrams for the system in question and carefully looked at them again, preparing for my meeting with the general manager. I knew he was a busy and important man. The New York office accounted for over 20 percent of the firm's revenues, so the general manager had a big role in the company. I took a deep breath and went into his office.

The general manager seemed neutral as he asked me what happened. "Did the system you installed seem to work OK?" he asked. "And if so, why is our client unhappy?"

"I don't know. I tested the whole system twice—not just once—before I left the site," I told him. "There's no reason he should be dissatisfied."

But the manager wasn't convinced. "You must have

done something to make the client unhappy," he maintained. "I think I'll visit them myself." I knew the client was a big customer and probably warranted such personal attention, but what would happen to me? Would I be fired?

Later the general manager called me. He'd talked to the client and found out that the man I had dealt with was working for a promotion. He wanted to look good, but he hadn't taken the time to understand my work. All he looked at was the fact that it took me longer than the estimated time to install the alarm system.

He had told the general manager that something must be wrong with the installation because it had taken me two extra hours to set up the system. And maybe since I had been over the estimated time, I must have skipped some crucial testing steps. By now the general manager knew I had done my job right. He soothed the client and called me to say, "I'm beginning to feel the client misjudged you." I hung up the phone with a big smile of relief.

After his inquiry into my work, the general manager began to stop by to chat from time to time. He seemed to like being around me. I wondered if he could feel the presence of the ECK in my life and actions.

After a few months, the general manager called me into his office. His face told a grim story. "Head-quarters is investigating me," he informed me.

His poor reputation as a manager was catching up with him. In the past, the manager had fired people or sent them home without pay before hearing them out. "They told me I should be more friendly, say 'good morning,' and such. Employees have been writing letters, saying I don't know how to treat people."

The general manager had one month to shape up—
or he would lose his job. So he sought my advice and
feedback. "Be truthful, Gerald. How do you see me?"

"My only interaction with you was fair," I replied.
"You didn't write me up; you found out I'd done my job
right. But you do have a reputation for being a poor
manager."

"Well," he pondered, "what would you suggest I do
to improve my reputation?"

I paused for a moment to invite the ECK into my
answer before I spoke. "I look for two things in a
manager," I said slowly. "First, a good manager likes
people and is open to them. He knows how to ask them
to do things with respect—politely and firmly. Second,
he sets clear goals and objectives that we can all share.
If everything is out in the open—what is expected and
how we're measured for performance—we can all relax
and do our jobs. Those two qualities—friendly firm-
ness, and clear, result-driven management—are all I
ask for."

"Well, I guess I can do that," the general manager
said thoughtfully. "Things could stand to change around
here." From that moment on, he began to open up a
little to others, asking employees for their advice and
talking more.

It took a few weeks before I noticed a change. One
day I thought to myself, *My boss isn't as edgy as he
used to be. The atmosphere is changing around here.*

Things were definitely looking up. We started to
get some feedback on companywide goals. Every week
or so, the general manager stopped by to ask me how
things were going. I felt like I'd become a company
barometer for him.

The month passed, and the general manager was

218

allowed to stay. After that, things really improved at work. Morale has continued to improve as one change after another has found its way into the company.

I've been with this firm for twelve years, always trying to consciously serve Divine Spirit in my thoughts and actions. This series of events gave me a chance to work more directly with the ECK in my job.

It has been a joy to help manifest more of God's love and presence at work. My coworkers are happier, my boss is happier, and I feel like my own self-image has improved as a Co-worker with the Mahanta. I attribute this to the presence of the ECK in my life.

The Same Love Song

Beverly Foster

rowing up, I spent every Sunday morning by my mother's side in the sanctuary of the Main Street Methodist Church. This was the church my mother had loved all her life. She found her spiritual strength in the mild sermons and familiar hymns. Every Sunday I sang the same hymns and listened to the same words, but they never satisfied me. When the minister talked about the Holy Spirit or the love of God, it just whetted my appetite to find out more.

Then I found Eckankar and stepped away from my old church. In this new religion, I discovered a living Master. Instead of just talking about them, he led me in real inner explorations of the worlds of the Holy Spirit.

My mother never understood my religion. I tried to explain to her that she too could have direct experience in the realms of heaven that her church talked about, but she always stopped me.

Eventually I quit trying to interest her in the ECK teachings, and she stopped waiting for me to join her again on Sunday mornings.

Then she became quite ill. Television preachers, visits from the new minister, and an old Bible brought

221

her comfort as she approached her death. All the while, I watched in frustration. I wanted so badly to explain about the Mahanta, my inner spiritual guide, who could lead her confidently from this world to the next. I wanted to share HU, the ancient love song to God that could bring her closer to the Holy Spirit, but her manner stopped me. Religion had been a closed subject between us for too long. Finally I gave up and asked the Mahanta to watch over her as she made the transition to the next world.

A few days after this Mama phoned me. That night she had dreamed about Minneapolis, my home and the home of the Temple of ECK. "You have a beautiful city," she said. The note of awe in her voice told me she had paid a visit to an inner city more beautiful than any physical one.

From that day on, Mama softened in many ways. The next time I visited her, she was eager to see pictures of the Temple of ECK. She even urged me to show them to the good churchgoers who came to visit her.

When Mama's last moments came, it was as if she stepped away from her body and then continued on a journey she had begun long before. I never saw the face of the spiritual guide who led her into her new life, but there was no doubt she was safe and protected. Soon after, I saw her in my dreams, bustling around a very busy corner of heaven.

Weeks later I traveled to an ECK seminar where I planned to take some time off to relax. After an early morning workshop, I took a drive for some sightseeing. I knew exactly where I wanted to go but kept circling one part of town. The map was of no use, and I put it aside.

I turned back to get on the highway but hesitated

at something unusual in the bright blue sky. I drove closer to see tall spires which I recognized at once. It was the tower of the television ministry Mama had watched from her armchair when she could no longer get out of the house on Sunday mornings. I drove to the church parking lot.

Mist from sprinklers under tall trees created a hushed sanctuary within the busy city. I crossed lush lawns to a small prayer chapel where bold brass letters spelled out, "My house shall be a house of prayer for all nations."

Then I walked around to the cathedral. A tour group sat on the left side of the vast sanctuary. Several aisles farther up near the front sat an old man in a wheelchair. I chose a seat and listened to the tour guide talk for a few minutes. Then, still not sure why I had come, I got up to leave. When I reached the door, a member of the tour group stopped me.

The old man in the wheelchair had once directed the choir, she said. Now he was nearing death. Today was his birthday. As a special tribute to him the organist was going to play a private recital on the three-story-high-and-just-as-wide pipe organ.

Wondering if perhaps that was why the Mahanta had drawn me to the church, I turned back and took a seat as close as possible to the old man's wheelchair. Just then the organist sat down with a flourish.

The first hymn he played was an old one. Mama and I had stood side by side and sung it many times when I was a little girl. The chords reverberated within me, opening my heart wide to the love we had shared. The song finished. Chapel bells and the organ's wheezing tones made a grinding transition to "Amazing Grace."

The familiar song echoed through the vast space. When the thundering sounds ended, I sat still for a moment. I felt happier than I had for a long time, privileged to have heard the concert. There was also a familiar, comfortable, out-of-place feeling I could not put my finger on.

That evening back at the Eckankar seminar they played "Amazing HU." This new ECK version of the old hymn was played on a hurdy-gurdy and sung by a choir in barbershop-quartet style. While the afternoon's organ version was stiff and plain, this version was witty and fresh with new life.

Then my excursion began to make sense. For all the differences in style, my mother and I had simply been singing our separate love songs to God all along. At last I could see the truth.

Whether these songs were accompanied by a massive organ or sung from an ECK stage, the tune was exactly the same.

As soon as this insight came to me, the feeling I had not been able to identify in the cathedral returned. This time I recognized it at once. Even across the vast distance we had created between ourselves, it was right there, fresh and sweet. It was the full weight of my mother's smiling approval.

Reclaiming a Friendship

Ed Adler

One day I had a bitter disagreement with my longtime friend Marion. We had been very close for years, and she was a warm companion to my wife and me. But Marion and I were both very upset over the issue between us, and we parted company.

I knew my wife wondered why I never called Marion anymore. As the anger cooled, I felt less upset toward Marion but decided we were on separate paths. From time to time I'd get a nudge to pick up the phone, but I'd slowly hang up without dialing her number.

I did send Marion a greeting card once that said, "Just thinking of you." There was no response. *I guess she doesn't want to reconcile either,* I thought.

About ten years had passed since I'd last seen Marion. One day I got a call that Marion's mother had died. The news of her passing was a shock; I could still remember her energy, charm, and beautiful soprano singing voice. Whenever we visited Marion, we had always enjoyed spending time with her mother as well.

"Why don't you go to the funeral, Ed?" a mutual friend suggested. "Marion will be there. She'll be so glad to see you."

I wasn't so sure. The next morning, I decided to

inwardly check the matter with Marion's mother.

I sang HU and went into contemplation. Suddenly I was fully awake, standing in the open vestibule of a magnificent ECK Wisdom Temple. There was a gentle breeze blowing that carried the scent of hyacinth. Very faintly in the distance, I could hear a beautiful, soprano singing voice. It seemed very familiar.

Moving toward me from inside the Temple was someone I immediately recognized. Although she looked about forty years younger, there was no mistaking the elegant presence of Marion's mother. She was dressed in a peach-colored gown decorated with a vivid orange-red scarf. She looked vibrant and happy.

We greeted each other warmly. She didn't seem at all surprised to see me. We talked for a while, then I asked her what was the most important thing she had learned. She didn't hesitate for a moment.

"Nothing matters but love," she said. "All your disagreements and confusing situations in life don't mean a thing. They're only temporary; love is eternal."

I knew then I would go to the funeral that day. I thought about the drive ahead. I always enjoy listening to classical music while I'm in the car, so I thought about what would be an appropriate choice for this special day.

As if reading my thoughts, Marion's mother said, "Play Sibelius's Third Symphony." I asked her why. She smiled. "Never mind, just do it." And the inner experience began to fade.

Later, when I got into the car, I pulled out my recording of Sibelius's Third Symphony and listened as the glowing music filled the car and the empty place within me. It was hard to fight back tears.

Marion was very grateful I'd come to the funeral.

In that special moment of reunion, all the darkness of the past just melted away. We couldn't talk fast enough to catch up on ten years, so we decided to meet for dinner the next evening with some mutual friends.

My wife and I were a few minutes late arriving at the restaurant. Marion was seated at the table; I noticed she was wearing a vivid orange-red scarf. Without saying too much, I commented on her scarf. She said, "It's funny, but I haven't worn this scarf in ages. I must have spent the better part of the afternoon tearing my house apart looking for it." I just smiled.

Then I asked her if her mother had liked classical music. She thought that was an odd question. "No, not really," she said. "She only liked Sibelius."

"Which symphony?" I asked.

"Well, actually the third was her favorite."

I laughed. Marion's mother had been right. Nothing matters but love. Death is certainly an illusion. She had been right there, in my contemplation, helping me reclaim a priceless friendship by seeing what was really important in life.

Inner Contract

E. K. Tyrrell

Several years ago I had a vivid dream. Its meaning eluded me for many months. In the dream, I found myself in a small study or library. A High Initiate in ECK stood behind a desk. I had never met her personally but had often enjoyed the many talks and workshops she gave at Eckankar seminars.

She smiled lovingly at me and slid a contract across the desk. I was to sign it.

As I was putting my name on the dotted line, I felt another presence in the room. I looked up and saw Sri Harold Klemp, the Mahanta, the Living ECK Master. He was standing at the other end of the desk in white shirt and trousers.

He gathered up a sheaf of contracts like the one I had signed. He did not look at me or speak. When he finished collecting the papers, he quietly left. Upon awakening, I had the feeling something very important was about to happen.

I wrote to the High Initiate I'd seen in the dream, describing in detail the room and my inner experience there. A short time later I received her reply. In her letter, she told me I had indeed described the study in her home.

She expressed gratitude that the Mahanta had used her as a channel for ECK. She suggested the dream might mean I should endeavor to be all that I could be. She stressed that any interpretation should be mine and mine alone. I knew there was more for me to learn from the dream, so I searched the Eckankar books for any reference to inner contracts. I could find no clues, so I gave up the search.

Not long after that, my husband of forty-five years (also an ECKist) was diagnosed with a terminal illness. We went through a long, dark period of testing and spiritual growth, as we prepared to say good-bye.

Love and constant help was given to us by our ECK friends. No task was too great or too small. Assistance was given before it was requested. One High Initiate, a nurse, stopped by after work almost every night to give me a rest in caring for my husband. Another ECKist, also a nurse, did everything to make him comfortable both at home and in the hospital. She also helped me and my family cope with the stress.

After my husband's death, his translation to another plane of existence, a memorial service was given in our home. The High Initiate who conducted it did so with great love and humility. My husband's family, though not ECKists, were much comforted by it, and remarked over and over on the beautiful service.

Several days after his passing, my husband appeared to me. He seemed as real as you or I, as he sat next to me in our favorite spot on the couch. He looked so well, so strong and healthy I could hardly believe my eyes.

Then all at once, he looked me straight in the eye and said, "Do you want to come with me now or finish your contract?" After having loved him for four-and-a-half decades, the pull to go with him was great. But somehow I also knew that we had learned as much as we could together. Now we needed to go our separate ways. Each of us would progress faster on our own.

Two years have passed since his death. I have learned many lessons about self-responsibility and self-discipline. Of course, I still had times of loneliness and doubt. One very bad night, I cried out, "What is this all about?"

In desperation, I opened *The Shariyat-Ki-Sugmad,* Book One. These are the scriptures of ECK. My eyes fell on these words: "Whether the chela is living on the Physical Plane or the Atma Lok (the Soul plane), he never feels he is in a separate world, or state. . . . He does not feel like either a citizen or an alien, but rather like a modern traveler who goes through each country as a tourist or for business.

"The entities of each plane look upon their existence as sort of a contract of service."

And further down the page: "Servitude on earth in the human form, or in any of the psychic planes, is a small price to pay if it purchases a ticket to the true Kingdom of God, which is by the way of Eckankar."

Here was the answer to my long-ago dream. I found that the joy that comes from truly serving God eventually banishes all fears and doubts for the Soul who is traveling home to God.

The Touch of Love

Elizabeth Kirby

My son works for United Airlines and had to stay in Chicago for a seven-week training that was very rigorous. I was concerned about him, but I managed to not call him on the phone every other day. Then, one night, I had a dream.

I dreamed that my son was eight or nine years old and was standing by a very wide boulevard. He had to cross from one side to the other, but he looked lost and scared. I went up to him and said, "Don't be afraid, Mom's here!" I held his hand and helped him cross the street. When I woke up I wondered what the dream meant.

Eventually, my son completed his training and returned home. I related my dream to him, and after I finished, he smiled and told me a story of his own.

Everything had been fine up until the sixth week, when the students had to practice for emergency situations. At this time, he found the course so demanding that he became agitated and unsettled. He found himself unable to sleep the night before an important practical exam.

After trying everything he could to calm down, he remembered once asking me to have the Mahanta help

233

him handle a situation that he didn't know how to resolve.

But all he could think of was his mother. He called out my name and started to sing HU the way I had taught him. After this he became calm and peaceful and soon fell asleep. He got only a few hours' sleep, but he passed the test with flying colors.

We compared notes and found that he had sung HU at the same time I had had my dream.

A Checklist for Forgiveness

Brenda Cooper

or as long as I could remember, there was a cold war between my father and me. No harsh words were ever exchanged; just a cool aloofness. I'd thought it was because Dad had been very strict and a tough disciplinarian. I harbored a lot of resentment toward him.

When I moved out of his house twenty years ago, I thought I wouldn't have to deal with my feelings about him anymore. I would live my own life and see him on holidays and occasionally in between, out of a sense of duty. I thought I wouldn't have to face this issue if I stayed away from him most of the time.

Then I started studying Eckankar. The ECK, Holy Spirit, gradually began to bring me to a realization— I was carrying a burden of unforgiveness. This load had become so heavy on my heart that it was almost physically painful. Once it surfaced, I agonized over this realization for weeks, then months. It followed me day and night, at work and at home. There was no hiding from it. I knew that if I was to move any further in my spiritual unfoldment, I had to resolve this.

I would have no peace until I forgave my father.

But what was this thing called forgiveness? It had always been an abstract idea to me, a concept I couldn't quite grasp. I didn't understand the mechanics of it. I knew God did it, and other people said they did it, but I always doubted that forgiveness was humanly possible. After all, we humans have incredible memories for the wrongs that are done to us. And even though we may say we forgive, do we ever forget? If we remember, have we really forgiven? I went around and around in my thinking, convinced that forgiveness was something that only God could do.

One morning I was driving to work, mulling over the problem in my mind, as I did continuously in those days. "I want to forgive him," I said out loud, "but I just don't know how!"

Then a still small voice said, "Take it as far as you can, and let God do the rest."

"Oh! That sounds easy," I said. I felt a little better just knowing that at least now I had a plan. Still, I wasn't quite sure what it meant. So that night I went home and contemplated on it.

I sat down in a quiet place, settled myself, took a few deep breaths, and sang HU a few times. I heard the words again: "Take it as far as you can, and let God do the rest." Not understanding exactly what that meant and being somewhat of a procrastinator, I sang HU some more. A few seconds went by, then minutes.

I finally blurted out, "OK! I forgive him!" I didn't feel any different. It occurred to me that if I wrote down the things that were bothering me, it might help.

Then something interesting happened.

Instead of getting a pencil and piece of paper, I visualized myself listing all the wrongs I felt my father had committed. Then I checked them off one by one, saying, "OK, I can forgive that, I can forgive him for that one, I forgive that," and so on. When I finished,

I wadded the imaginary paper into a ball and threw it up in the air—a gesture symbolizing my giving it all up to God. And then the miracle happened.

The paper ball went up, and confetti came down! In that same instant, the burden lifted. I felt lighter, as though something had been physically removed from me. Suddenly I was overwhelmed with a love for my father that I had never felt for him before. It washed over me in waves. And the joy! There are no words to convey it. It was "joy unspeakable and full of glory," as the Bible says. It filled me up and overflowed as tears rolled down my cheeks. What a relief!

I still occasionally think of one of those things on my checklist. But when I do, I just brush it out of my mind and say, "That's over. I've already forgiven him for that," or, "I gave that to God." The thought flees from my mind. I'm amazed at the happy childhood memories that have come to me—good things I had completely forgotten because the bad things were overshadowing them.

This was indeed an occasion worthy of celebration, complete with confetti! For it was finally over—the pain was gone. A relationship had been healed through God's precious gift of forgiveness.

New Life for
an Old Relationship

Zanna Ford

I sat down uneasily in the high swivel chair in my new hairdresser's salon. I hadn't switched stylists in years. What if she cut too much off? Cathy and I chatted awkwardly as she swathed me in plastic for a shampoo and asked after my health with faint, motherly concern. Why did she seem so familiar?

As the warm water coursed over my ears and she lathered my hair, I carefully probed for clues. I had a strong urge to help this woman, to give her love, or befriend her in any way I could. Why? Had I known her before, in another life?

Silently, I began to sing HU, a sacred word that stilled and focused my inner senses.

A gentle hum began to surround me, and a blue glow flashed in my peripheral vision, telling me of the presence of Divine Spirit. As they grew in strength, I knew I was off on an adventure to find the connection with this woman as she cut my hair.

"HU-U-U-U" I sang quietly to myself, as I listened to the radio she had playing in her shop. Cathy tilted my head down and began snipping. Suddenly the phone interrupted with an electronic peal. Since her hands were wet, Cathy left the caller to the answering machine.

A woman's voice came on the speaker, giving her message in clipped, British tones. A faint change in the ringing in my ears made me wonder. Had I known Cathy before in England?

Immediately, the radio began blaring a commercial: "The destination of choice is London!" I knew that Divine Spirit was providing me with important clues to my connection with this Soul.

As the haircut progressed, I continued to tune my senses to the Light and Sound, paying special attention to the inner screen of my imagination. Slowly a clearer and clearer impression of a past life began to form. It involved a close friend, with whom I currently had a very tumultuous relationship. This life had cropped up in vague dreams and experiences within my daily spiritual contemplations, but never before had I glimpsed the specific karmic threads of experience so clearly.

Yes, I had known Cathy before. She had given me bread when I was starving on the streets of Victorian London. No wonder I felt so kindly toward her.

Snip, snip went the scissors, as scenes from the past unfolded like a silent video. It explained so many of the difficulties I was passing through right now.

I was a young girl in the city of Dublin, Ireland. Born in a poor family, I had been helping my mother with the tubs of wash she took in, as well as caring for my numerous brothers and sisters. But as soon as I reached thirteen, my parents hired me out for a pittance as a scullery maid in a nearby gentleman's mansion.

My new life was a harsh one. I rose each day before

dawn to scrub the numerous fireplaces and lay fresh blazes, empty the chamber pots, sweep up kitchen scraps, and help Cook prepare for breakfast. And that was just the round of chores before dawn. My days were an endless circle of backbreaking work; I fell into my filthy attic bed each night around nine.

But if my meager lot in life was not hard enough, I was also cursed with the Irish beauty of my mother. It flowered early and faded quickly among the overworked poor women of our era.

My darkest day came when the sons of the house returned home from school. Although I was equipped with a sharp tongue and strong arms, they still found plenty of ways to make my life miserable, yanking me into closets or chasing me around the downstairs table.

My fate was set. At sixteen, I began to "go soft" on the younger son, who had blue eyes and a ready laugh. Although he was studying for the priesthood at Trinity College, I soon found myself pregnant with his baby.

Mistress turned me out, and my family refused to take me in. Near starvation, I begged a boat ride to England and set out on foot to find Trinity College. After several days of sleeping in ditches and asking the way, I arrived at the college gates.

I cautiously asked several students if they knew my lover, but each time I met with laughter and rebuff. So I sat down by the big iron gates to wait until he passed. Finally, as I lay near fainting, he walked by. I cried out, "My lord!" to him, and in confused embarrassment, he took me to a nearby pub for food and drink.

His eyes hardened as I told him of my predicament. I saw there was no hope of marriage, no hope of a safe and orderly life.

Before I left, he shoved just enough money into my hands to pay the train fare to London. I would eke out a miserable existence on the streets until my baby was born.

It was there that I met Cathy. She owned a wonderful-smelling bakery just down the street from my garret. Often I would go in just to savor the aroma of fresh bread and warm myself by her smile.

A capable mother of two, Cathy always had a kind word and a twopence bun for me. She was a touch of golden brightness in my bleak life. When my time came, I died in childbirth. I had prayed for just such a death each night for months, as I lay in my cold bed under the roof.

Alive for only sixteen-and-a-half years, I stepped once more into the Light and left my poor under-nourished body behind. As I looked back, I noted that the body of the baby was lifeless too—no Soul had chosen to give it life.

The scene swirled and faded.

Cathy spoke, and I started, as she handed me a round mirror. "Do you like the back?" she asked shyly. "Why, yes," I stammered. My mind was a blur as I thanked her, collected my coat and purse, wrote a check, and drove home in the gently falling snow.

So much was clearer now. The son of the house was, of course, my friend in this life. Much of the trouble between us had simply been left over from that painful episode.

None of these things were said—they just hung like delicate webs of karma between us. For some reason, meeting Cathy had unlocked the mystery. Now, how could I resolve these old wounds between this friend and me?

When I arrived home, I went upstairs and sat on my bed. Tears came, and I let out much of the pain that had been haunting me—pain that I had had no name for until now.

A huge burden had been lifted. Next I focused sweetly on the inner screen again, singing HU and thanking life for this gift of insight. I said nothing to my friend, but there was a new lightness and love between us. I mused to myself that it felt like the difference between tap water and distilled water: subtle, but real.

That night, a dream gave more glimpses of our mutual past. I had seen the life where my friend had hurt me. But now the tables were turned. Here's what I wrote in my dream journal:

I was an African girl, with gold rings in my nose and ears, gifts from my father (my friend in this life). I ran away to the next village when he hurt me.

I sold one of my rings for food and discovered it was worth much more than my father had told me. I stayed in this new village and married. My father came after me to recover his dowry, but the village hid me.

He cursed me—a threat I took very seriously. So I hired a witch doctor to kill him with black magic. When my father returned home to his stick-and-mud hut, he died of a raging fever within the week.

My new village then held me in high esteem, as one who was divinely protected. I became a witch doctor myself. I did some good with herbal remedies and healings, but also much evil.

In the dream, I felt a familiar heaviness which I associated with the black arts. It was a bad debt incurred from that life of negativity—repaid in the Irish experience.

I awoke that morning with a greater understanding of the mysteries of life. It did not immediately solve every problem in this troubled relationship, but this spiritual healing did make a difference.

My friend and I began to talk more and with an easier rapport. Trust sprang up where there had been resistance and pain. I knew the Mahanta, the Inner Master, had given me this gift of understanding. I truly love my friend and had done everything I could think of to heal our relationship. After I did everything I consciously could, the Mahanta stepped in to bring about the rest of the healing—one that made a real difference in my daily life and understanding.

7

Finding Eckankar

In many different lives, Soul gets the opportunity to leave Its little island. At first It stays because It's attracted by the antics of Its own world. When this begins to get old, then the voyage home to God begins in earnest.

—Sri Harold Klemp,
The Book of ECK Parables,
Volume 3

I knew that it was the true love of God and desire
for truth that had brought me to this point in my life.

A Visitor to the Class

Ann Archer Butcher

 any years ago, I was a teacher in a
small town in Indiana. Each day, I
taught a philosophy class for young,
inquiring high-school students. At
some point I began to pause at my door each morning before leaving for school and say a little prayer:
"Dear God, tell me what to teach them and show me
how."

Within a short time something very interesting
began to happen. In the middle of class, a long phrase
of philosophy would come into my mind. I would write
it on the blackboard and discuss it with my class.
Having no idea where the phrases came from, I finally
sent several of them to a research librarian. She told
me the quotes were from writers such as Plato,
Aristotle, and Socrates. But I was not one to memorize
long passages from philosophers.

Each day, whenever I asked for guidance from God,
this is what I got! After a while, the research librarian
said, "Sorry, I don't know where this new material is
from." Neither did I. But I knew this material was
precious and meant especially for us.

One day I asked for time off to go to the dentist,
and the substitute teacher arrived an hour early. "I'd

like to observe," he said.

He sat in the back of the classroom and was quiet until our discussion period. Then as usual, some great lofty thoughts came flooding through my mind. I began writing them on the board.

He raised his hand immediately and asked, "Where are you getting that material?"

I didn't know, but in order to give him an answer, I said, "I read it somewhere once." Class went on. I left for my dentist appointment, but when I came back the next day, I was suspicious. I wondered about this man and asked my students, "Did he teach what I told him to when I left?"

"No, he didn't."

"What did he do?"

"He wanted to read our journals, he wanted to hear about what we'd been learning. He asked a lot of questions about you!"

"Me?"

And they replied, "But don't worry. He wrote you a note and left you a gift."

I went to my desk and found a note. He said very nice things about what he had observed. I looked at my gift. It was a book. But the title startled me. *ECKANKAR—The Key to Secret Worlds* by Paul Twitchell. Secret worlds! I knew nothing about this. I had no metaphysical or esoteric background. What on earth was this word *Eckankar*?

In his note he wrote, "I think you'll find the underlined passages very interesting." Right on the blackboard, left over from the day before, was a long paragraph I had written. I was surprised to find it in this book. He had underlined it for me, along with other pas sages I recognized as being familiar. When he went through my students' journals, he had found many passages he recognized in this book.

I had no idea what was happening, but I continued my daily request for God's guidance. Then at the end of the school year, I decided to quit teaching and take a graduate-level program at Indiana University.

The university program was very intense. One day, I thought I deserved a treat, so I went shopping in my favorite dress shop. But when I got inside, there were no dresses to be found. There was only one man and a lot of books.

"Excuse me, but where did all the dresses go?"

"Nora's moved down the street. This is an Eckankar center."

An Eckankar center? I did not understand. I had thought Paul Twitchell, who wrote *ECKANKAR—The Key to Secret Worlds,* was like Emerson, or Thoreau, or Plato, or Aristotle, some great philosopher who lived and died long ago.

I asked the man so many questions that finally he said, "You know, there is an Eckankar regional seminar this weekend. Maybe you'd like to go."

On Saturday, I went to the Holiday Inn. I was a few minutes late, and the doors to the seminar were closed. I peeked in and listened carefully. Something in that room seemed familiar. There was a pull I could hardly resist.

I really wanted to go through the doors. But I waited. I listened a little more, and then I couldn't stand it. As I stepped into the room, the speaker paused. He looked down the aisle straight at me and said to the audience, "You know the woman I was just telling you about, the teacher. The one who was a perfect example of someone whom the Mahanta works with for years

249

before they ever know anything about Eckankar? Here she is."

Everyone turned and looked at me. I stood there, and suddenly there were tears streaming down my face. I knew that it was the true love of God and desire for truth that had brought me to this point in my life, to this place. I also knew that whatever this Eckankar was, it was calling me home to God, and I was going.

Temple Tour

Linda Evans

s I arrived at my first ECK Worldwide Seminar, I knew only to expect a wonderful experience. I was a new member of Eckankar, but I had already seen, heard, and felt many of the gifts of Divine Spirit.

The seminar that year was in Minneapolis, where the Temple of ECK is located. With great anticipation, I waited to tour the Temple on Friday morning. I had reserved a tour early in the morning.

It was dark when I arrived at the convention center and boarded the tour bus. As we traveled toward the Temple of ECK in Chanhassen I felt that this would be an extraordinary event, and I leaned forward in my seat as if to urge the bus to go faster. I expected the Temple to be beautiful, because I had seen photos and videos of it. But I had not expected the people on the tour to all look familiar, as if I had met them somewhere before.

After we had toured the building, admiring the lovely design, I waited for the bus to take us back to the convention center. I was standing outside, gazing at the golden stair-stepped roof which represented the steps toward God, when suddenly I felt a healing flood of love and gratitude flow through my heart. It was as if I were standing beneath a powerful waterfall. Tears streamed down my face as I tried to absorb all of the experience that I could. I didn't fully understand it yet, but I knew this visit to the Temple had changed my life forever. Soul was more determined than ever to return home.

Still in awe over my experience and more silent than usual, I returned to the convention center for the rest of the seminar. I met people from all over the world, and I filled my notebook with new spiritual exercises.

Every time I thought about my experience at the Temple, my heart swelled, and my eyes filled with tears. I couldn't speak of it yet. I didn't know how much it had changed me.

About a week after my return home, I was on my way to an ECK Worship Service when suddenly it hit me that a weight of sadness that I had felt all my life was gone! I had always envisioned this sadness as a heavy stone weighing down my heart. Because of the sadness, part of me had always been inaccessible to joy, love, and light.

I decided to try an experiment. For twenty-five years, I've sung blues songs without knowing why—or how I knew them. They just seemed to fit me. So I tried one of my old standards. Then I laughed out loud when I realized I didn't have any special feeling for the song anymore.

What a glorious blessing! I felt lighter and freer than I ever had in this lifetime.

That morning our worship service was about the baggage we give up on our way home to God. Now when I need a little reminder of the many gifts I've been given, I think of the Temple of ECK.

"I Met Him Seven Years Ago!"

Bimla Amar

A friend recently visited from Trinidad. She was supposed to stay with her sister, but for some reason, her sister was angry with her, so she stayed with us. She had come to London to get medical treatment for her son. The night she arrived, we sat up talking. After a while she asked me about my spiritual path, Eckankar. I described a simple spiritual exercise in which one can sing the word HU (pronounced like the word *hue*) for peace of mind and expanded awareness in life.

The next morning she came to me and said, "Bimla, last night when you were talking about Eckankar I was worried about your sanity. But the experience I just had proved to me that these teachings are true and helpful.

"After I closed my eyes and tried your exercise, I had a past-life recall that explained why my sister is angry with me right now. Tell me more about Eckankar. Do you have a book I can read?"

I supplied her with a book on Eckankar by Sri Harold Klemp, which she began reading. On the third day, she came to me and said, "Seven years ago, I was lying in bed, when a man with glasses appeared to me. I got scared and screamed. My son came and asked what was the matter. As soon as he spoke, the man disappeared. My son looked around and couldn't find anyone."

She said she didn't know why she wanted to tell me about this incident. During the day, my friend mentioned the man with glasses several more times. He seemed to fascinate her.

Before we went to bed, I told her that the Living ECK Master, Sri Harold Klemp, often wore glasses. I had a photograph of him which I showed her. When she saw it, she said, "This is the man I saw seven years ago!"

We were both very happy. She had wonderful experiences during the month she stayed with us. Then my friend's sister asked her to come stay with her. They mended their relationship, and the sister even offered to take care of my friend's son during his treatments, so my friend could return home to Trinidad. Before she left, I told her, "So many people are looking for truth. When Soul is ready, you always find the correct next step for you. I'm so glad you found Eckankar. You will know when it is right to tell others about it."

An Inner Call

Giovanni Riva

When I was a teenager growing up in Italy, life didn't seem to make sense. I had little self-confidence and a lot of fears. I also had many questions I couldn't find answers for.

When I completed school, to the surprise of my family I decided to leave Rome and go to Geneva, Switzerland. In Geneva everything was new and different. But still I felt lonely and confused. I wondered if it had been a mistake to leave my family. I continually asked myself, "What is life all about?"

Some time later, I had a strange experience that really shook me up.

I awoke very early one morning. As I lay in bed gazing at the garden outside my window and listening to the birds singing, suddenly my heart began palpitating, faster and faster. It felt like thousands of drums beating. I was filled with fear. *Is this what it is like to die?* I thought. I didn't want to die. Then the drums faded, I felt a light, electrical sensation between my eyebrows. It seemed to go through my body. I was immobilized.

My fear was beyond anything I had experienced. Then a sound came from within. It moved from one ear to the other, back and forth, faster and faster. Then, I felt myself separating from my physical body.

Suddenly a young man with blond hair appeared. He was surrounded by light. He was wearing a white robe and had a book in his hands. I knew he wanted to communicate. My fear was so great that all I could say to him was, "I don't want to die. There are many things I want to do here." The man made a motion of blessing, and the image changed. Now he was seated with his head bent, holding the book in his hands. He wore a dark robe.

Six months after this experience, I left Switzerland for South America. After one year something within was telling me that it was time for another change. So I traveled to California, and I decided to stay. I began college and a new career.

A recording studio in Menlo Park, California, hired me as a sound engineer. I enjoyed the work very much; it was interesting and varied. One of their clients was Eckankar, for whom they produced copies of audio-cassettes. While I made the copies, I listened to the talks by Sri Harold Klemp. What I heard fascinated me. It felt good, but I didn't quite know what it was all about.

During this time I also became aware of a sound within my head. It was similar to the sound near an electrical power line. This sound gave me a feeling of well-being. It felt quite uplifting.

A year later I changed jobs and went to work for a video-production company in Palo Alto. A curious coincidence was that this company was also hired by Eckankar, this time to make copies of their video-cassettes. For the first time I was able to see Sri Harold Klemp on video. Again, I liked what he was saying, but

AN INNER CALL

I still didn't understand the meaning for me.

One day I was duplicating a tape entitled *Soul Travel Workshop: The Golden Heart.* On the tape Sri Harold handed the microphone to a speaker who was to give a spiritual exercise. My attention was drawn to the speaker singing the word *Wah Z,* the spiritual name of Sri Harold Klemp.

I followed along with the exercise and had a flashback to my experience with the young man with blond hair who had appeared in my room eight years ago. *This is very interesting,* I thought. *There must be some relationship between my experience with the young man and this exercise.*

I rewound the tape and listened intently to every single word on it. It was a two-hour videocassette. *This is exactly the answer I've been searching for,* I thought at the end. But what is this Eckankar?

A couple of weeks later, a woman named Barbara was hired because our workload had increased. One afternoon as she came to relieve my shift, an Eckankar job was in progress.

"This Eckankar is something very interesting," I commented.

"Yes, I know," she said with a smile.

"Do you know something about it?"

"Yes, I'm an ECKist."

"Is that true?" I exclaimed. "How can I learn more about it?"

She calmly said, "If you like, you can go the ECK center in Menlo Park and buy a couple of books."

In a matter of minutes I was at the ECK center, picking out books to buy and read. I was very, very happy.

Sometime later, I went to an Eckankar meeting in

257

Palo Alto. On the wall I saw a number of paintings. Curious, I walked over to look at them. To my amazement, I recognized the man from my earlier experience in Switzerland. It was Gopal Das, who appears as a young man with blond hair. I learned this man was an ECK Master in ancient Egypt. He is still active on the inner planes as a teacher of ECK.

Suddenly everything was clear to me. Gopal Das's early-morning visit to me eight years earlier prepared me for this wonderful step in my spiritual life, my introduction to the teachings of Eckankar.

A Dream with Rebazar Tarzs

Theodore Carlat

I had recently broken up with my girl-friend and was devastated. I set out on a search to gain a better understanding of life. Why did my heart hurt so? And to come right down to it, why was I even here?

One night I turned on the television, and a talk show was on. A man was explaining his spiritual beliefs. "This is what I've always thought and believed," I said aloud. But I had never heard anyone talk about it before.

I hoped they'd give his name somewhere in the interview. But the show was over before I found out who he was or the name of his teaching. I thought about contacting the TV station to find out more, but it was already 1:00 a.m.

At six o'clock I woke so suddenly that I sat up in bed. Before I was even completely awake, I said a single word out loud: "Eckankar." I'd never heard the word before and didn't know what it meant. But I knew it was important and had something to do with my quest for answers about life. So I started calling bookstores, asking if anyone had ever heard of Eckankar.

A Hollywood bookstore clerk finally gave me a clue. "Yes, I've heard of it," he replied. "In fact we have a book here called *ECKANKAR—The Key to Secret Worlds*." I dressed quickly, drove forty minutes across town, and bought the book. A few days later I was still reading the book. That night I had an amazing dream.

It was a powerful and vivid experience that affected me for years. I felt the dream was far more real than anything in my everyday, physical existence. The distinctive presence of the place and the inner guide who appeared stayed with me each day for a long time.

In the dream, I was walking along a road, listening to someone talk. I knew I was being given important knowledge about my spiritual search. We reached a hill. I could see a series of small, golden knolls that stretched on and on to the horizon. Here and there, a few trees dotted the landscape.

The individual I was with drew my attention to the trees and said, "That is the forest." The trees were so sparse that his remark struck me and helped me remember the dream.

Next, we walked to a little cabin. I entered the door, but my eyes couldn't adjust to the darkness inside. All I could make out were many pairs of feet under a large table. Something important was being discussed at the table, but I couldn't quite grasp it. I just felt the love and significance of the situation. Then I woke up.

Years after I became a member of Eckankar, I came across an interesting technique in one of Sri Harold Klemp's monthly discourses. In the discourse, Sri Harold mentioned that we can go back to a dream experience during a spiritual exercise and explore the meaning of the dream in greater detail and consciousness.

So I traveled back to my dream, using a Soul Travel exercise.

I imagined the feeling of the dream and the presence of the individual who'd been at my side. Slowly I turned my head and saw the man. It was the Tibetan ECK Master Rebazar Tarzs. He was dressed in a maroon robe, and his voice was very resonant and distinctive as he said again, "That is the forest."

Then we entered the cabin. My first inclination was to assume I couldn't see. But then as I filled my heart with love and wished to know more, my vision cleared. A host of ECK Masters were seated at a table. There was Fubbi Quantz, Yaubl Sacabi, Gopal Das, and others I recognized from the ECK teachings. They were talking about my progress on my own path back to God.

Once again, the power of this dream profoundly touched my life. I knew without doubt that I had not found Eckankar. It—and the Vairagi ECK Masters who teach the ways of ECK—had found me!

A Special Gift

Janice Blair Taylor

reams have always held a special interest for me but never more than the evening I took my first conscious step toward Eckankar. The evening remains clear in my mind.

After working late I was preparing to go home. One other person was still there, someone I did not talk to often because I usually felt shy and a little uncomfortable around her. However this night I was drawn to talk to her.

Referring to an earlier palm reading by a friend, I said, "I was told I am a young Soul." I held up my hand to show her my proof. "And you are an old Soul," I continued, pointing to her hand.

She looked at me with a small, patient smile and calmly stated that we are all old Souls.

I was startled by her firm and serene response. "How can you be sure?" I asked.

She smiled again and began to tell me about Eckankar. We talked for hours. What she said seemed to mirror much of my beliefs about life and spirituality. I found comfort and joy in her words. She taught me to sing HU and suggested that I try it again at home.

When I had prepared myself for bed, I sat down to sing HU. I felt unsure and held no expectations.

After I fell asleep, I dreamed I was in school. It looked to be a high school, except the ceilings rose to great heights and the corridors were longer and wider than any school I knew.

I was standing in the middle of one such corridor looking around. In one classroom I could see my children. At the far end of the corridor, my husband was talking with a group of people being given an orientation to the school. As I continued to examine my surroundings, a dark-haired woman gently took my hand and placed some coins in my palm. I looked up, surprised to find her standing there. I quickly glanced down to the coins and back again to her in confusion. She smiled and told me there would be many teachers to help me along the way.

The coins in my hand were unusual, and I began to examine them closely. Of different sizes, each had a unique design. I took the largest coin and turned it over. I noticed the word *Eckankar* around the edge in large block letters. In the center of the coin was a beautiful three-dimensional picture of a forest and all its creatures.

"It's beautiful there," I whispered, amazed.

I looked up to thank the woman, but she was gone.

The next day at work my coworker casually asked about my evening. I told her about my dream experience, and her eyes began to sparkle with tears. I knew at that moment something special had happened. It wasn't until years later that I realized what a special gift had been given that night.

In times of doubt and wondering, I remember my dream and know that this gift of Eckankar did not come to me by accident. I am filled with love and happiness to be accepted into the spiritual community.

And many teachers, inner and outer, have been there to help me along the way.

Kathleen

B. Jean Wells

I met Kathleen at a seminar on death and dying. We felt an immediate rapport and decided to get together again to talk about where our lives seemed to be going. Little did I know that this budding friendship would propel us to the path of Eckankar.

Both Kathleen and I had had near-death experiences at an early age. We knew Soul existed without a body. We hoped to find out what happened to Soul after It left a body permanently.

The two of us visited many metaphysical groups but found no plausible explanations. It was during this period of searching that Kathleen told me her time might be running out. She had had a radical mastectomy four years prior to our meeting, and the doctors were not sure if all the cancer had been eradicated. One day she confided to me she was showing symptoms again.

We sat silently for a while, thinking of the ramifications, then quietly she began to speak.

"I have something to tell you," she said. "The year before I found out I had cancer, my only son shot and killed himself. He was seventeen. I never got to say good-bye."

I was speechless. There were no words to express the compassion I felt for her, so I just hugged her for a moment. It was then she told me of a haunting fear that her son as Soul might be forever doomed.

I suddenly understood Kathleen's pressing need to know what occurs after death, but more specifically after a suicide. She suggested we have tea and continue our conversation. I followed her into the kitchen. The morning paper was on the table. I began leafing through it, while Kathleen prepared the tea. Stopping on the community-calendar page, I scanned the events for that day, and the word *Soul* caught my eye. I focused on a small notice, reading it aloud: "Free introductory talk on the Ancient Science of Soul Travel."

Both Kathleen and I decided to go. The subject excited something within us; we could hardly wait until evening. We weren't disappointed. The speakers gave an overview of Eckankar. Their words struck a responsive chord within me, and I knew I had found the key for my spiritual liberation.

The next weeks were filled with activity. We read ECK books, discussed their contents, and found answers for many questions we had had. During this time I took Kathleen to her doctor appointments. The cancer was spreading. That meant more radiation and chemotherapy. She wanted time to pursue the study of Eckankar, so she opted to go through the treatments for the second time. Within the first month, she sent for her membership and began to study the discourses.

My life was to be profoundly enriched by the events that were to occur in the next two years. And Kathleen was about to make a quantum leap in understanding.

First she met with the ECK Master Rebazar Tarzs in the dream state. Then she began meeting with her son, the way he was at seventeen. She was able to hold him and say good-bye. The next time she saw him, he was about six years old. The last meeting she had with her son, he was a baby. Then Kathleen met another ECK Master, Shamus-i-Tabriz, and she was shown some of the Time Track. She saw her son was about to reincarnate into another physical body. This healed her fears, and she finally felt at peace about her son's suicide.

One morning Kathleen's only daughter called to share some very unexpected news: She was pregnant with her first child. The excitement of a grandchild carried Kathleen over some difficult days during her treatments.

We had received our Second Initiations and were finishing the second series of Satsang discourses when Kathleen's grandson was born. Over her doctors' objections she flew back east to visit her grandson. When she returned she was extremely ill.

But when I saw Kathleen the next day, I knew she had gained some spiritual insight. She smiled as she told me of holding the baby for the first time; as she looked at him, their eyes met with instant recognition. The baby kicked, smiled, and continued cooing for several minutes. She silently thanked Sugmad for this wonderful gift, for she recognized that her son had found his new physical home.

My Bridge to God

Tom Casad

he local Presbyterian church had a nine-month course to prepare high-school freshmen to join the congregation. Although I had not previously known about the program, my mother enrolled me at the start of my freshman year.

The group met after school once each week, guided by the church's youth minister. It was pleasant to meet outside of school with kids I liked, to discuss topics of interest to young adolescents, including aspects of Christian faith.

The following June, we were honored before the entire congregation as new members at a Sunday worship service.

This was a period of fulfillment for me, being recognized for the first time as a part of an adult community. I was happy to be associated with so many people whose company I enjoyed. But throughout the year, I had not taken a particular interest in God. That came during the next year, a year of heartache for me.

The youth minister also conducted a high-school fellowship program. During my sophomore year, I became an active member of this group. We met every Sunday evening to share friendship and to explore issues of Christian faith and service.

In contrast to the previous year, we talked about things more on our own terms now, rather than just accepting what we were told by the youth minister. As for issues of Christian service, the church provided ample opportunities for volunteer work in the community.

The youth minister led us on many Sunday projects, where we could translate our faith into action. A number of us met on our own during the week after dinner, sometimes going to visit other Christian groups. We all took our religion seriously and personally.

It happened that one after another of my friends in the fellowship group experienced being born again as a Christian. The elements of the born-again experience were simple: with sincerity, you prayed to Jesus for Him to come into your life. That was the same explanation each boy and girl gave me when I asked about what had happened to them.

I began to grieve as those months passed and friends I was so close to experienced something that we all valued but which eluded me.

We were all still loyal to one another, we all went to the same places, we all took interest in the same things. Yet so many of my friends went through this profound shift in their personal relationship with Christ. And I did not.

What kept me from having an experience like theirs were fundamental questions I had about God and life. What is a real spiritual experience? How could one reconcile religion with the rest of living?

I asked minister and layman, adolescent and adult, but no one could give me satisfactory answers.

I knew that to be born again, I had to be sincere,

but I could not be sincere about a teaching that was unclear within myself. From what I could find out from the people at my church, I had to quit asking and resign myself to a certain degree of ignorance.

Also during my sophomore year, I made friends with the college-aged custodians employed by the church for building maintenance and security. I got along so well with them that it seemed natural for me to join the custodial staff. The head custodian and I petitioned the church's business manager to hire me. Unfortunately, he considered me too young to be employed. This was another cause of sadness for me that year.

One night in February, as I was getting ready for bed, it struck me that my time had finally come to pray to Jesus with all my heart. I knelt beside my bed and asked Jesus, "Show me God!" Immediately a sense of peace came over me for the first time in many weeks, and I went to sleep.

In the next three months, events and relationships were unchanged with my family, school, church, and friends. We did the same things as before, but I was no longer distressed about God, Christ, and religion.

In May, to my surprise, the church's business manager mailed me a job application. He had changed his mind about hiring me as a custodian. I started work the next week on a part-time basis.

One afternoon, I was mopping the floor of the church social hall, working with a custodian I had just met. He had been working there for some time while attending college, but our paths had not crossed until I was hired.

As we worked, I began to talk about God. He shared some thoughts that made more sense than anything

I had heard before. When I asked him to tell me more, he offered to bring me a book. The next day he brought me *In My Soul I Am Free* by Brad Steiger.

It was the story of Paul Twitchell, the founder of Eckankar. I read the book quickly and with great enthusiasm, for it explained everything I had questioned. What a joy! Throughout the next year I read one Eckankar book after another. At the start of my senior year, I joined Eckankar.

I was so interested in what Eckankar taught that the significance of *how* I found the teachings did not impress me until I had the most wonderful dream.

I dreamed I walked out of a forest into a clearing. There stood a five-story wooden tower. I entered the tower and climbed to the top. From the top of the tower I looked down at the ground and saw a man. He was of average size with short hair, a beard, and knee-length white robe. I waved to him, and he waved back.

Then the man turned and walked off into the forest. The experience of love I shared with him as we waved was tremendous. In that long moment, I knew that he was Jesus, and that he had brought me to Eckankar.

8

ealth and Healing

Difficulties of health and other problems are part of going into the higher states of consciousness. Changes occur at every level of initiation. . . . the further you go, the more aware you become of these changes. . . .

Gratitude allows us to recognize that what we have is exactly what we need for our spiritual unfoldment. What we have right now reflects our spiritual state of consciousness.

—Sri Harold Klemp,
Be the HU

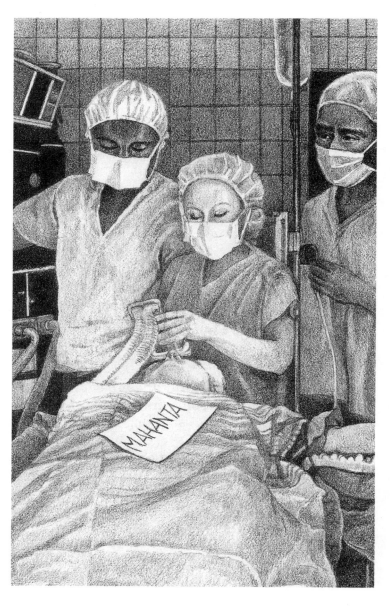

In the word *Mahanta,* I trusted that the love of
Divine Spirit would take care of me.

The Perfect Mosaic

Julie Olson

t was 1:45 in the morning on July 27, 1991, when the phone rang. As my husband, Paul, pulled himself out of bed to answer, I rolled over and thought, *Who could that be at this hour?* Suddenly, I knew exactly who was calling in the dead of night. From that moment on, I knew my life would never be the same.

Paul hung up the phone and came back to the bedroom. He told me that within the hour a surgeon would be removing two organs from a donor that matched my blood and tissue type. Soon I would be in the operating room participating in a great miracle of life. But the miracle had begun several months earlier.

I had struggled with chronic disease since I was diagnosed with diabetes at age twelve. By the time I reached thirty-four, diabetes had taken its toll on me. I had eye problems, and my kidneys barely functioned. Any movement took great effort, and I had to lie down and rest every few moments.

Earlier, I had recorded the following dream:

November 25, 1990

I was looking at a photograph of myself with a group of people surrounding me. The photograph was in black and white except for a golden

277

six-pointed star emanating from my forehead.
There was also a golden light over my abdomen.

After writing this in my dream journal I forgot about it entirely.

With the symptoms of end-stage kidney disease beginning, I had gone to the large university medical center near where I live. I learned that in the next few months I would have to begin dialysis to cleanse my body of built-up toxins.

At that time the doctors introduced another option: kidney transplant. My husband and I made appointments with all the proper departments and doctors and spent an entire day gathering information and asking questions.

Our last appointment that day was with the hospital's transplant coordinator. Her job was to orient me to the nature of kidney transplants. During the two-hour conversation, she brought up an idea that reached across the void between my dreams and reality: I could also have a pancreas transplant. A new pancreas would mean I would be cured of diabetes after my twenty-two-year struggle with the disease!

One of the ideas I had always found most intriguing in Eckankar was that of spiritual healing. Even though I hardly dared to think Divine Spirit would cure my diabetes, I always held out that hope. In the depths of my heart, I had wanted this healing for so long. Was it possible that the time had come for it to manifest?

In that moment with the transplant coordinator I saw the spiritual healing take place on the inner. I was willing to do whatever Divine Spirit required of me to see this healing all the way through to the outer. There were tears in my eyes as I expressed my desire to be whole and healthy.

"I have so much to live for!" I blurted out.

After a few days, I began to have second thoughts. The risks for the combined transplant were considerably more than for a kidney transplant alone. One afternoon as I sat on my bed, plagued by doubts, I idly reached over and picked up my dream journal from the table next to my bed and flipped it open. My eyes fell on the words "There was a golden light over my abdomen." It was my dream from months before. Now I realized that the golden light in my dream was coming from the area where my pancreas is.

I further interpreted the dream. The photograph, or finished picture, meant that the surgery had already taken place. The gold light showed that the healing would manifest from Soul all the way down through to the physical, the black-and-white picture in my dream. The group of people surrounding me was the team of doctors and nurses and ECK Masters of the Vairagi who would work so closely with me.

I felt flooded with a sense of well-being, knowing that Divine Spirit had shown me before I even knew about my surgical options that all would be well. This was my answer.

Many times later when I felt afraid or unsure of the outcome, I would think of that dream. The knowingness that all would be well was in that golden light over my abdomen. It was the promise of a spiritual healing.

The very next day after we received the phone call in the middle of the night, I was wheeled into the operating room. Three anesthesiologists leaned over me at the same time to ask if I was ready. I asked them which one of their faces I would be seeing last, right before I went out.

"All of us," one answered.

"Will you do me a favor? Right before I go out, will you say the word *Mahanta* for me?" I knew the Mahanta would carry me through the uncertainties of my coming ordeal.

"Wait, let me write this down," one of the anesthesiologists said, and he scurried to get a pencil. He wrote it out and then laid the paper right over my heart where he could see it and I could feel it. I felt the intense consciousness in the room and then heard the trio chorus, "Mahanta."

I know there is a big picture, a finished, perfect mosaic of how all things fit together in spiritual harmony and oneness. So often it has been this that I have trusted, knowing that while I may not have an inkling of the final outcome, Divine Spirit does. The ECK is always working for my greatest good and the good of all concerned.

In the word *Mahanta,* I felt the perfect mosaic and trusted that the love of Divine Spirit would take care of me.

The operation took eight hours and went without complication. Just hours after the surgery, I couldn't believe how much better I felt. And now, with my renewed health and energy, some days I don't know whether to sing, laugh, or cry with joy at this proof of the divine love of Spirit.

Getting Advice in Your Dreams

Jacquelyn Davis

*L*ast year, I went to the doctor for a routine checkup. The doctor told me I had a lump on the right side of my thyroid gland. He wanted to do some testing. I became very anxious.

The doctor reassured me. The lump on my thyroid wasn't normal, but it wasn't uncommon. He did a biopsy to extract some of the thyroid tissue and ran some tests. He wanted to see if the growth was benign or malignant.

The next day, the doctor called me. The growth was malignant. He recommended surgery.

I'd never had surgery before. I was so frightened the doctor urged me to take a few days to calm down and think about it. Then I could decide if I wanted him to remove the thyroid or perhaps visit another surgeon for another opinion.

Childishly, I decided if I didn't think about my thyroid, maybe the growth would go away. But the doctor called me after a few days and had his assistant book a 3:00 p.m. appointment. I reluctantly agreed, wondering how I would decide: to have the thyroid taken out or visit another surgeon for a second opinion.

I tried to settle my mind and contemplate. I asked

my inner guide, the Mahanta, what to do. Perhaps I would receive a sign during my spiritual exercise, some kind of indication that I was going to be OK and what I should do.

I sat in bed and tried to focus, but I was still very upset. I picked up a copy of the holy scriptures of Eckankar, *The Shariyat-Ki-Sugmad,* and simply held the book to my chest. I was so distraught I couldn't read.

The next thing I knew, I was asleep but awake in a dream. I was going to my appointment the next day. In my hand was a slip of paper with the location written on it. It said 3:00 p.m. on the third floor. So I walked into the building and stepped into the elevator.

Instead of going up or down, the elevator went to the right. This was strange! I got off the elevator and tried another one, but it also went to the right. So I went up to a woman sitting at an information desk. "I'm trying to get to the third floor," I explained, "but I can't get there."

She said, "See that man standing over there? He works on the elevators and can help you get upstairs."

I approached the man, but he said he didn't work on the elevators. Grabbing a guy who was walking by, he said, "This guy does. Ask him." The second man was in surgeon's garb, with a mask over his face. After hearing my problem, he took a panel off the wall near the elevators. It had many twinkling lights and wires inside.

He turned to me and said, "Well, there's a problem with the microparticles."

"Microparticles?" I asked.

"Yes, there are microparticles in here, and we have to get rid of them," he said kindly. "But don't worry, that's my job. I can take care of them." He worked in the panel for a few minutes and then told me to go back to the elevator. This time it went up to the correct floor, and I kept my appointment.

The next morning, I wondered what the dream was about. The word *microparticles* made no sense to me. And I was still unclear as to what I was supposed to do.

I went to my appointment with a heavy heart. The doctor came in and asked, "Are we going to do the surgery?"

I asked, "What exactly did your first tests show?"

"Well," he replied, "when we first did the biopsy, the growth looked benign. But then we did an isotope test with iodine. Microparticles showed up on the scan. They look like little sparkling lights on the scanner."

I looked at him in wonder and said, "Microparticles?"

"Yes, microparticles. It means we have to remove the growth and the right side of the thyroid."

Forgetting that my dream wasn't physically real, I blurted out, "So you're the man who does surgery to take care of microparticles."

He looked at me in amusement and said, "Yes, I guess I am."

I knew I'd gotten the guidance I needed from Divine Spirit in my dream. I told the doctor to schedule the surgery, and everything turned out fine. My health has improved, and I feel as if I have crossed a great hurdle in my life.

Gaining Freedom from Drugs

Henry Street

I found Eckankar at the very lowest point of my life. For about ten years, I had been smoking crack, the most harmful form of cocaine. I was in my late forties and had gotten to the point where I didn't care what happened in my life. Sometimes I didn't even care if I woke up in the morning.

Because of my drug use, we'd lost our family home and had been forced to move into an apartment. I'd lost my job and was working as superintendent of the apartment complex. My relationship with my children had totally deteriorated, and my wife had a serious illness that suddenly landed her in the hospital. She was paralyzed and not expected to live.

Every week, I was smoking more and more cocaine. It got so bad that my job was threatened; we were on the brink of homelessness.

One day in the middle of this I ran into a young woman who was a fellow Muslim. I started to salute her in the name of Allah, when she said, "I'm no longer a Muslim." For some reason this didn't strike me as odd. I asked her what she was now.

"I'm a member of Eckankar," she said.

The word struck a deep chord inside of me. I asked

her if it was Egyptian. I know now that the word *Eckankar* means "Co-worker with God," but at the time I didn't. Since I kept pestering her about this unusual word, she eventually brought me a couple of ECK books to read.

When I read *The Tiger's Fang* by Paul Twitchell, I felt as if I had traveled with him on many of the inner experiences he describes. I immediately became a member of Eckankar. And my life began to change.

One night I prayed to God for two hours about my wife. When I finished I knew in my heart that she was going to be all right. So I went to the hospital. She was still paralyzed, but a few days later she moved her little finger. She eventually got full use of her body back, and today she has only a slight difficulty with one leg. She walks with a cane.

I was still fooling around with drugs in those early days, so I asked the Mahanta to help me get free of them. One night I had a dream about the drugs. Usually when I dreamed about cocaine, I would wake up with an incredible craving for it. No matter what time of day or night it was, I would have to go out and find some.

This time I found myself in the dream state stacking rocks of cocaine in a smoking pipe. I was piling them high like ice cream in a cone. But just as I brought a match to the pipe, the whole image disappeared. I just shrugged my shoulders and walked away.

When I woke up, I was amazed at what had happened in my dream. Had that happened in my waking state, I would have normally had a fit—that was the power the drug had over me. But when I woke up from this dream, the desire for cocaine was totally gone. And it hasn't come back since then.

I knew I had to give back to life what the Mahanta had given me by freeing me from the power of drugs. In the neighborhood where I live, I started an antidrug program to help others fight drugs. I also work with Rutgers University on a community literacy program which involves people who are recovering addicts.

Today life is an adventure. I often meet people who are struggling with drugs. My gift is that I'm now able to share with them the gifts the Mahanta has given me.

"You Are Cured"

Hallie Shepherd

The year was 1982, right after my thirty-first birthday. My thirteen-year-old niece, Becky, had just come home from school with some great news. She'd won first place in an art contest and was headed to Texas for a national art show.

I was so excited, I chased her around the front lawn. We were like two puppies frolicking on a warm spring day, romping and rolling in the grass.

All of a sudden, I felt completely drained of energy. My muscles felt like those of a newborn babe. I was almost too weak to sit up. I felt zapped of all energy and strength. *Gee,* I thought, *maybe I'm coming down with a horrible case of the flu.*

That night we were going to take Becky out to dinner to celebrate her good news. So rather than let the illness take hold, I dragged myself into the bathroom. A nice, long, relaxing soak in the tub was my cure for stress and illness. I felt lightheaded as I lay there soaking. But I was determined to outrun this illness.

This strategy usually works for me, but it didn't this time. As I attempted to get out of the tub, I almost passed out. Every time I tried to crawl out, I got dizzy. Lights danced in front of my eyes, and I almost fainted.

I collapsed back in the bathtub and finally found the strength to pound on the wall and call for help. Paramedics and the fire department were quickly summoned. When the paramedics took my vital signs, they found I had almost no blood pressure. I was pretty close to death.

I spent a week in the hospital, while every conceivable test was run. I had CAT scans, I was poked and prodded, and the doctors took what seemed like pints of blood. I saw doctor after doctor; each tried to figure out what was making me so weak.

Finally they sent me home. The next day, my primary doctor called me. "Hallie," he said, "I'm afraid I have some bad news. You have a very rare condition called Addison's disease."

"What's that?" I asked.

"Addison's disease is a complete shutdown of your adrenal glands. It's rare and used to be fatal," he said. "Now it can be controlled by medications, usually some form of steroid." He then said I'd have to take cortisone every day of my life.

Needless to say, with such a strong remedy, I needed careful monitoring. The best doctors were a few hours away in San Francisco. So for three years, I faithfully traveled into the city every six months for careful monitoring by an endocrinologist.

I usually stayed at my brother Phil's house in Marin County, which is close to San Francisco. Phil was a member of Eckankar. In the 1970s I had also been a member, but I had later dropped away.

I was familiar with the ideas of Eckankar, and Phil kept me posted on new developments. I looked forward to seeing him each time I went to San Francisco. We would visit, and then I would sleep in his guest room.

One night, I had a very vivid dream. In the dream, the Mahanta, the Living ECK Master came to me. He bathed me in the most beautiful, radiant white light. It was like being wrapped in the warmest, softest cotton I could imagine.

Love and warmth gently showered down on me. Then the Mahanta whispered, "You are cured."

With startling clarity, I saw all my bodies—mental, causal, emotional, and physical—begin to shimmer and vibrate with white light. It looked like white soda pop bubbling and flowing through me. My bodies became perfectly aligned and in harmony with life.

Later that day I hurried to my appointment. When the doctor came in the room, I blurted out, "I don't think I have Addison's disease anymore."

He looked at me very skeptically. "What makes you say that? You must remember that only about twenty-eight cases in medical history have ever been reversed."

Now what was I supposed to tell this man of science? "Gee, Doc, I have this spiritual guide, and in a dream he said I was cured."

I didn't think that was the approach to take. So rather than explaining, I just asked the doctor to test me again. He grudgingly obliged.

I'll never forget the look on his face when he got the results of those tests. He went back over every test I had ever taken, to make sure I'd really had Addison's disease to begin with. Then he looked at me with a quizzical expression. "You are indeed cured," he announced. "We better start tapering you off that medication."

This gift of love from the Mahanta brought me back to Eckankar. It showed me that once you have accepted the Living ECK Master as your guide, you will always be under his umbrella of love and protection. As the Wayshower, he gives us the opportunity to resolve karma and work through the most difficult problems.

The Shariyat-Ki-Sugmad, Book One, (part of the scriptures of ECK) points out that the Mahanta does not perform miracles merely because we ask him to. I learned that the Mahanta gave me a gift of love because it was time for me to move forward on my journey home to God. I am so grateful!

The Gift of Life

Mike Hill

or a long time, life had seemed hard. I felt as if I was dragging my feet through every day. Then I had an experience that pushed me over the wall of illusion.

In mid-August, I developed severe headaches. Soon I was having trouble walking. Even when treading solid ground, I felt like I was balancing on a tightrope.

After several visits, the doctor sent me to the hospital for a CAT scan of my brain. The attendants laid me down on the table and proceeded with the scan. As it progressed I saw a Blue Light, signaling the presence of the Mahanta. Through a deep sense of knowingness, I realized that something was seriously wrong with my physical body. At the same time, I was sure that everything was going to be OK, that the experience would bring about a spiritual healing.

Later the doctor told me they'd found a cyst the size of a tennis ball lodged in my brain. It was putting so much pressure on my brain that I couldn't walk. It also affected my balance when I tried to stand.

I checked into the hospital that night for surgery in the morning. So much went on during the night before the operation that I didn't get much sleep. Attendants probed, stuck, and examined my body.

In the morning, the doctor came in and told me there was a good chance this tumor was cancerous and had spread to other parts of my body.

But I knew deep inside that I was going to be fine. After the operation, I was in the intensive care unit for two days. Then I was moved to a regular hospital room. That night, I had a beautiful light show from the ECK. The room was dark, and I was by myself when the walls lit up with a tremendous light display. It looked like huge fireworks going off all around me.

I closed my eyes and saw the Mahanta, Sri Harold Klemp, and the ECK Master Rebazar Tarzs outlined in blue light next to my bed. Then a happy baby floated next to them in the blue light, full of life.

A door opened at the foot of my bed. I knew it was for me. My eyes opened to a whole new world as I walked through the door in my inner vision.

After this profound inner experience, I fell asleep and dreamed a very special dream. A large group of ECKists were standing shoulder-to-shoulder in a circle, singing HU, the ancient name for God. It was very dark, and as we finished, we each went our separate way, still singing this song of praise for the Sugmad. Suddenly, a shaft of blue light arced from the ground to the highest point in the sky, and the sky exploded into bright blue.

In the dream, the light picked me up and sent me spinning into nothingness. I alighted in a beautiful land, like something in *The Wizard of Oz*. Color saturated everyone and everything. Brilliantly hued bugs and insect-like creatures in all colors covered the ground.

I've always had a fear of insects and spiders. But I lost all such fear. I wasn't afraid of life anymore. A short, hobbit-like man came up to me. "Can I do anything for you?" he inquired. "It's my job to help you in any way I can. Ask me anything."

"I'm fine for now, thanks," I told him with a big smile. Then I woke up.

I knew the dream was a wonderful confirmation of my reentry into life. Fear had kept me in a rut until that point. Facing the brain tumor had vaulted me into a new realm of possibilities and rich color. But the dream gifts were not over.

Then I had another dream. I was with some old friends from this life. We were struggling to get out of the bowels of the earth.

An old steel structure held us captive, and it took all our strength to make it outside. But it wasn't much better on the surface. The ground was shaking as a volcano erupted. Lava poured toward us as we fled to safe ground. This represented my old state of consciousness.

Then the dream shifted. I was in the company of ECKists, traveling in a much more peaceful and sane world. We climbed upward to a land of flowing waters and bathed in their freshness. As we rested at water's edge for a spell, I noted the huge mountains which reached up as far as the eye could see. I knew I had to explore beyond them. I was on a spiritual quest and would not stop. Then I woke up.

This dream reminded me of the spiritual purpose of my life every day. One by one, the doctors filed by to deliver the same message: "You don't know what a lucky man you are." Tests showed that the surgeon had gotten all of the tumor out. There were no other traces of cancer.

I don't consider myself lucky. Instead, I feel blessed.

This gift from the ECK and the Mahanta has helped me wake up to my fuller potential as Soul. I have never been weary of life since!

The Making of a Healing

Fay Elliss

'll never forget the day I was informed that my six-year-old great-grandson, Jimmy, had cancer. It had started in his jaw and had now reached his brain. An inch of jawbone had already been removed. Now the cancer had turned inward, beyond the surgeon's reach. Jimmy was being treated with radiation, but his chances of survival were not good. The news stunned me.

That day I started to evaluate my belief in ECK, the Holy Spirit. Was it real, or was I merely giving lip service? A great faith in Divine Spirit rose in me, and I asked for help from the Inner Master, the Mahanta.

Morning and night, I released Jimmy to the Mahanta's care. I would often see Jimmy on the inner, surrounded by the pure, white Light of God. I would turn him over completely to Divine Spirit, knowing he was in good hands.

After a few days, a transforming experience occurred. I awoke from sleep to find the room brilliantly lit.

I was disoriented as I sat up and looked around. It felt like I had suddenly awakened in an operating room at a hospital. The room was empty except for a long table covered by a white sheet. I stared and stared, wondering what it all meant. Five female doctors appeared on right side of the table. They were joined by five male doctors, who stood on the left side of the operating table.

Their uniforms were the whitest I have ever seen. They seemed to be standing at attention: so close to each other—arms touching—so precisely arranged.

I heard myself say, "I want Jimmy." A round, metal shape appeared from the ceiling. Brilliant streams of white light poured all around the sphere, and then a child-sized body appeared on the table. It was Jimmy, swathed in white bandages.

Jimmy was in the center of a huge light that poured down from the ceiling. I remember thinking: *He is surrounded by the pure, white Light of God!*

After I had taken the scene in for a few moments, it began to fade. I lay back in bed, and right over me were three lettuce-colored stems, about two inches in diameter and three feet long. I lay there thinking how strong the stems were. They seemed to be connections of love.

I began to feel their strength entering my body—and somehow I knew Jimmy would be all right.

Soon after, I went to California to visit Jimmy. I didn't know what to expect. I found my little great-grandson very listless. Although he was home, he had a feeding machine attached to him by a tube through his nose. His mouth and throat had been burned by the radiation treatments. He could not eat or swallow.

However, the very next day, for some unknown reason, the tube on the feeding machine broke. Jimmy's eyes started to shine with a most amazing light! He ran outside; he even got on his bicycle and rode around. At dinner he ate and ate.

To this day, many years later, Jimmy is healthy. He goes to school five days a week. As a precaution, he had a few months of chemotherapy. Then his doctors were amazed to pronounce him free of cancer. The doctors had planned to do reconstructive surgery on Jimmy's jaw. But to their amazement, a tooth started growing in that area, and new bone tissue eventually filled the gap left by the original surgery.

Before I left for home, Jimmy gave me a big hug. His arms went around my waist like two strong stems, and again, I knew: *He would be fine.*

I've learned that it never hurts to ask and be open to the gifts of ECK.

Send in the Clowns

Ed Adler

fter studying the teachings of Eckankar for over twenty years, I'm beginning to realize my present state of consciousness always tries to keep me in my present state of consciousness. Don't get me wrong! I've been blessed with more than my share of divine love, inner guidance, and perhaps some out-and-out miracles, as well.

But I have noticed that whenever my life is moving along smoothly and I feel I've solved all of life's mysteries, the ECK decides to test my true spiritual progress by tossing me a difficult situation.

Do I complain? Well, maybe just a little.

For example, there was that time I felt some sharp, lower abdominal pains. I ignored them at first, figuring they would go away. But they didn't go away. My father had suffered with colon cancer, so fear kept me from admitting that maybe there was a dangerous health problem here, something that needed immediate attention.

I really needed to see my doctor, but I dreaded medical examinations. I couldn't figure out why the examinations made me so anxious. Whenever any doctors had examined me in the past, they had been kind and considerate. I couldn't trace my unreasonable fear back to any traumatic event.

If I was going to procrastinate about seeing a physician, I thought I should at least check out my health situation on the inner with my friend and spiritual guide, Sri Harold Klemp. There was some tension at first, but I finally managed to relax enough to begin a spiritual exercise. As always, Sri Harold was close by. We greeted each other warmly. And did I complain? Well, maybe just a little.

"You know, I don't like what's been happening to my health, lately, Harold," I said. "This pain is making me very nervous. My life was nice and peaceful for a while, but now it feels more like a wild roller-coaster ride. Is all this really necessary?" I asked.

"You bet it is," responded the firm, inner voice. "It's true that the pain isn't much fun, but it's sure to get your attention. Maybe, if you're persistent, you'll discover the lesson in your problem."

"How about a little help?" I asked.

"Here's a little hint. Why don't you start by working on your diet?" the Inner Master answered.

Do I listen to that helpful voice? Usually—but not always. I might decide, instead, to do it "my way."

The pains in my abdomen were becoming more violent and insistent; I couldn't wait any longer. I needed to call the doctor as soon as possible.

"I'm sorry, but the doctor is too busy to see you right now," his nurse said when I finally called the office. "I can schedule an appointment for you in two weeks."

"Isn't that wonderful," I replied without much enthusiasm.

Somehow I got through those two weeks, but I did notice my anxiety level rising. The night before my medical examination, I lay rigid on my back, unable to sleep, staring up at strange shadows playing slow-motion tag on the ceiling. As the hours dragged by, I would occasionally glance over at the clock ... 1:00 a.m. ... 2:00 a.m.

And then, it seemed as though I awoke with a start. I couldn't see anything, but I was filled with anguish. The hairs on the back of my neck stood out straight, and the fierce, icy claw of fear began to squeeze my whole body, gripping it tighter and tighter. It felt like I was frozen in marble, unable to move a muscle.

Just when I thought I couldn't stand it for one second longer, a brilliant, white spotlight lit up a six-foot jack-in-the-box at the foot of the bed. The top of the box burst open, and out sprang a huge, smiling, papier-mâché head. It was fashioned in the likeness of my friend Sri Harold, and he was wearing clown's paint. Hovering over me at the end of its powerful spring within a few inches of my astonished face, the head gleefully shouted out, "Booo!"

I instantly realized that all my fears were as absurd as this extraordinary vision. Laughter quickly welled up inside me, and huge waves of relief shook my entire body, completely releasing the fear and tension that had been building for so long.

My wife, startled by my noisy laughter in the middle of the night, thought at first I had finally gone over the edge. I reassured her that, no, everything was truly fine. I was now confident that the upcoming medical exam would prove I did not have a dread disease.

Since the rising sun was just beginning to peek through the bedroom window, I decided not to go back to sleep. Instead, I did a spiritual exercise in order to contact my friend, Sri Harold. I was very relaxed now, so it was possible to make a strong connection.

"HU-U-U-U," I sang softly, and I began to feel Sri Harold's reassuring presence.

"Ed," he said, "I've been trying to work with you about your fear of medical examinations, but you've been a little tense lately. I had a tough time getting through. We don't need to spend a lot of time with this since it's very old stuff; but just watch this scene, and then let it go."

And there it was, the doctor's office of my childhood. But as I glanced over at the examination table, the image wavered and shifted. It wasn't the doctor's table I was seeing—it was a medieval torture rack. I was instantly filled with the memory I had so long suppressed. In a past life, I had been tortured to death during the Spanish Inquisition. But Sri Harold was right—it was old stuff. It had nothing to do with my life today. I could finally let it go. As I released it, I could feel the fear being washed away.

"Thank you," I said. "What a relief to understand all that torture business."

Then I remembered the sharp pains I was having in my abdomen. "Is it cancer?" flashed through my mind.

"No," he answered my unasked question, "you don't have cancer. Just stop drinking coffee."

"It's that simple?" I asked.

"It's that simple," he replied. And then he was gone.

I won't tell you there weren't any anxious moments in the doctor's examination room later that day. But the old terror was truly gone. And, of course, the doctor couldn't find anything seriously wrong with my intestines. I did ask him if drinking coffee could be responsible for the abdominal pain.

"No, I don't think so," he replied. "Not unless you've been drinking an excessive amount."

I told him I never drank more than two or three cups a day. But I had already decided to follow Sri Harold's suggestions and stop drinking even that moderate amount. Within twenty-four hours after giving up coffee, the pain stopped. It hasn't returned.

The next time I met with Sri Harold during a spiritual exercise, I thanked him again for all his help.

"But Harold," I couldn't resist adding, "a jack-in-the-box—that's outrageous!"

Who says the ECK always has to be serious?

9

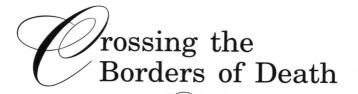

Crossing the
Borders of Death

When you gain power over the fear of
death, there is nothing that can hold you
back in this life. . . . All that a true spiritual teaching can give you is assurance of
the eternal nature of Soul, that you are
Soul and that you live forever.

—Sri Harold Klemp,
   The Book of ECK Parables,
   Volume One

My inner screen filled with brilliant blue, pulsating light. Then a golden light grew inside the field of blue. And my husband stood inside that light, happy and full of love.

Love Never Dies

Frances Blackwell

One Saturday morning in August, I was on my way to the post office when I took a wrong turn. Instead of turning left, I turned right and would have to double back through a series of turns.

As soon as I turned down the different route, I felt silence everywhere. I rounded a curve. There in the middle of the road lay a man. My first thought was, *He's a runner who's had a heart attack.* I parked the car on the side of the road and got out to see if I could help.

When I stepped out of the car, I felt as if I'd stepped into the presence of God. The area around the fallen man felt like a very holy place. Then I saw his terrible wounds and knew he'd been hit by a car and there wasn't much time.

I looked at him and said, "I'll be right back. May the blessings be." The latter is an ancient blessing in Eckankar.

I ran to the nearest house, yelling, "Call 911! Call for help!" They did. Then I ran back to the man and knelt beside him, singing HU, an ancient name for God.

The first notes came out as sobs, for my heart was ·

breaking with compassion. I heard the Inner Master remind me, "Frances, you have a task to do. Focus on it." So I centered myself, and the HU came out as clear as a bell, "HU-U-U."

The man's body suddenly stopped spasming. He turned and looked me in the eye. I knew Soul was recognizing the Light and Sound of God in the HU I sang. My inner hearing opened, and I could hear the man speaking. His only concern was for his family. "My wife, my family," he said silently, "please let them know."

I said to God, "How can I do this? This man doesn't have any identification on him."

The next minute, a man stopped his car and ran over. "Can I help?" he asked. Then, as he knelt beside me, he gasped, "Oh, my God, it's Stan."

"Do you know this man?" I asked.

He nodded yes.

"Please, go get his family. He wants his family to know."

The man hurried away. The injured man relaxed as soon as he knew this was taken care of. His next concern was voiced to me silently: "I need the blessings of God."

I said, "You have earned the right to walk in the presence of God. You have learned love and compassion and giving of yourself in this lifetime. You live forever in the worlds of God."

Soon the paramedics came and put the man in an ambulance. I continued to kneel at the side of the road, silently singing HU. A few minutes later, a small branch fell from a tree and landed gently beside me, and I felt waves of peace and love. I knew this Soul had translated from this world in the process we call death.

I left the scene sometime later, but for days I felt connected to this Soul. I was so touched by what had happened that I went to his funeral service. It confirmed everything that had been shown to me in those few precious moments in the middle of the road.

The minister spoke of how Stan had undergone a transformation in the last months of his life. He'd learned more about love and surrender and had a spiritual breakthrough while reading a particular story in the Bible.

The Bible story that touched him was about an angel who had come to a man in the middle of the road. The angel wrestled the man to the ground, and the man asked, "Who are you?" The angel said, "Why do you need to know?" And the man in the story answered, "I need the blessings of God."

That story struck my heart with love. After the service, I felt an urge to talk to Stan's wife, but I didn't want to overwhelm her with details of her husband's last moments. So I asked inwardly for help from Divine Spirit.

In that instant, someone called my name. It was a colleague of my husband's. He said, "Fran, I didn't know you knew Stan."

"I only met him in the last moments of his life," I said. "And the light around him was as bright as the morning sun."

"You've got to tell that to his wife," he said. "It will help her to hear your words." So he led me over and introduced me to Stan's wife; he mentioned I had found Stan and stayed with him in the road, and that I had an experience to share with her when the time was appropriate.

A few days later she called and invited me to come

to her house. Stan's brother and some other relatives were there. She wanted me to tell them what had happened.

"I hope I can tell it without crying," I faltered.

"It's OK," she said. "We've all been crying."

When I finished sharing my story, the wife said, "I'm so grateful that you were there for my husband. He let me know too that he was well and in heaven. After the funeral I went to sit alone in our backyard, and a butterfly hovered around me. It wouldn't leave. In my church, a butterfly is a religious symbol of the resurrection."

"In my church," I said, "we believe that Soul is eternal and lives forever." I felt she understood perfectly.

My experience with Stan's death was one of love and deep inner meaning, but I didn't know at the time that it was also one of preparation.

Just a few short weeks later, my own husband went into the hospital. Blackwell was an inspiration in his work as a jazz musician (a drummer), composer, and teacher—and his perseverance with life, because for the past twenty years, he'd lived with kidney failure and was on dialysis. His colleagues said he was a walking miracle.

I didn't know this was to be his last stay in the hospital, but I knew I needed to be close to him. I had a cot put in his room. There were many poignant moments during this time. One night I found him quietly crying.

"I don't want to leave you," he said. "Do you know how much I love you?" Not long after that he went into intensive care.

It is never easy to let go of a loved one. But the

312

transformation that took place on the roadside in early August eased my way. The doctors all tried to save my husband, but they knew they couldn't. I could see the unspoken words in their eyes. So I went into the hospital chapel and asked the Mahanta, "Please show me beyond the shadow of a doubt what my husband wants."

My inner screen filled with brilliant blue, pulsating light. Then a golden light grew inside the field of blue. And my husband stood inside that light, happy and full of love.

"Tell me what you want," I asked him.

"I'm ready to go," he said. "I love you."

I went back to the doctors. "There's something none of you have been able to say to me," I told them. "My husband is dying." We cried, and then we acknowledged that it was time to let go. I felt this set him free.

So we prepared for his leaving. His friends and family were there, and we had music from his latest recording playing in the room. He was surrounded by loved ones. In his final moments we all sang the HU. I saw the Mahanta take him into a heaven, one of the worlds of God. My heart was filled with gladness and sadness, both part of Divine Spirit, both part of divine love.

A few days later I was sitting on the edge of my bed crying. I missed my husband. Suddenly his presence filled the whole room and my heart with light and love. He sang a song to me:

Don't cry for me,
Though I've gone away.
I'll never leave your heart.
I'll speak to you in the Voice of God.
Forever, you walk in my soul.
Don't cry for me,

Though I cherish your tears.
They are the way your heart can heal.
I'm never far.
And you're always near,
Between a smile and a tear.
Don't cry for me,
You *know* the beat goes on
In the breath of all living things.
I'll sing life's song,
Sacred rhythm drum,
Beating time at its own game.
Don't cry for me—
I'm free.

A few weeks later, Laura, Stan's wife, sent me a card. In it she wrote that she had read about my husband's death and his courage. She said, "He was so fortunate to have you by his side."

I am grateful for the gifts these experiences have brought me. I'm discovering that love—all love—is God's love. And every act of giving with a loving heart brings us closer and closer to learning about a love for all life.

Celebrate life! Dare to love!

Love endures. Love doesn't change. Love lives forever.

Farewell to Brian

Tom Mapp

anuary 5, 1978, a cold gray day, found me poring over my books. I was trying to prepare for my comprehensive exams. This particular afternoon, study was more difficult than usual. I tried to concentrate, finally closing my eyes, only to find myself far away in consciousness.

I was in a place with light emanating from the very air, like a warm, friendly fog. I immediately recognized this to be the Astral Plane, which I had visited in my inner travels as a student of Eckankar. Next to me was my friend Brian, a blind scientist. "Brian!" I cried out, and just as on the physical plane, Brian recognized me by my voice.

"Tom!" he responded, "what's happening?"

I answered matter-of-factly, "Brian, I think you just died."

Brian's physical body was hundreds of miles away in Philadelphia, and he was sick with cancer. When I had last seen him, six weeks before, Brian was not expecting to live much longer. As I left I had said to him, "I'll see you again." I had said it not to give him some false hope that he was going to fight off the disease, but rather to affirm a strong feeling that I would see him again. And so it happened, although not on the physical plane.

Continuing in the experience, I saw the scene in Philadelphia by perceiving the emotional states of nearby people. I thought I recognized Sue, Brian's wife, quiet and calm. I thought I recognized Brian's sister, also calm, somewhat farther away. The tranquil nature of the scene there made me question my assumption that Brian's physical body had died.

So I said to him, "Oh, maybe not." And we zipped back to the place where we had met only moments before.

Brian wanted to know where we were. I told him it appeared to be the Astral Plane. Brian wanted to know more about the Astral Plane. "You move around by thinking yourself to other places," I began, and we talked for a while.

In this place with the luminous air, there had been no other features of landscape. But then I noticed that there were other beings nearby. We tried to approach them, but they kept their distance, although the closest one radiated loving energy. I guessed that these entities had previously died themselves and that they were keeping their distance because Brian had not died yet.

As quickly as it began, the experience ended. I opened my eyes on the physical plane and saw my desk and textbooks. About fifteen minutes had elapsed.

That evening, calls began arriving to tell me that Brian had just died. But my experiences with Brian were not yet over.

The next night I saw Brian briefly during my spiritual exercises. I told Brian that he did not have to be blind anymore. Two days later during another contemplation I met Brian again, this time for a longer encounter. Brian looked stronger and more upright, without the odd tilt of his head which I associated with his blindness—and he wasn't blind! He was excited about what he would be doing next.

Brian, ever a scientist, wanted to give me some information to verify our meetings. The passing of information proved to be difficult. Apparently my mind has a censor, only allowing certain information to be stored. Brian could tell me his address where he grew up, and I could hear that on the Astral Plane, but I could not get it into my lower mind for recall later.

After some effort and frustration, we got through the name of Brian's aunt. Brian told me that the loving entity I had seen in our first inner meeting was his aunt who had died several years before him. I said good-bye to my friend, and I have not tried to contact him again.

A month later I met with Sue and a few others from our old group of close friends. Sue was able to verify the name of Brian's aunt.

Sue also told me that the moment I had been with Brian on the Astral Plane, Brian had fallen asleep. Before sleeping, Brian was able to talk to her and respond coherently, but after that nap Brian only babbled. A transition had occurred at that time.

My experiences with Brian gave power to my belief that there is a life after the death of our physical bodies. This assurance has been of great comfort to me.

Answers from a Dream

Joann C. Carbone

I had always wondered about death. As a student of Eckankar, I knew that Soul lived on after this life. But would death itself be scary or painful?

One night I had a dream that was just as vivid and real as my everyday life. I was riding through the lush, hilly countryside with my husband, Dan. Brandy, one of my golden retrievers, was in the back of the Jeep. Without any warning, the car veered off the road. Suddenly we were hurtling through space toward the bottom of a cliff! I remember bracing for the impact and thinking, *What a painful way to die!*

Before the car struck the ground, both Dan and I found ourselves standing on top of the cliff. We looked down at the car as it went up in flames. There was no pain. As Soul, we'd left our physical bodies before the impact occurred.

Confused and dazed, Dan and I turned to each other and hugged. We were OK.

Then we looked around as if to say, "What's next?" We didn't know what to do or where we were.

We slowly turned away from the sight of the burning car and surveyed the landscape behind us. A short way ahead was a lovely one-story resort or motel. As we approached it, a lady scurried around the corner of one of the buildings.

She carried a book or notepad in her hands. When she saw us, she appeared flustered for a moment. Then she checked her book again and smiled. "We didn't expect you for another second," she laughed, "but welcome! Let me take you to a comfortable place where you can wait until your Master takes you to your new home."

We followed the pleasant woman. She reminded me a little of Edith Bunker on the old TV series *All in the Family*. Sweet and a little scattered. Suddenly I stopped.

"What about my dog?" I blurted out. "Brandy was with us in the car!"

Our kindly hostess smiled again, turned, and consulted her book. Then she looked at her wristwatch. "Oh yes, your dog, Brandy. He will be along right about now."

Just then, Brandy trotted around the corner of the building, wagging his tail in an enthusiastic greeting.

As I reached down to pat him, I woke up in bed. For a long time, I didn't move or speak. I thought about this dream gift from the Inner Master. Now I knew what death might be like.

There was no fear. There was no pain. It was a smooth transition from one frame of reference to another. As Soul, my husband and I had simply turned our backs on one life and started another. I thanked Wah Z, the Dream Master, for this experience. It has brought me a deep feeling of peace and reassurance. Now I feel I can live my daily life with less fear and more joy!

Helping Another Across

Deborah Williams

My dearest uncle, who lived in Florida, died recently of a rare cancer of the blood. I called him often during the last few months of his life.

One day I was driving alone on the freeway when I heard someone call my name. I don't usually hear voices, but this one seemed familiar. I had a feeling that someone I loved was with me in the car.

When I got home, a message told me of my uncle's death just a few minutes before.

I knew instantly that the voice I had heard in the car had been my uncle's. I hadn't recognized it at first because it had been the voice of a youthful man in his prime. Chemotherapy and radiation treatments had made my uncle's voice old and raspy, painful to listen to. I knew this experience was to give me proof that Soul lived on forever.

I decided to fly back to Florida with my father to attend the funeral. This wasn't an easy decision for me. I had many painful memories of Florida from a previous marriage. But when I thought about my uncle, all I felt was love. I asked the Inner Master if I could be a vehicle for love during the visit and maybe help my family and friends.

The church was filled with people who had come to honor my uncle. After the service, we went back to my aunt's house. There I met a close friend of the family.

He was very striking, with his gray hair and the bluest eyes I'd ever seen. He sat down next to me and said, "I know the church says that when you die, that's the end. But I just can't buy that. What do you think?"

I took a deep breath and said, "You know, I agree with you. Soul lives on. It lives on forever."

"Well!" he said. "How do you know that?"

"I've experienced it," I replied calmly. I told him about my experience with my uncle. He had visited me after his death to say farewell and give me love.

"Are you a psychic?" he asked, fascinated.

"No," I laughed. "But I might be a little more open to the idea of life after death than most people. I belong to a spiritual path that teaches you awareness through spiritual exercises. It's Eckankar, the Religion of Light and Sound of God."

Then I wanted to turn the conversation around and see what he thought. "Why are you asking these questions? Have you had some spiritual experience too?"

The man smiled and began to tell me a story. He used to travel around the world with my aunt and uncle. One time they went to Greece. He walked into the Olympic ring as a casual tourist when suddenly he saw crowds of cheering people. Their roar surrounded him. He looked down and saw himself standing in an athlete's body.

"It took all my willpower not to bring my hand to my chest, just like the athletes did in ancient Greece," he exclaimed, eyes aglow.

"No one could ever take that experience from me," he concluded. "I'm a Catholic, but I'm also questioning how that happened. I want to know more."

We went on to talk about Eckankar and even sang HU together. I told him, "If you sing HU for twenty minutes a day, your life will unfold and be uplifted. You can become more sensitive to God's messages."

Our conversation wound down after that. He said in parting, "It was wonderful to meet you again. I don't know why I say that, except somehow I know we've met before." Chills went up and down my spine.

He left the house within minutes. I stood watching him go, realizing we'd both gotten what we needed: proof of Soul's immortality, and a chance to serve Divine Spirit.

An Unusual Reunion

Decy Orrick

On February 3, 1987, an old friend from college, Bruce, went to a public park, put a gun to his head, and ended his life.

Bruce's death was my first exposure to suicide, and for the week following his funeral, I walked around with a knot in my stomach and a profound feeling of hopelessness and sorrow. Thankfully, the passage of time helped ease the pain.

Then one night in the dream state, I found myself back in my college fraternity house where I had spent many happy years. I knew immediately that I was somewhere in the Astral Plane because I noticed several subtle differences in the building. There was some sort of reunion in progress and many of my fraternity brothers were going from room to room greeting one another.

As I made my way along the corridors I shook hands with many old friends. I had to smile to myself when I saw the alumni association president sporting a mustache which he would never wear in the physical universe. I was a little surprised that no one seemed to realize that I was not truly a part of this scene in a real sense. I felt I was playing a role in a very special drama. Then I saw Bruce.

Immediately, I gave Bruce a warm hug. I felt tears of joy stream down my face after our embrace, but for some reason I don't think he could see them. I looked at him and said, "I love you."

Calmly Bruce replied, "I know," and suddenly I knew that Bruce needed to talk to me some more.

"What do you know about reincarnation?" he asked.

Instantly I knew that Bruce was about to undergo a rebirth in the physical world. As a student of Eckankar, I felt a responsibility to let him know what I had learned about death and rebirth.

We sat down and had one of those heart-to-heart talks like we had enjoyed fifteen years earlier. This time, however, we spoke about the immortality of Soul, the sacredness of the human vessel, and of Eckankar. I realized that Bruce owed a heavy karmic debt for having taken his own life. For this reason I knew that I had to share my thoughts about developing a love for all life.

We spoke a very long time and then we both sat back. Bruce gave me one of his crazy, cockeyed smiles which had always made me chuckle, and said, "Thanks, Decy." Then I awoke in the physical.

I learned that the truth of Eckankar exists on all planes at all times. I am grateful for being allowed to bring these memories back into the physical to confirm this truth and to have the companionship of an old friend once more.

Messages from Hal

Pat Tennant

My husband, Hal, struggled with cancer for a year before he died. During the final stages of his illness, Hal refused to discuss the possibility that he might die. We had said all the important things to one another, and I longed to talk to him about what he was experiencing. He was a perceptive person and was aware his body was getting progressively weaker, but to the end he firmly believed that he could overcome this enormous obstacle.

After Hal died, he hovered near our six grown children and me for quite some time. I had always believed that death ended all earthly emotions, but that wasn't so. Hal was suffering from the separation as much as we were.

During this emotional time, the children and I recognized a common thread in our dreams—Hal was saying a loving good-bye to each person, and he urged each one to remind me how he felt about me.

This story tells it best.

One day my daughter-in-law, Diana, who lives two thousand miles away, found on her list of things to do, "Phone Hal." She didn't know another Hal, and so she went into contemplation wondering if there was something she could do for him. There was.

His message was to send me a white orchid with a special message which she memorized. She immediately placed the order, and within hours the florist arrived at my door with a white orchid and card that read, enigmatically, "From Diana and Friend."

The Inner Master realizes that I can be a slow learner, so when he wants me to pay attention there will often be a violent thunder and lightning storm lasting no more than five minutes. That happened as the flower was delivered, and I realized this was something even more special than a thoughtful gesture. I sat down to think about it.

Through the years, I've enthusiastically attempted to grow orchids, with limited success. Hal used to bring me a new orchid for special occasions, and I realized, after some prodding from the Master, that the orchid was a special message from Hal. He had chosen Valentine's Day, the anniversary of the day we were engaged. I ran to the phone and called Diana, and she gave me his loving message.

That was when my healing began.

A short time later I found the courage to ask Hal to go on, even though I knew I'd never stop missing him. He did leave then, and one child reported that in a dream she found her father pursuing his fascination with computers on another plane and having a wonderful time.

A Death That
Changed My Life

Rhonda Mattern

A married a French ECKist in 1986. I remember thinking how bizarre, yet
wonderful, it was to spend my entire
wedding reception sitting in a corner with my
new mother-in-law, discussing Eckankar in French.

My mother-in-law, whom I will call Sophie, was
very concerned about her son's involvement in
Eckankar. During our conversation, she interrogated
me about each of the wedding guests.

"That man over there in the nice suit. Is he in
Eckankar?"

"Oui, Sophie."

"And the woman from Togo; I hear she's a lawyer.
Is she involved in this too?"

"Oui, Sophie."

"And the doctor from Versailles? *He's* in ECK?"

"Oui, Sophie."

She was incredulous. How could all these normal
people be involved in something she thought was so
strange?

Over the years, Sophie and I had many heart-to-
heart talks about ECK and other subjects. She even

read an ECK book or two, and though she became more comfortable with Eckankar, she remained skeptical. My husband and I divorced in 1992, but we remained good friends. I stayed in contact with his parents, planning to visit them after the 1992 ECK European Seminar.

A few weeks before my trip to Europe, I got an urgent call from my ex-husband. My heart raced as I tried in vain to make sense of his news: His mother, Sophie, had committed suicide.

My mind went in five hundred directions at once. Sophie, vibrant and beautiful. Sophie, the woman with everything: the right car, the right husband, the right house on the French Riviera, the right clothes.

I hung up the phone in a daze. For hours I paced from one end of my apartment to the other, crying uncontrollably. Somehow I couldn't accept the fact that I would never see her again.

"Wait a minute!" I said. "I *can* see her again!"

Conscious Soul Travel has never been my strong point. Although my years in Eckankar have brought me many incredible out-of-body experiences and lucid dreams, I can rarely bring them on at will. However, in this moment of despair, I felt a new determination to brave the inner planes and see Sophie one last time.

I lay down on my bed and sang HU for a few minutes. Try as I might, nothing happened. I felt ashamed that after eighteen years in Eckankar, I still hadn't mastered the art of Soul Travel.

Once again, waves of sadness and loss washed over me, emotions that my mind labeled as negative. As I tried to push back these feelings, my mind drifted to a passage in one of Paul Twitchell's books. In it, Paul finally succeeds in initiating a meeting with his teacher,

Rebazar Tarzs. The secret, Paul discovered, was to travel on a vibrational field between himself and his teacher on the inner planes.

Suddenly I realized that the key was not putting aside my feelings but using them as a way to travel to Sophie. My feelings were beautiful, deep, and totally appropriate to the moment. They were a wave issuing from my heart, a wave I could ride into the higher worlds.

With this in mind, I began focusing on the love I felt for Sophie. I felt myself being lifted in a dizzying, spiraling motion. Before I knew it, I was standing on a cloud, and Sophie was beside me looking rather confused.

A cloud, I thought. *How corny. This can't be real. Where are the temples, the Masters? This is just my imagination.*

Sophie was astonished to see me. She spoke to me in excited French.

"Rhonda, it's you! Am I still alive?"

"No. Well, *yes.* I mean, you died, but as Soul you're still alive."

"Why are you here? Are you dead too?"

"No, I wanted to come visit you."

"So this Eckankar, it's all true, then?"

"Oui, Sophie."

In the conversation that followed, Sophie and I discussed the guilt she felt on committing suicide. The whole time I was talking to Sophie, part of me was standing back criticizing: This can't be happening. I must be making it up. I don't really have the ability to consciously Soul Travel.

Suddenly I saw Wah Z (Sri Harold Klemp's spiritual name) by our side, glowing in a blaze of white light.

I told Sophie that I would like to introduce her to someone very special. She saw Wah Z and said to me, "Oh, it's the head of Eckankar. C'est la grosse légume [the big vegetable]." This struck me as an odd statement, but so much was happening at once that I simply brushed it aside.

The three of us stood in a circle and hugged. I could hear sounds swirling all around us and felt a love that words cannot describe. I wanted to stay in that moment forever, but try as I might, I couldn't hold on to the experience. Suddenly I found myself back in my bedroom.

Rooted once more in the physical world, I immediately started to doubt my experience. Each time a doubt would crop up, I'd hear the words *la grosse légume*. After a number of rounds of this, it final ly occurred to me that a message from Divine Spirit was trying to get through.

I called a French friend. "Is *la grosse légume* a standard expression in French?" I asked. He explained that "the big vegetable" was the equivalent of "the big cheese" in English. That made sense: Sophie loved to joke and tease. I could picture her seeing the Mahanta for the first time and referring to him as "the big cheese of Eckankar."

Suddenly I froze. Wait a minute. I didn't know that expression in French. But Sophie did. That meant she *was* there. My experience must have been real!

As the weeks and months pass by, the mind still questions: Maybe I heard *la grosse légume* in conversation once and filed it away unconsciously. Maybe I saw it in a book. Maybe I knew it once but forgot it.

But as Soul, I know the truth. Last month, once again, I rode the waves of love and visited a dear friend on the inner planes.

10

Past Lives, Present Lessons

When the Inner Master shows you a karmic picture from a past life, it is mainly to give you an insight into yourself as you are today—the most perfect spiritual being you have ever been in all your lives. That is who you are today.

—Sri Harold Klemp,
The Eternal Dreamer

Please Wah Z. How can I let go of fear, and love more completely?

Past Lives, Present Healings

Zanna Ford

uring my wintry drive to work, I began to notice two bright yellow road signs. The first was on my regular route: Deaf Child. The other, on a less-direct but sunny road, read Blind Approach.

It was a lonely time. A relationship had just drawn to an end. And a coworker I loved very dearly had closed the door on our friendship. She claimed I was ruthless in my pursuit of what I wanted. She no longer felt comfortable—or even safe—around me.

When I looked at these twin pains with honesty, I had to acknowledge a deep, irrational fear and resistance to love. Some inner door was jammed shut, and I felt panicky at the thought of letting anyone too close. I asked the Inner Master, the Mahanta, to show me a way around this obstacle to love. I remember saying the words aloud, "Please Wah Z. How can I let go of fear, and love more completely?"

That's when I noticed the signs. I knew they were connected to my request, but I didn't know how. After a few weeks of wondering, I set off on a weeklong visit to Australia. I'd wanted to go there since I was ten.

When I boarded the plane in Los Angeles, things looked good. The uncrowded flight afforded a whole row of seats for sleeping. Attendants passed out head-sets for the three movies and offered an array of meals. I settled with a nice fat book, a fruit plate, and a pillow. Before long, I fell into a deep sleep. As I drifted off, I noticed my throat was a little scratchy but put it down to the dry air on the plane. Nothing to worry about. The hours passed quickly.

"Please place your seat backs and tray tables in the upright position as we begin our gradual descent into Sydney," announced the steward. I roused and stowed my thin airline blanket and pillow.

Suddenly an aching sensation swelled behind my ears. My throat was alarmingly sore now, and my sinuses were plugged. I began to whimper and then scream as the plane dropped like a brick over Darling Harbor. I pressed my hands over my ears as my ear-drums crackled, gave way, and burst, causing excru-ciating pain.

By the time the plane taxied to the gate, I was dizzy and stone-deaf. Waves of nausea washed over me. Blood dripped down my cheeks from my throbbing ears. The alarmed flight crew pressed me with damp towels and tried to call for a wheelchair and emergency aid. I refused, trying to be stoic about the pain.

I staggered out to the terminal and sat down to wait for my luggage at the baggage claim carousel, then stood swaying in customs for a half hour to clear my bags. When it was my turn to speak to the customs officer, I couldn't make out a word he was saying. With a chill I remembered the sign: Deaf Child.

Fortunately, a friend was waiting at the gate. She immediately called her teenage son, Jim, to take me to the doctor. The physician was very kind, reassuring me that I wasn't going to lose my hearing. Within thirty minutes I had a prescription for an antibiotic, a pain reliever, and a strong decongestant. All that was required now was a week of bed rest.

What a great way to spend a week in Australia, I thought glumly.

For four days I tossed in my bed, fading in and out of consciousness. My hearing was totally blocked. Periodically I'd crawl to the cool tiles of the bathroom floor to ease my fever, then return shivering to the woolen covers. I was loose in time, thinking about all that had happened since I left the U.S., wondering if it had anything to do with my fear of deep love.

The more I thought about it, the more I saw that my inner block seemed to have two threads: unworthiness on one hand and distrust of myself on the other. There was a closely held belief from the past that I was not deserving of love and that if I let someone in too close, I would hurt them.

As I slept, a past-life visit to Australia slowly came into focus. At first, glimpses came in my dreams. Intrigued, I enlarged upon them with long spiritual exercises, where I sang HU and asked for insight. Slowly the details came, as if I was watching a familiar, yet strange movie.

The year was 1747. I was born in London as a male named Nathan C. Boothe.

A cruel upbringing left me with little compassion for my fellow Souls. At age thirteen I was impressed into service as a sailor, with a job to transport spices and other goods for profit. To insure compliance, the service locked me in leg-irons at night until I accepted my lot as an ill-treated deckhand.

I grew to snarling manhood, fighting my way to a position of authority on deck. My voyages crisscrossed the seas from Cape Horn to exotic Cathay. I had a love of fine teak and Kauri wood, strong ale, and women. But my defining characteristic was ruthlessness.

Twenty-five years later one of my specialties was to deliver prisoners to the penal colony in Australia. We put them aboard ship in leg-irons while still docked in London harbor. After a few months of bread and water, the prisoners lost any will to fight. That's when we set sail for the Southern Cross. Out of a load of eight hundred, a little more than two-thirds usually survived.

If a prisoner crossed me on the voyage he was immobilized in double irons below deck. If he did it a second time, I had him killed. I was deaf in that lifetime to the influence of Divine Spirit: I loved the power of my position. I even ignored the opportunity to jump ship and find love with a woman who cared for me. I had decided to wallow in a low opinion of myself that justified cruelty to others.

In the spring of 1793, we dropped off a load of prisoners and enjoyed a few weeks' leave in Australia, then headed out of Sydney past Norfolk Island for the return trip. An ill wind from the north blew the ship back on a reef, smashing the hull. As water swirled around me, I realized with shock I'd never learned to swim. I died a horrible death, sharks closing in to end my misery.

After that vision, my dizziness faded a bit.

I sat up in bed and turned on the TV to watch a program about sightseeing in Sydney. The program featured the historic seafront area, preserved from the 1700s, called "The Rocks." I knew I had to visit this place; maybe it would complete my inner healing and give me a place to start on my outer renewal.

Just getting dressed and down to the lobby left me out of breath. But I got on a bus and stumbled out when the driver announced The Rocks.

Instinctively I headed for a dark waterfront tavern that looked like the kind Nathan Boothe would have enjoyed. A board in the window advertised beef curry with rice.

Totally out of character by now, I stood at the bar and pounded for attention, ordering a plate of the curry. Two men tried to ignore my rudeness; finally one of them slapped a plate in front of me. I ate the curry with great contentment, feeling like I had finally knit the fabric of Soul's inner and outer experiences together in this dark tavern. Now that I had a feeling for what it had been like to be Boothe, I might be able to release the lingering effect of his pain in my life today.

I walked back out into the tropical sunshine and waited at the corner for the light to change. Still near-deaf and unused to cars careening by on the left side of the road, I had to concentrate to cross safely.

As I stared intently at the traffic signal, I heard a gurgling noise. My ears suddenly drained. Everything was terribly loud: the clatter of shoes on the cobblestones, the birds, people calling. And an insistent beeping sound like the beeping of a loud alarm on an electronic watch.

Excuse me," I said to the businessman next to me, "what's that beeping sound?"

"It's for blind people. The traffic light is letting them know how much time they have to get across the intersection. The beeping speeds up as the light begins to change."

As soon as I heard this piece of Golden-tongued Wisdom, I had to smile. Life was guiding me across a difficult road. I'd just released my deafness from the past, where I hadn't been willing to hear and accept God's love and guidance. Now after many lifetimes I was getting a chance to change. God was signaling me out of my spiritual blindness.

On the final day of my visit, I spent a few hours at the National Maritime Museum where I sat listening to tapes in a replica of a ship, an old clipper. Actors read prisoners' accounts of the harrowing journey to Australia. A wave of acceptance washed over my heart as I truly heard the pain I had inflicted on myself and others.

I saluted the salt-pitted anchor at the entrance of the museum and flew home. Now the second half of my work would begin.

In the weeks that followed, I began to notice how traces of my spiritual deafness and blindness had threaded through most aspects of my inner and outer life. When someone got too close, I would lash out in word and deed; whenever I cared about a job or dream too much, I would somehow push it away. It happened in meetings at work, in projects I wanted so badly yet would sabotage.

My shock grew as spiritual understanding opened: I'd been holding back love in so many ways!

Each day I sang HU and asked for help to heal this area of my life. I asked Wah Z to help me trace the threads of ruthlessness and self-hatred that had dogged my relationships and actions in this life. Each time I identified a thread, I imagined the healing balm of Light and Sound seeping into the age-old cracks and wounds of my heart.

As time passed I began to notice a change. One day, my once-dear coworker began to talk with me in a friendly way, the expression of distaste gone from her face. A breakthrough came when she recommended me for an important project.

"Things are somehow better with you, aren't they?" she commented. We hugged and vowed to work together in harmony.

As love and relaxation gradually eased into my heart, I made a new friend, and a new relationship began to blossom.

It is not common to glimpse past lives directly. But if you are sincere, you can ask to be shown more about love. Then look for the assistance of Divine Spirit, which comes in ways unique to each Soul. It brought me unexpected gifts and the miracle of change.

A Past-Life Recall

Sean Talbot-Saver

he dreams first began when I was around seven years old. Breathtakingly colorful and vivid, the same dream would be repeated two or three times a year. Fresh scenes were added to it each time.

In the dream I was standing in a beautiful green forest that felt like home. There was a nip of the year's first frost in the air. I was walking away from some red railroad cars. Dogs and horses milled about a growing crowd of people. Then the crowd stepped from the forest into a large clearing, and the dream faded.

In my midteens I experienced this familiar dream from a new, outside perspective. As if watching from above, I watched the group of people moving into the clearing. They were short and stocky, with dark hair and eyes. The women wore long skirts with peasant blouses, their long hair covered by scarves or shawls. The men were dressed in coarsely-woven shirts and pants. All had grim expressions, and I felt a wave of sadness from some of the young women in the group.

As I seemed to fly gently toward the scene, my attention was drawn to a young girl who appeared to be about four years old.

She was small and thinner than most of the other

children. Her black hair was cut short; cropped bangs in the front emphasized her round face and large dark eyes. She was draped in what looked like a man's coat.

Suddenly I was looking out of the little girl's eyes. When I awoke, I realized I had been viewing a past life from the dream state.

As the dream expanded over the years, I pieced the story together. I experienced two perspectives in the dream—that of the little girl and that of Soul, the peaceful observer. Whenever I participated in the scene as the little girl, I could recall earlier memories from that life. I remembered happy times: playing games with the other children in the clearing and celebrating the upcoming wedding of my fourteen-year-old sister around the campfire. I felt that we were Gypsies living in Romania. The year was about 1942.

On the cold gray morning that I saw so often, we were awakened by a group of light-skinned soldiers dressed in gray uniforms. They marched us into the clearing that was usually my playground. The men were taken somewhere I could not see. We children were separated from our mothers, who were led to the other side of a large creek bed. I saw my mother with her arm around my grandmother. My sister was crying softly. I knew somehow that we were all going to die, yet I was not scared. Everyone was incredibly calm. My mother had an expression of grim strength. My grandmother was so sick I felt she would be relieved to die. The only sadness I felt was for my beautiful sister who would never see her wedding day.

As I gazed serenely at the soldiers, I noticed a very unusual man mingling amongst them.

He did not look like anyone else. He was very tall and slender, with wide shoulders. He was dressed in light blue trousers and a long flowing shirt of a pale blue that almost appeared white. He had a brown leather bag slung over one shoulder.

The man had striking features and bright blue eyes. His skin was darker than the soldiers, but lighter than ours. His most striking feature was his beautiful shoulder-length, strawberry blond hair. His movements were graceful as he glided through the crowd. In my child's mind, I wondered if he was someone who kept records for the soldiers or if he was Czechoslovakian.

Mercifully, I was looking at this man as gunfire sounded across the creek. The women were dead. The rest of the scene unfolded so quickly. I looked over at their bodies, and then again at the man, who was suddenly right before me. He knelt down in front of me, looked deeply into my eyes for a second, then cradled my head to his chest. Somehow he conveyed the message to me, "Don't worry, it won't hurt." I heard a loud noise like a bang and simultaneously experienced blackness and an odd pressure in my chest. I knew only the loving presence of the man in blue. Had the bullets passed through him too?

Once I had the full realization that I had been a Gypsy killed by Nazis in my last life, I did not have the dream about the clearing for years. But occasionally I would see this beautiful man in other dreams. I loved and trusted him and always felt safe in his company. I thought maybe he was somebody from another past life—possibly a loved one or relative.

Then one day, after I had begun studying the teachings of Eckankar, the dream returned. This time I looked closely at the face of the man in blue and recognized him from a portrait I had seen. My friend from the dream world—my protector in this previous life—

was the ECK Master Gopal Das.

Once this final piece of the puzzle dropped into place, the dream never returned. But now I know that the guidance of the spiritual teachers known as ECK Masters can span many lifetimes. The Spiritual Exercises of Eckankar and the guidance of the Living ECK Master have helped me not only recall other lifetimes but also understand how they affect me today.

A Trip to the Mental Plane

Jean Louise Lindahl

I am an operatic singer. When I sing, the sound surges through my body, my instrument. The vibrations make me feel like a crystal about to break. It is an exquisite feeling.

The downside—as so often portrayed in the media—is a sensitive, artistic temperament. An artist can feel things intensely and translate the human experience to others through music, art, writing, or theater. My question was, How does an artist maintain balance?

Lately, I'd been facing some stormy waters psychologically, and my dream life reflected it. I felt I needed balance, something stronger than the usual dream experiences to ferry me over these rough seas.

Then I discovered a brief reference in an Eckankar publication to a clinic for healing on the Mental Plane. That very night before falling asleep I asked to visit the Mental Plane and receive a healing session at this clinic.

The next morning I awoke feeling lighter, as if a heavy burden had been removed, but I had no conscious recollection of any dream experience. I was grateful for whatever had occurred during the night, but I knew my problem hadn't disappeared. I wanted and needed more in-depth work, so I kept asking to go to the clinic. For two more weeks I asked and yet had no recall of being there.

Finally the Dream Master drew back the curtain of my resistance, and one morning I awoke with the following, intensely vivid dream experience fresh in my mind:

I dreamed I was given the name of a doctor. Above all else, I wanted to be certain that he was the right doctor for me. I skeptically called him on the telephone. The more we talked, the more I relaxed. Soon I was convinced that he was someone I could trust. In the dream, I made an appointment to see him in person.

I eagerly arrived at the appointed time, filled with hope and expectation. The room was filled with therapists, the doctor, and four nurse-assistants. Through various methods they began to reveal qualities about my inner nature that were incredibly accurate. I was amazed at the sophistication of their diagnostic techniques.

I had the strong impression that these therapists had lived through the same inner struggle I now encountered. They had themselves proceeded through a healing analysis and emerged whole. Now, in turn, they were treating others struggling with the same dilemma.

After these preliminary realizations, the real work began. They revealed my own nature to me, aspect after aspect. At one point, I tried to retreat from the acute pain of self-realization and felt a fog fill the room. The fog had a remarkable source; it was issuing from my own eyes! I strove to look through it, to see again, and I felt the fog gently lift.

A parade of past lives was shown as the dream

continued. In one of the past lives, I saw myself as an operatic singer with a successful, international career. I had carried my inner urge to its fullest expression and lived the artistic life I had always aspired to.

But I couldn't understand why so many things in my present lifetime stood in the way of attaining this once again.

Two burning questions imprinted themselves on my mind: What is the relationship between the artistic/creative person and psychological imbalance? And if my aberrations are removed, will I retain my artistic abilities?

When I asked them about this, the therapists laughed and laughed. But they were kind enough to answer my hungry mind: The weaknesses would go, my talents would stay — only now, they would be more free than ever before to manifest.

Though I felt I had learned a lot, the session was not over yet. The therapists kept revealing more, until the realizations became finer, deeper, more piercing. I felt myself slipping, losing consciousness. The therapists handled this deftly, and I felt them gently bringing my attention into focus.

As I slowly came back, they applied pressure to the exact point where the acute realization and severe pain originated. They used a technique somewhat like acupressure. As they pressed the point, the energy centered there was released and dissipated like fog.

In the dream I realized why for years I had carried a quote by Felix Mendelssohn in my wallet: "God, art, and life are but one."

I'd come back in this lifetime to take that philosophy one step further: Art is but a step on the long, well-traveled path back to God.

As I was released from the pain of centuries, I left the inner clinic, understanding that this was the first of a series of sessions that were a part of my spiritual healing.

I awoke from the dream with lingering, vivid memories and deep gratitude regarding what had occurred. I felt a renewed desire to face life directly again, without fear. What an incredible gift from the Mahanta!

Close the Slipper Shop

Alyce Simonet

*S*omething within me needed to hear violins that evening. Checking the newspaper, I discovered a string concert at the campus where I had earned a college degree. I felt that I had to hear these violins or I would burst. I went by myself, knowing this was to be a very private experience, somehow vital to my spiritual future.

As I walked into the fine-arts building, many old feelings poured in. I remembered another April, this time in 1961, the year in which I was finishing a college degree. It was a time of loneliness and hurt, of being careful about how I was dressed, desperately hoping no one would notice my weight gain. I was pregnant and very unwed, and in 1961 that was a crime in the eyes of my social world.

The night of the concert I relived that earlier time in my life—but now without the hurt. The love in the music soothed my inner being. Oh, I needed that, with all my heart. The love was so profound that I had to leave at the intermission, for I would not have been able to drive home if I had taken in one note more.

On my way home I talked out loud with Wah Z, the Inner Master, reviewing my feelings about the concert.

Suddenly a comment from a friend came to mind: She felt I had never really loved her, because I had never given her a pair of slippers. I'd made hundreds over the years.

"When did you start making slippers and afghans?" the Inner Master's voice came to me.

The housemother at the home for unwed mothers where I had gone after graduation taught me to make heavy afghans, and of course, to make slippers with the remaining yarn.

I told Wah Z about this, and his reply was unexpected: "Close the slipper shop!" My heart knew that each time I made a pair, I was reliving those painful old feelings.

The day after the concert, I wrote a note to the daughter I had given up for adoption. She had never forgiven me for allowing her to be adopted, and I had not seen her since she was eighteen. Now, twelve years later, my note simply said, "I love you! Thank you for selecting me as your birth mother."

Today I received the note back in the mail from the post office with the stamped message, "Forwarding Time Expired." Burning the card in the fireplace, I felt I could finally drop the burden I had carried all these years. The book of my heart is turned to a new page.

A Special Feeling of Love

Kathie Matwiv

I work as a nurse in a ward for the termi-
nally ill where patients die every day. As
an ECKist, I am given a golden opportunity
to practice divine love and compassion.

When I first met Mike, one of the patients, I knew
we had a karmic link that had brought us together in
this place. I had particularly strong feelings of unconditional love for him. I wanted to make his last days
as comfortable as possible.

One day I was wiping his face as he slipped in and
out of consciousness. I wondered what past life had
brought us together.

As I looked at his face, relaxing and thinking of the
Mahanta, I heard the sounds of single-shot rifles. My
Spiritual Eye opened, and I saw myself as a young
soldier being shot in the chest. Another soldier, whom
I recognized as Mike in this life, ran up to me. He lifted
me over his shoulder and carried me to a ditch. He
spoke soothingly to me of God as I died.

Now, in 1992, our positions were reversed. The
brief vision explained my special feeling of love for
him. When he died a few days later, I was there, singing HU to him and soothingly telling him of the divine
Light and Sound, and the Inner Master, the Mahanta.

I was even given the opportunity to comfort his mother and brother.

I was grateful to repay a debt of gratitude with true spiritual understanding.

An Important Decision

Ingrid Haller

s I flew home from the ECK European Seminar that year, my heart was still closed from the emotional difficulties in my life. The seminar hadn't lifted the heaviness. Most of the hour-and-a-half flight back to Zurich I spent in the airplane's bathroom, sick from what I later learned was food poisoning.

I spent the next five days in bed; the pills the doctor had prescribed didn't help. My weight dropped dramatically in those five days as my condition worsened. I became so weak I could barely walk to the bathroom.

My life was miserable; I was disappointed in everything. I knew what I needed most was love, but I didn't understand anything about it. During this time, my mate brought me food and drink, but he let me go through my difficulties alone. One day he came in the room and said, "You have to decide whether you want to die or live!"

This shocked me because I hadn't realized I was letting myself slip into such a deep depression that it could end my life. His comment snapped me out of my apathy, and I called a friend who is an ECKist and a medical doctor. She said to go to back the hospital.

During the next five days, I stayed in a strange

semi-conscious state, not aware if I was alive or dead. For a while, I seemed to be watching many television screens. On each screen was an image of myself. Most were hard to accept.

These screens stayed in my vision whether my eyes were open or closed. Every time I had an emotional reaction to what I saw on a screen, I would feel a horrible pain in my stomach. This forced me to be neutral, to learn how to see myself from Soul's point of view and not to react to myself with hatred anymore.

After a time, the many TV screens faded to just one. I began to watch the absorbing drama of one of my past lives in detail. I was a Catholic nun of about thirty, the same age as I was now, in this life. I was on my deathbed. A circle of six to eight nuns stood around me. They were all very kind and loving.

All at once I was lifted out of the nun's body. I could suddenly see what kind of medicine would save my life.

I returned to consciousness and asked the nuns to go look for this medicine. They refused kindly and with sweet smiles, saying that it was not fitting with Catholic ways to use the herbs. I felt terrible anger, knowing I would die because of their ignorance.

Next, I fell into light sleep and had an important dream: Many ragged men were stumbling out of a glacier. They were bleeding and their ghastly screams rent the air as they ran in all directions. The men were shouting that they had been buried for forty years.

When I awoke, I knew the men symbolized my own pain and emotional hurts. They had been frozen in my being before this life even began. Now they were coming to the surface to be healed.

Soon after, a man dressed in gray came to me while

I was in a half-sleep. He had a gray face, beard, and aura. I was very weak but instinctively turned my back to him. Later I realized that he was the Angel of Death. By turning my back, I had decided to live.

Over the next few weeks, I rested and sorted through my dramatic healing experiences. As a child, my mother had tried to tell me about her Christian beliefs. I always wondered why I was the only one of her three children who refused to hear anything about it. Each time I stepped into a Christian church, a feeling of great sadness would come over me, forcing me to leave. Now I understood why.

I knew that in my life as a Catholic nun, I had started to work my way back home to God. My bitter disappointment had led me to the truth of the Mahanta, the spiritual guide who could take me into the deeper secrets of love.

When I revisited the experience of dying in that life, I discovered with a shock that one of the nuns around my bed then is a family member in this life. We'd always had difficulties and fights. Now our relationship is slowly healing. She too is starting to seek a deeper meaning in life.

In this experience the Mahanta helped me to heal my emotional body from afflictions that had held me back in this life with a poor self-image and anger. Now I am much happier and lighter as I pursue my understanding of giving and accepting love in daily life.

Parent Lake

Mary Carroll Moore

've always been uneasy about being alone in the wilderness, even though it pulls me with its intense beauty. My childhood summers were spent canoeing lakes in the Adirondacks where my grandmother owned a summer camp. Living in Minnesota, about six hours' drive from the Boundary Waters wilderness area, I imagined, with pleasure, paddling remote lakes under cloudless skies.

Yet behind this desire to enjoy nature at its most untamed was a persistent sense of its lurking danger.

Several summers ago my husband and I started packing for our first canoe trip. I was blissfully unaware how my underlying unease had gotten hold of our planning, but it began to show in the heaps of food I wanted to bring. Nothing seemed enough. Every trip to the store brought home more freeze-dried packages, another bag of fruit or candy bars, a couple more boxes of emergency rations.

The pile grew in a corner of the living room—more than a week's worth of rations for a family of five.

Driving north that weekend was a gentle process of shedding the familiar cities and sights. We passed patchwork fields and neat farmlands, going deeper into the unknown territory of the wilderness. We stopped to visit farm stands and eat in a roadside restaurant.

The day was warm and pleasant, and the bright blue canoe shone on the roof rack in the sunlight.

As we neared the wilderness that afternoon, I grew drowsy and lethargic, lulled by the gentle sounds of the car. In my half-sleep, the scent of the pine woods filled the air, and a strange dream crossed my vision.

* * *

I stood in a sunlit forest clearing, dressed in greasy buckskin, the tight loop of a beaded band on my upper arm. I knew I was alone, and it frightened me very much. A tight band also gripped my heart; for some reason I knew I must be very quiet. The name *Monegwa* came to mind.

The car jolted, and I woke suddenly, a cold, constricted feeling in my chest.

We arrived at Snowbank, the first lake, toward evening. Our plan was to spend the night at a shoreside campsite, then portage the canoe to a second, more remote lake the next morning. But I convinced my husband to push on, in the few hours of light left in the summer evening.

I made it sound easy: a relaxed paddle to the portage trail, maybe a mile to carry our gear and canoe, then another lake to cross as the sun set behind the trees.

The remote lake is Parent, isolated and accessible only by air, paddle, or foot.

As we loaded the canoe, I joked about the abundant food supplies, then silently added more packages to the space beneath my canoe seat, not sure why it was so important but wishing I'd brought even more. We set off across Snowbank, enjoying the slanting rays of evening light and the sound of other canoeists in the distance. When we reached the portage trail on the far side, we discovered the canoe was too heavy with supplies to lift out of the water, so we unloaded it and began carrying the first of many boxes and bags up a root-strewn dirt trail that led to Parent Lake.

My first glimpse of Parent Lake gave me an unexpected shock. It looked eerie in the setting sun, a bank of dark clouds casting an almost greenish light over the surface.

Much rougher than Snowbank, the water was thrashed by a sharp wind that caused the waves to lap aggressively against the rocky shoreline. Our paddles pushing through the water like heavy spoons in molasses, we slowly worked our way across the rough lake. The shoreline, studded with deformed pines and ravaged by the wind, hung dark shadows over the lake's surface in the twilight.

It seemed to take forever to reach our campsite, and as we pulled the canoe onto the rocky beach, I was again overcome by an almost incapacitating drowsiness and great sadness.

What was going on?

The uncomfortable feelings paralyzed me until I was unable to perform the simplest task, even unpacking a pot to boil water for tea. The sun was setting rapidly now, and I sat hunched on a fallen log while my husband set up the tent and started the cooking fire.

The feeling that overcame me, shutting out all others, was that I would die soon, in this place, and no one would know.

The stupor continued through the evening. That night, before I fell into a light sleep, I listened for a

361

long time to a pair of loons calling, laughing, across the lake.

The comforting sound counteracted the deep sadness I felt and relaxed my heart. I seemed to remember someone I loved telling me a story about loons — God's gentlest birds — protecting the frail beings in this world. I drifted to sleep listening to their almost-human cries and smelling the strong piney scent of the trees that encircled the clearing.

* * *

In my dream I am again Monegwa, and I am sitting on a fallen log, stiff with misery. I have walked all day to this remote clearing on the shore of a small lake. I am very far from my home territory, which is good because my parents want to kill me. I have observed them commit a heinous crime against the tribe. They have lied to the elders, and I am blamed. My grandmother has secreted me out of the camp at night, taking me to a trail that stretched into the distance.

Seven years old, hardly a man, I must go into the wilderness alone and try to survive.

Sitting in the clearing surrounded by pines, I remember my grandmother's parting words. She has told me to listen for the loon, the bird of laughter and joy, my protector in this life. The loon, she says, will remind me that there are those in the tribe who still love me. Leaving her I feel great sadness, and fear pulls at my heart. The harsh beauty of the wilderness offers me little comfort.

Because I am weak with sadness and unable to stir myself to find food or make a fire, I die in the clearing a few days later.

* * *

The dream was only a faint memory as we packed up early the next morning and paddled away from the pine clearing on the shore of Parent Lake. The further we went, the better I felt. Our canoe glided swiftly over the now-glassy water, and the portage trail was sunlit and mostly downhill. The first thing I heard when we arrived at Snowbank was the clear, happy sound of children's laughter echoing from a nearby cove.

You go along in life, and you may have a problem or a feeling you don't understand. It's often irrational and out of proportion to present life. If the window opens on a past life that caused the problem, you may have a chance to gain a broader perspective. Then you can learn the lesson and get on with your life today, released from one more bond with the past.

The window that opened on Monegwa's life and death at Parent Lake didn't fully erase my unease with being alone in the wilderness. I simply have more peace now with unexplained emotions. When they come, I know that fighting them is not the answer. I stay aware of the situation, try to surrender, maybe get some sleep, or do a Spiritual Exercise of ECK to gain perspective. Sometimes I get an inner cue to take action to realize the meaning of the problem.

After a time, there is usually a healing, and happiness comes again in the present moment.

11

ivine Love

Soul knows what It wants even if the human consciousness does not. This is one of the ways the ECK reaches the human consciousness. Soul has often met the Mahanta, the Inner Master, months or even years before the individual comes in contact with the teachings of ECK.

From the time this first meeting occurs on the inner planes, there is an intense longing that cannot be explained. But in ECK we know that God is love, and this longing is a desire for the love of God. With the love of God comes a joy and happiness that can only be known through personal experience.

—Sri Harold Klemp,
The Eternal Dreamer

"Where do we come from? Who are we? Where are we going?"

The Art of True Surrender

Robert Claycomb

A new supervisor had been assigned to oversee the work at one of my jobs. He was a very pleasant person, but he had strong opinions about how things should be done. He was methodical, organized, and used to a highly structured and hierarchical system of thinking.

I've always had a lot of respect for people with these attributes. But some of the changes he was proposing really disturbed me.

I was sure some of them would undo the heartfelt efforts of many of the workers, including myself. Several times I tried to explain this to him, but it was like hitting my head against a brick wall. No -response.

The situation bothered me so much, despite my ECK training in detachment, that I began to think of quitting the job.

One night, as I was brooding about the problem at work, I turned on the television news. The coverage was of the Persian Gulf conflict. As I listened, I was surprised at the alternating currents of fear and pride, fascination and concern, worry and wonder that surrounded me. I was like an oarless boat on a rough sea. And I was completely without detachment.

One of the film clips showed a soldier huddled under his blanket during his watch in the Saudi desert. He had a faraway look on his face. For a brief moment I was beside him, chilled by the desert winds. It reminded me of a painting I'd once seen by the artist Paul Gauguin. In one corner of the painting was the title in French: "Where do we come from? Who are we? Where are we going?" This was how I felt about both my job and the war.

Perhaps I would have to be willing to fight for what I knew to be best at work. I began sharpening my sword for the battle, preparing all the aspects of my argument. It kept me busy for an hour or so, until I grew tired and went to bed.

That night I dreamed I was speaking with Paul Gauguin. I stood beside him as he painted one of his models, a young Japanese girl. We began to talk about the war. "It is not like the other wars, this one," I said. He continued to brush the canvas with delicate strokes, as if not listening. Then he turned, eyebrow arched, and replied, "No, it is not. It is an inner war."

My body was tingling when I woke up the next morning. All day I thought about this. I knew that the conflict I was feeling was really inside of me. I decided to leave my job if necessary. But first I would give up my inner resistance to the new supervisor. I would say, "We can do whatever you want."

That evening I got a call from my supervisor. What he said surprised me greatly. This was not the same person I had been at odds with. He explained that he really only wanted to be sure that the work was serving the company. Then he said to me, "We can do whatever you think best."

That night as I turned on the news again I was

mulling over all that had happened. The key had been true surrender, being willing to let things be as they are. It is a way of giving divine love.

I was getting a new picture of detachment. It did not mean standing constantly apart from your feelings, but accepting them in the light of this love.

That night they were interviewing another soldier in the Middle East. "I just want to complete my mission and go home," the military man said simply. This time I agreed wholeheartedly with him.

Redreaming Your Life
with Love

Debra Hickman

One weekday morning, I went to my daughter's school to volunteer as a parent-helper. Before starting, I decided to stop by my daughter's classroom and dress a wound on her finger. I had forgotten to bandage it before she left for school. We went to the rear of the room where a group of second-grade students were clustered around the assistant teacher's desk.

As I was bandaging my daughter's finger, one of the girls in the group looked coyly at us. Then she brashly said to my daughter, "Amy, that picture you made today was really ugly!" Stunned, I turned to face the child, hoping it was a misunderstanding. But this time she looked directly at me, repeating the comment louder.

The group's attention was fixed on us; the children were waiting for our reaction. We said nothing. The assistant teacher broke the silence. "That's enough, Sarah!" she ordered.

As I left the room, I assessed my parenting skills. Why had I said nothing? I was hurt for my daughter and felt defensive.

At bedtime that evening, the intensity of the experience faded. But I was still confused. Through the teachings of Eckankar, I had found that divine love eventually heals any painful situation. I was also learning to resolve some of my daily conflicts at night in my dreams. I decided to try that approach, to work things out while I slept.

I began softly singing HU, the ancient name for God. As I fell asleep, I entered a dream in which I saw my daughter's antagonist, Sarah. I approached her with critical words, but she matched each remark with an equal rebuke. I realized this would never work and remembered divine love.

I began to sing HU in the dream. Immediately, the girl and I hugged, an embrace of love and light. Although I don't remember exactly what we said to each other, I do remember thinking that she looked very pretty. The divine love we shared dissolved any negative feelings. When we parted it was with humor.

A few days after my dream, my daughter came home from school. She cheerfully told me Sarah had come up to her that day in class and said, "Hey, Amy, remember that time when your mom was here and I said your picture was ugly? I was just kidding. And Amy, your mom is pretty!"

Not all conflicts in my life are resolved this quickly or this easily. But I am finding that if I hold divine love as my ideal, while singing HU, my conflicts will work out for the good of all concerned.

Night School

Barbara Ely

ecently, my older sister and I had a quarrel. We had worked for many years to develop a loving relationship, but after just five minutes of argument, all I could remember were the things that had separated us since childhood. I left with a hurt that wouldn't go away.

That night before sleep, I decided to go to a Golden Wisdom Temple in the dream state. Maybe I could learn something about my relationship with my sister. So I inwardly asked the ECK Master Tindor Saki, "Teach me wisdom in speaking."

The second night, I dreamed I was dancing with a man I had loved deeply when I was young. I kept getting out of step. I would shuffle and quickstep, trying to find the rhythm again. I felt this great love for him, but I kept thinking, *It takes a while to get back in step.*

I woke with these words in my heart, "It takes a while to get back in step." I realized that even though we were out of step, our love was not lost.

I also realized what the dream was teaching me. To have differences with others is simply to be out of step with them or life. I searched my negative feelings for my sister to find the loving rhythm that would bring things back in step.

If a picture is worth a thousand words, an inner experience like this is worth even more.

Lesson from a Mouse

Joyce Snyder

It was a brisk, autumn day. So many things had been happening in my life that I was having a hard time adjusting to the rapid changes. I had come home from work feeling weary and dejected and now stood in my kitchen looking out the window at the trees in the woods next to my house. They too were changing.

I stared at the pile of dirty dishes in the sink, and for a moment I felt overwhelmed. I didn't know where I'd find the strength to deal with them, let alone any of the other problems that had arisen.

Just then, out of the corner of my eye, I caught a movement on the stove next to me. I turned and saw a tiny mouse sitting on one of the burners. That was the last straw! My patience, which had been stretched taut as a tightrope, snapped. I let out a bansheelike scream—not in fear of this little mouse, but in sheer frustration from all the tension and stress I'd been under lately. As I continued venting my feelings, the mouse seemed frozen on the spot.

"Get out of here," I shouted at him. I didn't want him on my stove or in my house. I just wanted him to go back wherever he had come from. "What am I supposed to do with a live mouse?" I yelled at him.

Panicked, he hopped from burner to burner, trying to escape. He didn't know how to get away from me. He surely must have wanted to. After a few minutes of out-of-control screaming and frustrated tears, I caught myself and thought, *This is ridiculous. There must be a better way to handle this.*

The Living ECK Master has said that within every problem lies the solution. We just have to use our creative ability to find it. So I stopped shouting and began singing HU, an ancient name for God, to calm myself. The mouse and I stood two feet apart, staring at each other — both of us trembling with emotion. His little body was quivering with fear as his heart raced madly.

Slowly my anger evaporated. When I recognized his terror, in that moment I felt love and compassion for this Soul in a little mouse body.

I kept singing HU softly while looking at the mouse. I felt calmer and knew he too was feeling less terrorized by me. I began talking to him quietly, explaining that I didn't want to hurt him. I told him he couldn't live in my house, but my garage was OK.

Next I had an idea which I carefully explained to the mouse. I opened a brown paper bag and lay it on its side at the edge of the stove. He watched all this warily. I told him that if he would get into the bag, I could carry him safely outside and no harm would come to him. I continued singing HU to myself.

The second I finished explaining all this to the mouse, he turned and ran into the bag. Quickly I carried the wiggling bag outside and released the mouse.

I was shaken by this experience. On the surface it was just one more stressful situation typical of many that had been happening to me lately. But I knew there were important lessons to be learned from it.

The amazing power of HU had neutralized a frantic situation. Only when I—and the mouse—had calmed down could a solution be found. Releasing my inner tension had allowed me to find a creative way out. I was grateful for this opportunity to see how the ECK helps us and the tiniest of Its creatures.

How to Sidestep Trouble

Lucy Hansen-Addy

Our dog Larsey arrived in the house as a lovely puppy, adored by everyone. As Larsey grew up, however, we saw her gradually change from a calm, loving puppy to an ill-tempered dog. By the time she matured, she had become a menace who occasionally snapped at my own children.

Then came Bobby, a Doberman pincer given to us by a very dear friend. Everyone was worried: Would Larsey allow the helpless puppy to survive? Initially, we kept them apart. Then we decided to bring them together while we stayed close to intervene if need be.

Larsey bared her fangs and shook with rage. She sprang at the puppy, who quickly laid on his back, quite motionless.

Bobby was so still we wondered if he was hurt. Meanwhile, Larsey jumped all over him, barking and growling. But the puppy showed no reaction.

After some time, Larsey turned and went off, angrier than ever. Bobby happily sprang up and ran off too. From that moment on, Bobby adopted a consistent approach to Larsey. He never resisted her or responded to her attacks.

Even though Bobby grew to twice Larsey's size, and

we knew that a fight between the two dogs would leave Larsey in big trouble, Bobby still refused to fight.

One morning I woke up to find my next-door neighbor very angry. I could hear her outside, yelling at my children. She was particularly angry with my five-year-old daughter. I listened carefully and realized she did not approve of something that the girl had done the previous day. I waited for the woman to calm down.

Her tongue-lashing then began to include me. She hurled insults and insinuations at our house. I tried to control myself. But my silence seemed to aggravate the situation. She shouted even louder.

At that point, I decided to go out and give her a piece of my mind.

Just as I was getting out of bed, the two dogs rushed into my room. This was quite unusual. Quick as lightning, Larsey turned and jumped on Bobby. Bobby just threw his huge body on the floor. He waggled his tail and tried to play instead. It was very clear that he was giving patient love to his assailant.

I sat transfixed by the dogs. In the end, there was no fight, as usual. Bobby met every aggressive move from Larsey with love.

I immediately realized I was watching a waking dream, which is the language of God. I knew I had to avoid a confrontation with my neighbor.

To calm down, I sang HU, the love song to God. When I was feeling better, I went to see my neighbor to talk things over with her. In my new frame of mind, I was able to bring harmony to the situation.

Together, we talked about how troublesome children can sometimes be. When we parted, both of us were laughing heartily.

Back inside my house, I thanked Wah Z, the Inner Master, for the guidance — and for having made it possible for me to sidestep anger and see Bobby as one of my teachers of divine love.

The Chemistry Teacher

Dennis Madden

y wife and I were visiting her parents in Iowa. My wife's former chemistry teacher was ninety years old that day. He was having a birthday party at a hall downtown. We were invited.

Normally I don't like to socialize much. But when I heard about the celebration, I could feel Divine Spirit moving me. I became excited about going. So we got cleaned up and drove over to the hall. When we arrived, there was a long line of people waiting to greet Leonard and congratulate him on his ninetieth birthday. When it was my turn, my wife introduced me to her former teacher. He shook my hand for a long, long time. Then he didn't let go. He kept shaking it.

As he held on to my hand, I had a sudden knowingness that he was sensing the love of Divine Spirit flowing through me, a student of Eckankar. It made me feel very privileged.

When Leonard finally decided to stop shaking my hand, he then grabbed me by the shoulder with his other hand. He held me like this for a long while as he talked to everyone else. Eventually the reception line dwindled, and I went to the refreshment table. There my wife and I met Leonard's daughter and granddaughter. His daughter did the same thing her father had done: she took my hand and wouldn't let go.

She held my shoulder for a while too. I felt she was also sensing the divine love. Then she put her hand in mine very trustingly, as a child does. I very gently closed my hand on her fingers and felt the flow of love. I knew the ECK had touched her heart.

My wife and I sat down to eat some cake and talked with many people. As we were getting ready to leave, my wife stopped to say good-bye to a few friends. I stood next to her and felt myself drift away from the physical reality and into an inner awareness of life.

I saw the room with my inner eyes. Everyone's heart was open and glowing. Light flowed from each attendee and joined in the center of the room just below the ceiling. It made a beautiful ball of white light.

I could see and feel the ECK, the Holy Spirit. It was enveloping these Souls, aiding them and supporting them on their way back home to God.

The Crayfish

Nancy Truglio

When I was a graduate student, I lived in a quiet apartment complex that was landscaped with several streams. I always loved the sound of running water, and frequently I would take a walk by a stream just to listen or to study the life going on there.

It was like looking into a different world. The waters were home to crayfish, who showed up each spring. By summer, they had grown pretty big, and the large population caused a good deal of competition for food. Many of them did not survive. Eventually, they would thin out until the whole process began again the next year.

One summer evening, I heard a strange sound at my door. When I opened it, I was surprised to see a crayfish standing there. He marched across the carpet without hesitation and then stopped to stare at me. I really didn't know what crayfish ate, but I offered him the only thing I had: raw hamburger.

He proceeded to eat, and as he had his meal, the air stilled around us. I felt we could understand one another.

He had been hungry. There was not enough food to feed all the crayfish in the stream. He had left the water to brave the long walk to this house because he knew he would get food here.

When he was done eating, I carried the crayfish back to his stream. Watching as he disappeared into the water, I knew that something very special had taken place.

The night seemed to be unusually peaceful, and I felt a curious joy come over me. Although I did not recognize it for ten more years, the Mahanta had been with me, granting me the opportunity to aid another Soul in need.

The Secret Power
of Divine Love

Joann Casad

It is springtime in the park. The new leaves on the trees are vibrant green. Daffodils and narcissi dot the banks of the small lake where ducks have gathered to swim. The flowers' exhilarating fragrances beckon memories. Sounds of quacking ducks, songbirds, and laughing children are carried through the air; and my heart expands as I breathe deeply of the love of life.

Children feed the ducks while proud parents watch from nearby benches in the warm spring glow. Angela, my four-year-old daughter, takes bread from my hand and runs off to join in while I sit with the other parents.

Angela enthusiastically flings pieces of bread into the swarm of quacking ducks. Soon her little arm loses its rapid rhythm. The bread is gone. She begins chasing the baby ducks, attracting the annoyed attention of many parents, who turn to glare at me.

I know Angela will probably start to wail if I physically intervene. Instead, I start to silently sing HU, an ancient name for God. I often do this in times of stress to help me remain calm. I ask what I should do, and open myself to guidance. Divine Spirit whispers, "Be patient."

I smile apologetically at the concerned parents as though everything is all right. Soon Angela stops chasing the ducks and wanders toward me with a pouted lip.

I put my arms around her and ask, "Why were you chasing the ducks?"

"I want to take one home," she says angrily.

"Well, Angela, if someone was chasing you and trying to take you away from your mother, would you want to go?"

"No," she admits, looking down at the ground.

In a moment of inspiration, I ask, "Does the little duck know how much you love it?" as I stroke her hair.

She gives no response, so I continue. "If you tell the duck you love it and you will leave it with its mommy, maybe it will let you pet it."

She looks up at me with her beautiful hazel-green eyes: pools of familiarity and knowingness. Suddenly she blurts, "OK," and quickly runs to the ducks.

Angela squats down and puts her hand on the ground. Then, to the surprise of everyone, including me, a baby duck walks right into her palm!

The parents and I gape as she pets this tiny, fluffy baby duck. Time stands still for the exchange of love.

Then the little duck hops off her hand and goes back to its mother. Angela, beaming with joy, runs to me with outstretched arms. She hugs me tightly for a long, long time, while parents and children applaud and cheer.

Love touches everyone and everything, and my heart soars on this glorious spring day. I silently thank the ECK and sing another HU.

The Last Train

Robin Perlman

*I*t was past midnight. I waited for the last train home after a long evening of work. My breath hung in the cold, winter air as I sighed with exhaustion and relief.

A man stood beside me, yelling angrily to himself. He had long, wild, unkempt red hair and massive scars on his arms and face. The odor rising from him caused me to move away.

As the train pulled in, I gathered my belongings and stepped inside; the glaring fluorescent lights contrasted starkly with the evening. The man stumbled into the train after me and sat directly in front of me. He turned around and continued ranting. I was his captive audience.

This is all I need, I thought to myself. The man yelled about his brother and how much he hated him. He moved quickly from one topic to the next. At times, it was difficult to understand the words. I closed my eyes and silently sang HU. When I opened them, I was moved to listen with my heart.

He looked at me and asked, "Would you marry me? I mean, if you had the heart to, would you marry me?"

I paused before responding, "Well, I'm not really looking to get married, but if I was, yes. Yes, I would,"

I replied. Inwardly I understood the question behind the question. I knew that Soul was really asking, Am I capable of being loved? I gave him unconditional love, just as it is given to me during my ECK spiritual exercises each day.

I asked, "Have you ever been married before?"

"Yes," he said, "but my wife was killed in an automobile accident."

During the course of our conversation, I learned about this Soul's earthly journey. Among his many experiences, he had been in Vietnam and witnessed the violent deaths of many of his friends. He had almost died himself.

"Boy," I said, "you've really experienced some pain in this lifetime, haven't you?" He nodded.

"Do you think there is a reason for all this?" I asked.

"Yes, there has to be," he said.

Just then, the train stopped at my station. I stood up and realized that the man's speech was now articulate. As we gazed into each other's eyes, I saw his were clear and focused. Soul had recognized Itself, and we had both received a gift of love.

12

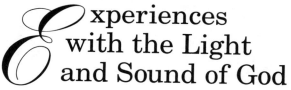

xperiences
with the Light
and Sound of God

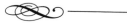

The water of life is actually the ECK, which is the Light and Sound of God. As you drink of It, visualize the Light and Sound rushing through your being. Know that once you drink of this, you will never be the same. You will always thirst for the waters of heaven.

—Sri Harold Klemp,
The Spiritual Exercises of ECK

As if in a dream, I turned off all the equipment. But the HU song was still playing!

Hearing the
Mysterious Sound of God

Anita Krotz

I have a good friend, whom I knew was a member of a religion called Eckankar. One day she loaned me an audiocassette set about a very healing word called HU. She didn't tell me much about it. She just said, "Listen to this, and see if you like it."

So I took the tapes home. The next morning, I listened to the first audiocassette. It was very interesting to hear Sri Harold Klemp, the spiritual leader of Eckankar, tell stories about how singing HU, an ancient name for God, has helped people. He also told a little about the history of this spiritually charged word. I practiced a couple of the short exercises he gave; they were very easy. I liked them so much I decided to play the second audiocassette, where thousands of people sing HU together.

The sound of the HU Song was very soothing and pleasing. It ended, and I went about my day. I turned my tape player off and played a CD on my CD player.

The next thing I remember was being vaguely aware that the music had ended. The house was quiet. Then to my surprise, the HU Song came back on! How was that possible?

I went back into the other room to check my stereo equipment. I carefully stared at the tape player. Nothing was moving. As if in a dream, I turned off all the equipment.

But the HU Song was still playing! I looked around my house and listened to the sound vibrating in the room. I wondered if it was coming from a lawnmower or an airplane outside.

But no, the sound exactly matched the HU I'd just heard. In wonder, I walked around and around the room, trying to figure out if the sound had any particular source. It seemed to surround the room.

The HU lasted for about two minutes and then slowly faded away. I remember feeling uplifted. My heart was singing the rest of the day. I didn't know it then, but it was my first miracle of hearing the divine Sound of God. My mind didn't know what to make of this experience, so I carefully tucked it away as a precious memory.

About two months later, my friend invited me to an Eckankar seminar in Anaheim, California. I said to myself, "I'm going to go. I don't know anything about Eckankar. I'm not really looking for a spiritual path, but I like to learn new things." And I remembered the sound of HU ringing around the house.

The seminar was wonderful. There was so much to choose from: roundtables, workshops, and main-program talks on fascinating subjects. I learned about inner guidance, meeting the ECK Masters, and how to put more divine love into my thoughts, words, and actions.

On Saturday evening, I listened to Sri Harold Klemp, the Mahanta, the Living ECK Master in person for the first time. Right before he began his talk,

I looked around and wondered about the people in the seats around me. What did they have in common? They were so different—from all races, nationalities, and walks of life. What did they see in this spiritual leader? It was fascinating, very different from any meeting I'd ever been to before.

Something happened to my heart when Sri Harold spoke. It was the same feeling I had had when the sound of HU filled my house. I just knew I was hearing truth and love.

It uplifted my heart again—and this time, my mind was able to trail along a little. Three weeks later, I became a member of Eckankar, and it's been the most life-changing step I've ever taken.

Needless to say, the HU is very important to me. I sing it every day, with gratitude and love. I will never forget how the HU filled my house the first time I played that audiocassette from Eckankar on my stereo. As Soul I know I recognized that sound, and I'm grateful for this gift from the Mahanta.

A Guardian Angel
and God's Golden Music

Deborah Bryk-Serva

My best friend, Karen, and I were inseparable throughout grammar and high school. We played together in the afternoons, and many nights I slept over at her house.

I was the oldest of seven children; she was the youngest of three. The age gap between Karen and her next older sibling made her house a quiet place for me to escape my brothers and sisters. We used to talk about spiritual experiences a lot. I remember her telling me about being out of her body. Karen had lost her father when she was very young. She sometimes mentioned that he visited her, and that they talked together.

Karen and I remained friends until I went away to college. A few years later, we had a falling out. I felt badly.

Karen got married and moved away. A few years later, I found Eckankar. Karen and I didn't have much contact. Then she called me nine years ago when her mother died. I had had a dream experience with her mother and so had Karen. We talked about it, and she was comforted that we'd both seen her mother in the dream worlds.

Karen knew about Eckankar, but she was raised in Christianity and still seemed satisfied with its teachings. We had no further contact until two years later. When my daughter was born, Karen called to congratulate me and we talked briefly. At the end of the conversation, she said she felt a little sad that we weren't as close as before. I agreed, and again, we drifted into silence.

Then about a month ago, I was asked to give a talk at an Eckankar seminar. The title was "Hearing the Golden Music of God." I was very busy with my job as a pediatric cardiologist and asked Divine Spirit for help. "Please give me a sign if I'm supposed to give this talk," I said. "I have only one week to respond. Do I have anything to say about the golden music of God?"

By the end of the week, there was still no strong feeling of what I should do or what to say. Then at 10:30 p.m. the phone rang. It was my friend Karen.

She was a little timid about calling; it had been so long since we last talked. But I was very glad to hear from her. She had moved to Kentucky. I would have had no way to contact her. As we chatted, she brought me up to date. She now had three children and was working as a nurse in a rehabilitation hospital.

Her days were spent with people who had spinal-cord injuries, her evenings in a nursing home with the elderly. In both jobs, she said, she tried to let people know there's more to life than just the physical world.

"I tell them about my dream experiences with my mother after she died," Karen told me, "to show them there's more than what we see in this world. The people I deal with have had severe and sudden injuries or are so very old. They're often very frustrated."

"Karen," I asked, "do you still have experiences in your dreams?"

"Yes," she replied. "I go to this place where there's a huge pool of water. I swim in it, and I always wake up feeling wonderful. I don't want to come back, it's so nice.

"What about you, Debbie? Are you still in Eckankar?"

"Sure," I replied. I was getting up the nerve to mention the HU to her. "You know," I began, "there is a word you can sing to open yourself to God's love. Then God can touch us through daily experiences."

"Oh," she exclaimed, "I know what it is."

"What's the word?" I asked.

"Well, it's HU," she said firmly.

I was taken aback. But I supposed that she'd heard about Eckankar and HU somewhere.

"How did you hear about it?" I asked.

She got very quiet. I had to pry it out of her. Finally she said, "Well, *he* told me."

"Who?" I asked, suddenly excited.

"He's been working with me for a while. You would call him a Master, but I call him my guardian angel."

As I sat back on the bed, tears came to my eyes and chills ran up and down my arms and back. I was amazed. I'd heard stories of people getting information about ECK on the inner, before hearing about the outer teachings of Eckankar. But this was someone I'd known since we were kids.

I realized with a shock why she'd called me. I was going to try to share HU, but she already knew about it. I ended up receiving a wonderful gift from her. It was my sign from Divine Spirit—a story for my talk on hearing the golden music of God.

When I told Karen, she laughed and said, "I felt I was supposed to call you all week long! I wondered if you were dying or something. I couldn't figure out why I was thinking of someone from the past so strongly."

I asked her, "What do you do every day that might have brought you such a wonderful insight?"

"I don't really know what you mean," replied Karen. "As I go about my day, I just say, 'Not my will, but thine be done.' I repeat it over and over as I do my work. That's when I hear this HU in my mind. I try to treat each person with love, dignity, and respect.

"A lot of the people with spinal-cord injuries have lost the use of their limbs. Some personal-care situations are very uncomfortable, and they often get upset. So I tell them, 'Listen, I'm not male, I'm not female; I'm a nurse, and I'm just here to help you.' It's our mutual job to learn how to cope. I try to make light jokes and keep them comfortable and unself-conscious. I think of it as divine love."

We talked a little more about HU. I told Karen about the audiocassette set "HU: A Love Song to God." One audiocassette talks about HU; the other is a recording of thousands of ECKists singing HU together at an international ECK seminar.

She was eager to have a copy, so I said I'd mail one to her. We also decided to become pen pals. The HU has served to bring us closer together. Through her connection with Divine Spirit which prompted her to call me, we have healed the old wounds of the relationship. Now we're willing to move on and find a new harmony.

Needless to say, I shared Karen's story at the seminar. She taught me a lot about the qualities of love and giving that allow us to hear God and the benefits of listening to the golden music all around us, all the time.

My Neighborhood Improvement Plan

Steve Whitelaw

hrough a series of unforeseen circumstances, I found myself living in a house I thought I had sold two years ago. The problem was, the neighborhood had gone downhill—way downhill!

Big trash dumpsters sat in the street, and trash was scattered everywhere. Gang graffiti covered every surface. From a window I could watch drug deals taking place along the street all day long. My housemate once checked to find out what they were selling. Cocaine and heroin only, they replied—nothing soft like marijuana. My neighbors were afraid to confront these young hoodlums. If they did, they found their tires slashed or windshields broken.

So one day I wondered to myself, *Why do I deserve this? What kind of waking dream am I participating in?*

If adversity brings spiritual growth, I decided glumly, I was a really lucky guy. But after contemplating the situation, I decided I could be an active cause or creator in my own waking dream. I vowed to turn the situation over to Divine Spirit. Each morning in my spiritual exercise—and all through the day—I began to visualize the ECK, or Holy Spirit, pouring into the area. I watched as It scrubbed the neighborhood sparkling clean with fresh life and divine love. This was not of my doing or willpower. I was simply trying to be an active, conscious vehicle for Spirit.

Two weeks later, things began to change.

One weekend a group of fifteen to twenty young neighbors, armed with brooms, rakes, trimmers, and paintbrushes, worked to clean up the trash and paint over all the graffiti.

With the cleanup under way, I decided my next step was to maintain my right to move freely on my street. The ECK gave me another idea: to walk, skateboard, and ride my bike (with discretion) about the neighborhood.

At first I found I had to do extra spiritual exercises just to get my courage up. Thoughts of an early death passed through my mind. But confrontations were rare, and they quickly dissipated. I found that silently singing HU really worked wonders in preventing negative situations.

This situation has proved to me what an uplifting effect the ECK can have on an area whenever someone is willing to be a vehicle for Divine Spirit. Things are slowly improving in my neighborhood. I feel safe now, and I'm organizing a neighborhood watch program to keep the situation moving in the right direction. I'm also working with a local homeowners' group for change here.

Moving back to my neighborhood gave me the unexpected opportunity to grow and learn as I worked to improve my everyday environment—inside and out!

Soul Travel Surprise

Doug Munson

I sat with my sister, her boyfriend, and about forty other people in an Eckankar workshop on past lives, dreams, and Soul Travel. As thrilled as I was to be with my sister again after an absence of a few years, I still felt a little empty spot. I missed my wife, April, and our two boys. They weren't able to make the trip to the ECK Worldwide Seminar with me.

At about two in the afternoon, we were asked by the facilitators to try a Soul Travel exercise. "Place your attention above and between your eyebrows. This point is called the Tisra Til, the Third Eye. It's a place where Soul—you, as a conscious, individual spark of God—resides.

"Now take a deep breath, and join us in singing HU. It's pronounced like the word *hue*. HU is an ancient name for God; it's also a love song to God. Now imagine a place you would like to be right now, just for a moment or two."

I knew at once where I was going.

Everyone sang HU. The sound filled the room like a celestial symphony. It spirited me to Minneapolis, to the couch in our living room. I sat there for a second with my hands folded, then I got up and moved around, looking in on the boys playing and April, busy with household chores. Although it was in my imagination, it felt real, in a way. I felt warm and comfortable to be with them again for the moment. Then we were called back to the workshop. I checked with my sister and her friend to see if they had enjoyed their experience. They had. Then I had to run off to a meeting.

We met the next morning to hear Sri Harold Klemp speak, then they treated me to a walk along the beach and a quick tour of Hollywood before they drove me to the airport for my afternoon flight home to Minneapolis.

That evening I was greeted at the airport by my family with hugs and highly animated stories about the week we'd spent apart. As we drove home from the airport, I told April about being with my sister. I wanted April and the boys to know how much I'd missed them while I was away, so I told her about the Soul Travel workshop. I said, "I Soul Traveled home Saturday." She looked at me, wide-eyed, and said, "What time was that?"

"Oh, a little after two, California time," I replied.

"You know," she said, pointing to my younger son, "around four o'clock our time, this little guy said, 'Mommy, I just saw Dad in the kitchen with you out of the corner of my eye. He was standing next to you with his hand on your shoulder.'"

Good Morning, America!

Mary A. Brattesani

I volunteer two days a week in the intensive-care nursery at a children's hospital in Oakland. Many of the babies are premature and very sick. Their mothers have often used crack cocaine or heroin during their pregnancies, and the babies are undergoing withdrawal from drugs or suffering from other serious health problems.

One day, I arrived at my post to find a film crew from the popular television show *Good Morning, America*. They wanted to produce a segment for their show on volunteerism in America.

They asked if they could film me taking care of the babies.

I had never been on camera before. I was very concerned about making it through the ordeal of taping and taking direction from the producer. As the film crew was setting up, they had me sit in a rocking chair with a baby. People and bright lights swirled around us, agitating the infant and unnerving me.

The more the baby fussed, the more nervous I got, until I thought I was going to lose my own composure and cry! There's nothing like the sound of a wailing baby to express tension and fear—and I am very afraid of public speaking.

In desperation, I did the only thing I could think of that might work: I began to sing HU, an ancient name for God, as a love song.

I leaned over and softly sang HU to the baby. We both began to calm down. But I forgot that a member of the crew had already attached a microphone to my smock. And I didn't know that the camera had quietly started. Suddenly I was startled to hear the producer say, "Whatever you're doing, Mary, don't stop. It sounds really nice!" The producer was so taken with the sound of HU that he changed the focus of the piece to include it.

When my segment was aired on TV, background music had been added. It was a lullaby and the sound of HU!

I thought this was a once-in-a-lifetime experience, to share the beauty and spiritually uplifting sound of HU with so many listeners. But not long after that, a local TV crew came into the nursery. The attitude of this crew was a little different. They wanted me to look cute and cuddly with a baby, and then move on to the next assignment as quickly as possible.

A sick baby doesn't necessarily feel like being cute. I could tell the reporter wasn't getting what he wanted. In my increasing discomfort, again, the only thing I could think to do was to sing HU.

When this segment was aired on the five o'clock news, the TV anchor started by saying, "Here we're going to meet one of the volunteers at the local children's hospital. And she sings to soothe the babies."

The next thing you hear is the sound of HU.

Not just the media seems to love this song of HU. It suits the babies too. They and I will often calm down and listen to the divine Sound Current that runs through this beautiful name for God. It's a form of prayer and upliftment that really works for me.

What Is That Sound?

Leslie Leider

My first experience with the Sound Current—a manifestation of Holy Spirit—was about a month before I became a member of Eckankar. I think I had been hearing It for quite a while before it actually registered in my consciousness.

When I was watching TV in the evening, I would become aware of a background noise. It sounded like the hum that a tuning fork makes.

I thought it was coming from something electrical. I would search high and low for the source of the sound, but to no avail. I would turn off the TV, unplug the refrigerator, put my ear to the clocks—but I couldn't find it. It was driving me crazy!

Eventually, I would just give up and return to my TV show, trying to ignore the Sound. Sometimes it was pretty difficult, as the Sound became all-pervasive. After this happened several times, my frustration began to mount. I kept asking myself, "What am I hearing?" Finally I got the crazy notion to just sit down and think about it until I figured it out.

After thinking about it, I decided that I did not have tinnitus, a ringing of the ears. The Sound I heard was the Sound of life itself. It was some undercurrent of energy that sustains all that exists. It just wasn't heard by most people.

They were probably capable of hearing It, I thought. *But they just didn't.* I recognized that there was something special about my ability to hear It, but I didn't know what. Was God trying to tell me something? I guess I equated my odd skill with some kind of psychic phenomena like seeing auras. However, I possessed no other talents or tendencies along those lines.

After mulling this over, I felt pretty sure my conclusions were true—at least for me. Having figured this much out, the Sound was less annoying to me, and I more or less accepted It as a fact of my life.

Shortly afterward, I saw a couple of spots for Eckankar on TV during the wee hours of the morning. I knew of Eckankar at that time. Eight years earlier, a woman I worked with in the Air Force had told me about it.

She had never mentioned the Light and Sound, however. I had been fascinated by what she did tell me, but I hadn't recognized Eckankar as the path for me. Back then, I was at the very beginning of my own spiritual search and had some shopping around to do.

Over the next few years, I looked into a variety of teachings and eventually came across one that satisfied me for about two years. I eventually realized that something was missing. I had no idea what it was, but I did know that I had to keep searching. Little did I know when I experienced that unusual sound that what I was seeking was making Itself known to me!

After seeing a second TV spot, I decided to learn more about Eckankar. Within a day or two, I made a lunchtime trek to the local ECK center in my town, where I purchased four books. Before I had even finished the first one, I knew that my search had come to an end. I read about the ECK and Its twin aspects, the Light and Sound of God.

What I learned about the Sound Current confirmed my own conclusions. Now I knew It to be the Voice of God.

During my first six weeks as a member of Eckankar the Sound was incredibly loud. I could hear It over the noises of traffic as I drove down the street. It varied only in intensity. Sometimes It almost hurt. But knowing what It was, I loved It.

When It finally quieted down, I wondered what I'd done wrong. Sometimes I thought It was gone, but It wasn't. I had only to redirect my attention to It. Eventually, I came to realize that I am always connected to It.

The Sound of God is a constant in my life now. It gives guidance and nourishes Soul. I feel blessed to be able to experience the Holy Spirit as I do. I'm on my way back home to God.

A Spiritual Exercise
That Changes Lives

Joyce Darcangelo

I managed the occupational health center for a company in Calgary, Alberta, Canada. In January, one of our employees fell into a very severe depression and attempted suicide three times, which landed her in the hospital.

After about two weeks of treatment, the psychiatrist in charge of her case started sending her out on short visits, and she came to see me. This woman was a recovering alcoholic and drug addict. I had assisted her through several crises at the health center, so she had come to trust me.

As we talked, she told me that she didn't have any control over her urge to take her own life. There were voices in her head. She was simply waiting to get out of the hospital so she could give in to the compelling urge and end her life.

We talked for a while, and she asked me what I thought would happen after death. I told her that I believed we live on and that it's best to face our problems now, in this life.

I don't generally speak of Eckankar or my own spiritual studies to others. But I felt a strong inner nudge that this woman would benefit from a simple spiritual exercise.

I asked her if she would like to try one with me.

At first she said, "No, I don't think so, but I do want to talk for a while longer."

"That's fine," I responded, letting the matter drop.

About ten or fifteen minutes later she said, "I think I would like to try that spiritual exercise you mentioned."

So we went into an empty office and closed the door. I explained how to sing HU: I told her to sing this sacred sound for a few minutes while relaxing and focusing her attention within herself.

The exercise had unusual results. The woman was so anxious that after a few moments of singing HU she would start talking to me. She said that she was getting a severe pain in her head and that the noise that she felt there all the time was getting louder. It would not stop.

"Don't stop singing HU," I suggested. "Just open up to the love of God that is in the HU."

And so we continued to sing HU for a few minutes; then she was suddenly quiet. It seemed as if the whole office was deeply quiet in those few moments. I could feel the silent healing of Divine Spirit as I continued to sing HU for a few more minutes.

When I opened my eyes, the woman was asleep. After a while I gently woke her. She looked up at me and exclaimed, "You know, the noise has stopped! I've never felt so much space in my head."

She continued: "I saw something too. I saw a black cloud surrounding my mind. As we sang HU, I saw the sun gradually begin to peek around the edges. How can I keep this feeling?"

I told her how to call on the spiritual teacher and

comforter, the Mahanta, for help. She could also keep HU in her mind all the time, and for twenty minutes a day, she could sing HU aloud while looking at that light as it burned away the black cloud. "You can also visualize the spiritual force as a blue light whenever you need help to overcome your urge to harm yourself."

A few days later the woman phoned me and said, "I've talked to my doctor, and I'd like to come back to work half-days. I feel I'm ready—may I?"

So I said, "Yes, I can arrange that."

Two days later, she started her first half-day shift from 7:00 to 11:00 a.m. Before she began, she asked if we could sing HU. So every day for a week, we practiced this exercise together. Now sometimes she sings HU at home as well.

I still haven't told this woman much about Eckankar, but before I left for an international Eckankar seminar, she unexpectedly came to my office and said, "I wish you a very beautiful seminar. I want to thank you very much for the spiritual techniques. I'm handling things in a way I never thought I could handle them. I feel better than I've felt in years!"

The effect of HU on the crushing noise in her head was a dramatic reminder for me of its healing power. This experience was also a great confirmation to my inner nudges!

The Purple Light

Debbie Joy

*O*ne of the first things I learned in Eckankar was not to compare my experiences or my spiritual growth with anyone else's. And for a long time I fooled myself into believing I wasn't. But I also had strong and disturbing feelings every time I listened to someone else describe a vivid out-of-body or Soul Travel experience.

In my contemplations I would see a beautiful purple light. It pulsed with life and seemed to grow bigger while I watched. But I worried that nobody I knew of had ever said anything about a *purple* light. I had only read that the Light of God was blue or white. So I would try to push the purple light aside so the right color could come in.

Needless to say, it didn't work. Whatever else this purple light was, it was persistent.

Two years passed, and I was at an Eckankar seminar. I was still concerned that I hadn't seen the right color light after so much study and effort. I also didn't have the vivid Soul Travel experiences so many people talked about.

I was in a workshop that day at the seminar. After much sharing from the other participants about their experiences of Light and Sound, the facilitator said something that changed my way of thinking. "Whatever you see in contemplation, whatever you hear or feel, is it," he said. "Stop looking out there for something that looks like a cookbook description of a spiritual experience. Look instead at what you have. You've got what it takes!"

The rest of the workshop and the seminar is a blurred memory. Instead of listening to more of everyone else's experiences, I began to spend time looking at my own. I read back through my journal and found more had happened than I could believe: a realization that came to help me solve a problem with my boss; a unique concoction that helped add needed variety to my diet; less heavy emotion when dealing with difficult family members; dreams showing my growing ability to do things for myself—and that glowing purple light!

Maybe my experiences aren't as vivid and extraordinary as other people's. But they are mine. The ECK, this loving life force from God, is working with me in every aspect of my life. I now have the awareness that ECK sees into the unique heart of each of us—and touches us each in the right way.

Glossary

Words set in SMALL CAPS are defined elsewhere in this glossary.

ARAHATA. An experienced and qualified teacher for ECKANKAR classes.

CHELA. A spiritual student.

ECK. The Life Force, the Holy Spirit, or Audible Life Current which sustains all life.

ECKANKAR. Religion of the Light and Sound of God. Also known as the Ancient Science of SOUL TRAVEL. A truly spiritual religion for the individual in modern times, known as the secret path to God via dreams and SOUL TRAVEL. The teachings provide a framework for anyone to explore their own spiritual experiences. Established by Paul Twitchell, the modern-day founder, in 1965.

ECK MASTERS. Spiritual Masters who can assist and protect people in their spiritual studies and travels. The ECK Masters are from a long line of God-Realized SOULS who know the responsibility that goes with spiritual freedom.

HU. The most ancient, secret name for God. The singing of the word HU, pronounced like the word *hue,* is considered a love song to God. It is sung in the ECK Worship Service.

INITIATION. Earned by the ECK member through spiritual unfoldment and service to God. The initiation is a private ceremony in which the individual is linked to the Sound and Light of God.

LIVING ECK MASTER. The title of the spiritual leader of ECKANKAR. His duty is to lead SOULS back to God. The Living ECK Master can assist spiritual students physically as the Outer Master, in the dream state as the Dream Master, and in the spiritual worlds as the Inner Master. Sri Harold Klemp became the MAHANTA, the Living ECK Master in 1981.

MAHANTA. A title to describe the highest state of God Consciousness on earth, often embodied in the LIVING ECK MASTER. He is the Living Word.

PLANES. The levels of heaven, such as the Astral, Causal, Mental, Etheric, and Soul planes.

SATSANG. A class in which students of ECK study a monthly lesson from ECKANKAR.

THE SHARIYAT-KI-SUGMAD. The sacred scriptures of ECKANKAR. The scriptures are comprised of twelve volumes in the spiritual worlds. The first two were transcribed from the inner PLANES by Paul Twitchell, modern-day founder of ECKANKAR.

SOUL. The True Self. The inner, most sacred part of each person. Soul exists before birth and lives on after the death of the physical body. As a spark of God, Soul can see, know, and perceive all things. It is the creative center of Its own world.

SOUL TRAVEL. The expansion of consciousness. The ability of SOUL to transcend the physical body and travel into the spiritual worlds of God. Soul Travel is taught only by the LIVING ECK MASTER. It helps people unfold spiritually and can provide proof of the existence of God and life after death.

SOUND AND LIGHT OF ECK. The Holy Spirit. The two aspects through which God appears in the lower worlds. People can experience them by looking and listening within themselves and through SOUL TRAVEL.

SPIRITUAL EXERCISES OF ECK. The daily practice of certain techniques to get us in touch with the Light and Sound of God.

SUGMAD. A sacred name for God. Sugmad is neither masculine nor feminine; IT is the source of all life.

WAH Z. The spiritual name of Sri Harold Klemp. It means the Secret Doctrine. It is his name in the spiritual worlds.

421

FOR FURTHER READING AND STUDY*

The Secret of Love
Mahanta Transcripts, Book 14
Harold Klemp

Your life is what you have made it. If you can learn from the lessons you've created for yourself, you'll find greater happiness, peace, and freedom from fear. Harold Klemp's true-life stories and practical insights will help you expand and be stretched. Through small acts of love you'll find yourself—and God.

The Spiritual Exercises of ECK
Harold Klemp

This book is a staircase with 131 steps. It's a special staircase, because you don't have to climb all the steps to get to the top. Each step is a spiritual exercise, a way to help you explore your inner worlds. And what awaits you at the top? The doorway to spiritual freedom, self-mastery, wisdom, and love.

35 Golden Keys to Who You Are & Why You're Here
Linda C. Anderson

Discover thirty-five golden keys to mastering your spiritual destiny through the ancient teachings of Eckankar, Religion of the Light and Sound of God. The dramatic, true stories in this book equal anything found in the spiritual literature of today. Learn ways to immediately bring more love, peace, and purpose to your life.

How to Master Change in Your Life: Sixty-seven Ways to Handle Life's Toughest Moments
Mary Carroll Moore

In your life, you always have a choice. You can flee from change, a victim of *fate.* Or, as the hero, you can embrace each challenge you face with courage and grace. Included are sixty-seven powerful techniques to help you understand change, plan the future, conquer fear and worry, and resolve problems of the past.

*Available at your local bookstore. If unavailable, call (612) 544-0066. Or write: ECKANKAR Books, P.O. Box 27300, Minneapolis, MN 55427 U.S.A.

There May Be an Eckankar Study Group near You

Eckankar offers a variety of local and international activities for the spiritual seeker. With hundreds of study groups worldwide, Eckankar is near you! Many areas have Eckankar centers where you can browse through the books in a quiet, unpressured environment, talk with others who share an interest in this ancient teaching, and attend beginning discussion classes on how to gain the attributes of Soul: wisdom, power, love, and freedom.

Around the world, Eckankar study groups offer special one-day or weekend seminars on the basic teachings of Eckankar. Check your phone book under **ECKANKAR**, or call **(612) 544-0066** for membership information and the location of the Eckankar center or study group nearest you. Or write **ECKANKAR, Att: Information, P.O. Box 27300, Minneapolis, MN 55427 U.S.A.**

☐ Please send me information on the nearest Eckankar center or study group in my area.

☐ Please send me more information about membership in Eckankar, which includes a twelve-month spiritual study.

Please type or print clearly   940

Name _____
       first (given)   last (family)

Street _____ Apt. # _____

City _____ State/Prov. _____

423

ABOUT HAROLD KLEMP

Sri Harold Klemp was born in Wisconsin and grew up on a small farm. He attended a two-room country schoolhouse before going to high school at a religious boarding school in Milwaukee, Wisconsin.

After preministerial college in Milwaukee and Fort Wayne, Indiana, he enlisted in the U.S. Air Force. There he trained as a language specialist at Indiana University and a radio intercept operator at Goodfellow AFB, Texas. Then followed a two-year stint in Japan where he first encountered Eckankar.

In October 1981, he became the spiritual leader of Eckankar, Religion of the Light and Sound of God. His full title is Sri Harold Klemp, the Mahanta, the Living ECK Master. As the Living ECK Master, Harold Klemp is responsible for the continued evolution of the Eckankar teachings.

His mission is to help people find their way back to God in this life. Harold Klemp travels to ECK seminars in North America, Europe, and the South Pacific. He has also visited Africa and many countries throughout the world, meeting with spiritual seekers and giving inspirational talks. There are many videocassettes and audiocassettes of his public talks available.

In his talks and writings, Harold Klemp's sense of humor and practical approach to spirituality have helped many people around the world find truth in their lives and greater inner freedom, wisdom, and love.

International Who's Who of Intellectuals
Ninth Edition